LITERARY PATTERNS, THEOLOGICAL THEMES, AND THE GENRE OF LUKE-ACTS

Charles H. Talbert

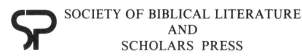

SOCIETY OF BIBLICAL LITERATURE
AND
SCHOLARS PRESS

Distributed by
SCHOLARS PRESS
University of Montana
Missoula, Montana 59801

THE GENRE OF LUKE-ACTS
Copyright © 1974
Society of Biblical Literature

Library of Congress Cataloging in Publication Data

Talbert, Charles H.
    Literary patterns, theological themes, and the genre
of Luke-Acts.

    (Monograph series—Society of Biblical Literature;
20)
    Includes bibliographical references and index.
    1. Bible. N. T. Luke and Acts—Criticism,
interpretation, etc. I. Title. II. Series:
Society of Biblical Literature. Monograph series; 20.
BS2589.T34 1975   226'.4'06   74-78620
ISBN 0-88414-037-7

PRINTED IN THE UNITED STATES OF AMERICA
PRINTING DEPARTMENT, UNIVERSITY OF MONTANA, MISSOULA, MONTANA 59801

Foreword

What is attempted in this book has grown out of research done during two years of post-doctoral study. During 1968-69, at the University of North Carolina at Chapel Hill and at Duke University under the auspices of the Cooperative Program in the Humanities, and during 1971-72, in Rome under the auspices of the Society for Religion in Higher Education, I was able to read in the areas of modern literary criticism and Classics. Without the time and enrichment supplied by these years this volume would never have been born.

I have profited greatly from the careful reading of earlier drafts of this work by friends in Italy, England, and the United States, as well as from the stimulation derived from the faculty and students of the Baptist Theological Seminary at Rüschlikon, Switzerland, where some of the material was presented in a week of pre-Easter lectures in March, 1972. My family and I will long remember the graciousness of Professor Gunter Wagner and his colleagues.

A word of appreciation must also go to the Graduate Council of Wake Forest University for a grant to cover the cost of typing the manuscript.

This work is dedicated

TO

MY PARENTS, AUDREY HALE AND CARL E. TALBERT

WITH GRATITUDE

Acknowledgments

Material from LUKE AND THE GNOSTICS by Charles H. Talbert, copyright © 1966 by Abingdon Press, used by permission.

Material from "An Anti-Gnostic Tendency in Lucan Christology," by Charles H. Talbert, NEW TESTAMENT STUDIES, 14 (1968-69) 259-271, copyright © Cambridge University Press, 1968, used by permission.

Material from "Artistry and Theology: An Analysis of the Architecture of John 1:19—5:47," by Charles H. Talbert, CATHOLIC BIBLICAL QUARTERLY, 32 (1970) 341-366, copyright © 1970, used by permission.

Material from "The Kerygma of the Book of Jonah," by Georges Landes, INTERPRETATION, 21 (1967) 3-31, copyright © by Union Theological Seminary in Virginia, used by permission.

Material from "The Redaction Critical Quest for Luke the Theologian," by Charles H. Talbert, in JESUS AND MAN'S HOPE, 1.171-222, published by Pittsburgh Theological Seminary, 1970, copyright © PERSPECTIVE: A Journal of Pittsburgh Theological Seminary, 1970, used by permission.

Material from "The Lukan Presentation of Jesus' Ministry in Galilee," by Charles H. Talbert, REVIEW AND EXPOSITOR, 64 (1967) 485-497, copyright © REVIEW AND EXPOSITOR, 1970, used by permission.

Note: Abbreviations follow those used in the *Journal of Biblical Literature* (list in Supplement to vol. 90 [September, 1971] 70-76).

Contents

I. GAINING A PERSPECTIVE 1

II. LUCAN PATTERNS (1) 15
    Gospel-Acts Parallels 15
    Correspondences between Acts 1—12 and 13—28 23
    Correspondences between Luke 9:1-48 and 22:7—23:16 26

III. LUCAN PATTERNS (2) 35
    Parallels between Acts 1:12—4:23 and 4:24—5:42 35
    Correspondences between Luke 4:16—7:17 and 7:18—8:56 39
    Parallels in Luke 1—2 44
    Parallels in Luke 3—4 45

IV. LUCAN PATTERNS (3) 51
    Luke 10:21—18:30 as Chiasmus 51
    Acts 15:1—21:26 as Chiasmus 56
    Correspondences between Luke 24 and Acts 1 58
    Correspondences between Luke 9 and Acts 1 61

V. THE PATTERNS IN THE LIGHT OF THE LUCAN
    MILIEU 67
    The Classical World 67
    Israelite-Jewish Aesthetic 70
    Early Christianity 75
    Questions Raised by the Survey 77

VI. LUCAN HEILSGESCHICHTE AND THE PATTERNS
    OF LUKE-ACTS 89
    The Popular Image of the Philosopher in Antiquity 89
    The Early Catholic Decadence Theory 99
    The Relation between John and Jesus 103

VII. THE PATTERNS AND LUCAN CHRISTOLOGY 111
    The Ascension 112
    The Baptism 116
    The Occasion 118

VIII. LUCAN PATTERNS AND THE GENRE OF
    LUKE-ACTS 125
    Analysis of Laertius' *Lives of Eminent Philosophers* 125
    Comparison of Laertius' *Lives* and Luke-Acts 129
    Genre, Patterns, and the Lucan *Sitz im Leben* 134

CONCLUSION 141

INDEX OF PASSAGES 145

INDEX OF AUTHORS 157

CHAPTER I

Gaining a Perspective

The author of Luke-Acts is not only a theologian. He is also "a consumate literary artist"[1] with a "mind that is tuned to the aesthetic."[2] This artistry is reflected, for example, in the remarkable variation in Luke's style in the separate parts of his two volume work. In the Gospel we find a preface written in irreproachable literary Greek followed by the infancy narratives written in the style of the LXX.[3] This very transition has been though to prove the author to be a conscious artist.[4] In the Acts also the author chooses the style which is suitable for the different periods, places, and persons he is describing.[5] He imitates the LXX in the first part of Acts and in the missionary speeches to Jews due to his feel for the Palestinian context of the earliest church.[6] His speeches also employ old titles for Jesus and ancient kerygmatic formulae in accord with the archaizing tendency of antiquity.[7] At other times, less solemn, the author is capable of "painting a scene easily and expansively, dwelling lovingly on details, in almost conversational tones."[8] Luke simply varies his style in terms of the situation he is depicting and the tone that situation requires. Indeed, it is the opinion of H. J. Cadbury that Luke's sensitivity to style is even more far-reaching than that of the literary men of antiquity who understood the imitation of classical models of style.[9]

Another characteristic of Luke-Acts which has come to be recognized as a facet of Luke's artistry is his tendency to balance some feature of his work with another which corresponds or is analogous to it in some way. This method of composition is found, for example, in the correspondences between the Gospel and the Acts, in the parallels between Peter and Paul in Acts, and in the parallel panels of Acts 1—5.

Recognition of such data in the Lucan writings goes back at least to the early nineteenth century.[10] Though variously interpreted, this data was regarded as highly important for the interpretation of Luke-Acts. F. C. Baur, for example, saw the correspondences between Peter and Paul in Acts and explained them in terms of the Lucan tendency as he saw it. Acts, he thought, was an attempt to reconcile the hostile Jewish and Gentile wings of the church. The Peter-Paul parallels were constructed by Luke in the interests of such a reconciliation. If the chief apostles to whom the conflicting parties of the church looked were themselves not in conflict, why should there not now be harmony in the church?[11] Adolf Harnack, in reaction to Tendency Criticism,

1

denied that Luke purposed a detailed parallelism in the history of the two apostles in Acts. The correspondences presented themselves naturally and did not have to be sought. They reflect the history of the apostles.[12] Harnack's importance in the interpretation of such data, however, lies primarily in his explanation of the parallels in Acts 1—5. Functioning as a source critic, Harnack explained the parallels in Acts 1—5 as doublets. After the analogy of source critical work on the Pentateuch, the parallels were clues to sources used by the author, namely, Jerusalem Source A and Jerusalem Source B.[13] In *The Making of Luke-Acts,* Henry J. Cadbury offered a stylistic explanation for the very same type of data. There is a Lucan fondness for pairs of words, doubled vocatives, parallel pairs of birth stories, parables, and miracles, as well as the wide parallelism between the careers of his heroes, Jesus, Peter, Paul, and Stephen.[14] Whether the explanation of the data was in terms of tendency, sources, or style, from Baur through Cadbury the correspondences were regarded as highly important to a proper understanding of Luke-Acts.[15]

In the last generation the responses to the phenomenon of parallels in Luke-Acts have been mixed. On the one hand, there has been some continuity of effort with research in the period from Baur to Cadbury. First, in addition to the confirmation of some of the insights of past research, there has been an accumulation of evidence for more formal patterns expressive of the principle of balance in the various parts of the Lucan writings. For example, Rene Laurentin has argued that the birth narratives in the Third Gospel are arranged into parallel cycles of John and Jesus material.[16] M. D. Goulder asserts that the travel narrative in Luke falls into two sections which correspond to one another in inverted order.[17] J. G. Davies has shown that there are remarkable correspondences between Luke 9 and Acts 1.[18] In a study of the Galilean ministry of Jesus in Luke, I have offered evidence that would indicate that Luke 4:16—8:56 also consists of two panels which roughly correspond to one another.[19] Some of these studies have not only pointed out the formal patterns but have also used them as clues in the interpretative process. None has been more effective in this regard than Paul Minear who has used the similarity of style in the birth narratives and the rest of Luke-Acts to argue that Luke 1—2 are integral to the total work. The duality of Lucan expression here functions as an interpretative key.[20]

Second, the totality of Luke-Acts has been seen from the perspective of its formal patterns expressive of the principle of balance. Among German speaking scholars Robert Morgenthaler's work pursued Cadbury's stylistic explanation with a passion.[21] Luke-Acts is a work of art, organized from its smallest components to the whole in terms of the "law of duality." The meaning-function of this duality in the Lucan writings has its roots in the Israelite-Jewish principle that true testimony must be established by the mouths of at least two witnesses (Deut 19:15).[22] Since the Lucan two volume work is witness, the duality expresses artistically the principle of true testimony.[23]

Among English speaking scholars M. D. Goulder has attempted most thoroughly to understand Luke-Acts in terms of its balanced formal patterns.[24] Operating out of a perspective gained from his tutor, A. M. Farrer, Goulder argues for a multitude of correspondences at every level of the Lucan work, many of which had been seen by research over nearly two centuries. For example, the Acts is parallel to the Third Gospel. The explanation for these patterns is that Luke is writing typological history, the life of Jesus providing the types of the life of the church. It is the Pauline doctrine of the body of Christ which is finding formal expression in the patterns and cycles of the books. Christ is alive in his body, the church.[25]

The lack of persuasiveness in the works by Morgenthaler and Goulder is closely connected to two problems. Neither stands in the main stream of work on Lucan theology. The theological positions to which they try to relate the formal patterns are, therefore, deficient when viewed from redaction critical perspectives.[26] Moreover, neither works from a comparative literary stance. Their presentation of formal patterns and their understanding of their functions are limited by their failure to use comparative materials from the wider Mediterranean world of Luke's time.[27]

Helmut Flender has attempted to use Morgenthaler's thesis about a Lucan "law of duality" as a point of departure for his study of Lucan theology.[28] In contrast to Morgenthaler, however, Flender asserts that this Lucan technique is determined by a certain priority of theological concerns. When, for example, the correspondences constitute complementary parallelism, it is because Luke wishes to present his material from several different points of view rather than causally. When they constitute climactic parallelism, they are used to place side by side what belongs both to the old and to the new world of God. When they constitute antithetical parallelism, they show Luke's awareness of the gulf between God and the sinful world. Unfortunately, it is not really clear how Flender is able to move from his stylistic data to their supposed theological roots. Flender's work, typical of much recent research concerned with the formal patterns, has not been able to delineate successfully the function such patterns have in the Lucan writings.

On the other hand, there is a significant discontinuity between past and present research. For one who has immersed himself in the history of research from Baur through Cadbury, perhaps the most striking feature of Lucan research today is the peripheral position of the formal patterns or parallels in current discussion. In contrast to such figures as Baur, Harnack, and Cadbury, for whom the correspondences were a key to something significant about Luke-Acts, the main current of research today goes its own way with little or no concern for this facet of Lucan artistry. It is given only a passing nod in the work of our generation's two most influential Luke-Acts scholars, Hans Conzelmann[29] and Ernst Haenchen.[30] Kümmel's recent survey of the current scene confirms the impression one gets of the irrelevance of this facet of the Lucan artistry for the main stream of redaction critical study of Luke-Acts.[31] Study of Lucan theology today goes on, for the most part, divorced from a consideration of the formal patterns expressive of the principle of balance which control large segments of the Lucan writings. This is in sharp contrast to an earlier time.

Such disinterest is problematic on at least two accounts. In the first place, study of the formal patterns of a document is needed as a control on the potential subjectivity of the redaction critic. L. E. Keck's review of *John the Baptist in the Gospel Tradition,* by Walter Wink, ably illustrates this contention.[32] The major limitation of the work, Keck claims, is one shared with most redaction critical work. "Wink does not sufficiently analyze literary structures within the Gospels. This invariably atomizes the text in the quest of details traceable to the evangelist . . . ." Keck maintains that redaction criticism should pay closer attention to "the way the materials are structured into larger units and sections." Apart from a concern with the "architecture of the text," the "relentless tracking down of motifs that crop out here and there is not subject to adequate controls by the text as a whole." Such a warning can only be viewed as the verbalization of a concern common to every practicing redaction critic and every discerning reader of redaction critical works. The conquest of subjectivity in the employment of the redaction critical method demands an awareness of the smaller patterns and the larger architectonic designs which govern an author's arrangement of his material.[33]

In the second place, at a number of other points in NT research today scholars are manifesting a genuine concern for just such formal patterns and architectonic designs. It is somewhat surprising that interest in the architecture of Luke-Acts is on the decline at just the time when interest in such a problem is on the upswing elsewhere in NT study. For example, both Gaechter[34] and Fenton[35] argue that Matthew as a whole is organized as a chiasmus. Gaechter, moreover, exposes both the numerical and the chiastic patterns which control the several parts of the whole. Citing similar patterns in the Apocalypse of John, he then infers that these patterns point to a Semitic milieu for the Gospel.[36] A further example of renewed interest in the architectonic dimensions of an author's artistry is Albert Vanhoye's study of Hebrews.[37] In it he has exposed an elaborate patterning of the epistle, including the balanced forms of chiasmus and inclusion. Similarly, Edward Malatesta's work on the Epistles of John explains the letters in terms of balanced patterns.[38] With interest like this in the formal patterns through which a document is organized, it is strange that the patterns of Luke-Acts, long recognized by research, are regarded today as peripheral to Lucan study.

Although such studies as those just mentioned call our attention back to data we are currently overlooking,[39] they do not seem to offer adequate guidance for our own study. First, both Vanhoye and Malatesta set forth the formal patterns and then stop. The patterns are treated in isolation from the totality of the document's achievement. There is no attempt to discern the pattern's function in the text as F. C. Baur, for example, did.[40] Second, Gaechter works on the formal patterns in isolation from the document's milieu and hence can make the questionable inference that balanced patterns like chiasmus point to a Semitic setting for the material. Indeed, no NT scholar seems concerned to set the patterns in their larger Mediterranean context to see what light this would shed on the whole matter.

In light of the previous discussion two observations need to be made. (1) Redaction critical work cannot be done in a satisfactory way without attention to the formal patterns that make up the architecture of a writing. (2) Investigation of the formal patterns and architectonic designs of a document must not be done in isolation either from the writing's overall achievement or from its environment.

What is needed is a method of operation which will allow us to investigate certain of the formal patterns of Luke-Acts—in particular, those expressive of the principle of balance—in such a way as to see them within Luke-Acts as a whole and in the author's environment. It seems to me that there is an approach to ancient literature characteristic of much classical scholarship which fits this need. This is an approach which may with some justification be called "architecture analysis."[41] The remarks about this method which follow are organized as answers to two questions: (1) What is architecture analysis? (2) In the approach of architecture analysis are there sufficient controls on scholarly subjectivity to justify the use of the method?

What Is Architecture Analysis?

Architecture analysis is a variety of the species style criticism within the genus literary criticism. We can clarify this approach to the study of classical literature if in the first place we illustrate its three major emphases from some recent work on Homer, Herodotus, and Vergil. (1) Certain classical scholars have been concerned to discern the formal patterns or architectonic designs that control the arrangement of the material in its larger units. Cedric H. Whitman's *Homer and the Heroic Tradition*[42] reflects this interest in the formal aspects of the *Iliad*. He argues that the poem as a whole forms one large concentric pattern and that within the whole are a vast system of smaller ones giving shape to the separate parts. He regards the principle of balance around a central point, such as is implied in concentric circles, as the dominating structural principle of the *Iliad*.[43] John L. Myres' *Herodotus: Father of History*[44] (which works out in Herodotus ideas appearing in his earlier *Who Were the Greeks?*[45]) and Henry R. Immerwahr's *Form and Thought in Herodotus*[46] treat the narrative prose of Herodotus in a formal way. Myres' emphasis is on Herodotus' employment of a pedimental mode of composition[47] on every scale, small and large.[48] Taken together, these two scholars call attention to the widespread presence of architectonic designs in Herodotus.[49] In his *Structural Patterns and Proportions in Vergil's Aeneid*, G. E. Duckworth argues that formal patterns dominate this epic.[50] There are three such patterns which control the organization of the whole: (a) alternating rhythm where even numbered books are those with the greatest tragic impact and odd numbered books which are lighter and serve to relieve the tension; (b) parallelism of halves where Books 1—6 are paralleled by Books 7—12; and (c) a tripartite division where three groups of four books each are related to each other in an ABA' pattern. The same principles, moreover, are at work in individual books or parts of books just as they are in the ordering of the whole.[51]

(2) The conviction in significant strains of modern literary criticism that literature and the arts belong together as parts of a culture and that they manifest in different media the underlying unity of a *Zeitgeist* finds expression in the classical scholar's concern to see the formal patterns that control the organization and give unity to a writing in their relation to the larger cultural context of the document. Noting that the relationship between Homer and geometric painting has long been recognized, Cedric Whitman observes that in Homer there is a circular composition with scenes framing scenes in concentric rings around centerpieces "exactly as central motifs are heavily framed by borders in geometric art." Indeed the patterns in the *Iliad* are the "acoustical analogue" to what is found in visual art. The clue to understanding this Homeric technique in the *Iliad,* Whitman thinks, lies in the recognition of the tendency to adjust oral technique to the psychology underlying the geometric symmetry of the late eighth centry B.C.E.[52] John Myres links the ABA' patterns that dominate Herodotus to the arrangement of sculptured figures in the pediments of Greek temples and to the bilateral symmetry of Greek painting. Indeed he presents the arrangement of certain sections of the *History* in pictures as though they were sculptured forms on a Greek temple.[53] This pattern he believes goes back to a certain sense of rhythm characteristic of the Greeks.[54] Duckworth compares two of the architectonic designs of the *Aeneid* with similar patterns in the *Ara Pacis Augustae.* This altar may be seen either as two parallel groups of three friezes each so that there are Roman and Julian-Augustan halves or as a tripartite division divided according to legend, history, and symbol. In what is surely the most controversial aspect of his book, Duckworth argues that the roots of such patterns are to be found in the Golden Mean ratio characteristic of classical culture.[55]

(3) The classical scholar's effort to point out the employment of such architectural patterns for both aesthetic and didactic ends follows the tenet of modern literary criticism that the connection between form and content in literature is so vital that it is meaningless to consider one of them without constant reference to the other. No one else goes to such lengths in this repsect as Cedric Whitman. He contends that architectonic patterns may be either functional or non-functional. Examples of both may be found in the *Iliad.* However, he is adamant in his assertion that though pattern may have been originally mnemonic and functional, such a purpose is clearly superseded when it becomes the structural basis for a fifteen-thousand-line poem. It has become an artistic principle, a scheme abstractly architectonic.[56] Myres thinks that generally pedimental structure is an aid to meaning because it focuses attention on the center of the work. Here is where the emphasis in meaning is to be found.[57] Immerwahr claims that Herodotus "is a classic example of the

doctrine that thought appears primarily in the organization and structure" of a writing.[58] Though he does not work out his contention, Duckworth claims that the architectural features he isolates "are not merely an adornment for their own sake but are devised to emphasize and make more significant the meaning of the poem . . . ."[59] Duckworth's major dependence throughout his book is upon R. S. Conway's *The Vergilian Age*[60] and, if I understand him aright, he would follow Conway on the question of the relation of form to meaning in the *Aeneid*. Conway argued that the crowning book which Vergil has placed in the center to unite all that stand before it and all that stand after it is Book 6.[61] If so, it would be in line with the findings of Lawrence Richardson, Jr., who in his *Poetical Theory in Republican Rome* concluded that in the composition of narrative poetry in this period, the climax of the action falls at or near the center. In this procedure the Roman poets were following the basic compositional rules of tragedy which determined the position of the climax near the center of the action. The climax falls near the center and the denouement near the end.[62] However Duckworth may understand the exact relation between the architectonic designs uncovered in the *Aeneid* and the epic's meaning, he does make explicit that the "fact that many hearers . . . would not be conscious of the proportion is no argument against their existence . . . . A great poet or artist or musician always puts more into a work than is ordinarily realized."[63]

On first glance one can discern basic similarities between architecture analysis and modern redaction criticism of the gospels. Both regard the writer of a document as a genuine author, not just as a collector or editor. Both are concerned with a writing in its present form as a completed product and with its sources only in a secondary way. Both are concerned to understand the stance of the author of the final form of the writing by studying indications of the author's creative handling of the material. Beyond such obvious similarities, however, the difference between the two approaches is basic. The primary concern of architecture analysis is to detect the formal patterns, rhythms, architectonic designs, or architecture of a writing. That is, this approach is concerned with style insofar as it shapes the final product by the arrangement of the larger units of material, especially the whole. As part of its auxiliary concern to interpret the significance of the style, architecture analysis concentrates not only on the pattern's analogies in the visual art of a document's context and its roots in a cultural *Zeitgeist* but also on the question of the architecture's potential didactic significance, that is, on its relation to the meaning of the writing. At the same time, within this approach style has a certain autonomy. Its significance is neither eliminated if the style is found to serve only aesthetic ends nor exhausted in or by the possible message it conveys. The *way an author expresses himself* is regarded as a valid quest in and of itself. Redaction criticism's primary concern, however, is to detect the unique theological views which the evangelists have imposed upon their materials insofar as these can be discerned in their seams, interpretive comments, summaries, modification of material, selection of material, omission of material, *arrangement,* introductions, conclusions, vocabulary, christological titles, and other means.[64] Arrangement, then, is but one avenue among many by which the goal of redaction criticism may be attained. In redaction criticism there is no concern for formal patterns as such. Only if the arrangement is found to be theologically motivated has it been considered noteworthy. For example, if the twofold division of Galilee-Jerusalem found in Mark is due to "literary and stylistic motives, Redaktionsgeschichte is not involved, but if this scheme is due to a theological motive, then Redaktionsgeschichte is very much involved."[65] There is, moreover, no concern by the redaction critic to show any link between the architectural patterns discerned and a cultural *Zeitgeist.* Rather, the theological views of an evangelist are usually presented as being in opposition to some group which is believed to be corrupting the faith, often because some mode of thought, viewed as alien to authentic Christian existence, is influencing the group unduly. Discontinuity rather than continuity with culture, then, is the normal emphasis of redaction criticism. In redaction criticism the *distinctive theological* content of an author's self-expression is the desired objective of one's quest. Architecture analysis and redaction criticism, therefore, represent materially different approaches to literature.

The two methodologies should not be regarded as mutually exclusive, however. Rather they should be understood as mutually enriching. Redaction criticism needs architecture analysis as a complement to its own efforts as a guard against scholarly subjectivity. Architecture analysis needs redaction criticism in order to be able to deal effectively with the relation of a formal pattern to meaning. We may conclude, therefore, that in the study of early Christian sources, architecture analysis is an appropriate complement to redaction criticism.

What Controls on Scholarly Subjectivity Are Possible?

The specter which hovers over any approach to the New Testament writings that focuses on the architectonic patterns giving unity to a particular document is a phantom named scholarly subjectivity. The excesses of certain scholars in this respect have been enough to cause respectable researchers to shy away from such subjective enterprises.[66] Regardless of the fruitful possibilities inherent in the employment of an architectural analysis approach to the New Testament, it is unlikely that it will attract many adherents unless it can be shown that there are real controls available to inhibit the scholar's subjectivity.[67]

In applying architecture analysis to the study of the New Testament, there are two safeguards. One the one hand, there are the *internal* controls, indications within the text of the writing itself that point to the existence of a given pattern. (1) It should be possible to exhibit a pattern controlling the arrangement of large units throughout an author's work, and in units of all sizes. At least in the classical sources where similar architectural designs are found this is almost always the case. (2) Where possible—e.g., in the

Gospels—one should be able to show that the pattern is located in the redactional activity of an author rather than in the tradition. Insofar as this is possible, architecture analysis possesses as great a safeguard against subjectivity as does redaction criticism. It is, of course, more difficult to use this control in an epistle because of the lack of tradition behind the text. Anywhere that redaction criticism can be used in the epistles, however, architecture analysis will find the separation of tradition and redaction an aid in the fight against subjectivity. On the other hand, there are *external* controls, indications outside the text that may render a proposed pattern probable or improbable. (1) For a convincing case, one would need parallels to the architectonic designs proposed for a New Testament writing from the literature of the writing's larger context. Architecture analysis assumes that writings in antiquity used certain conventional patterns for the organization of their materials. If the patterns are conventions they should be evident in more than one document and should be found in a wide cross-section of writings in a document's milieu. (2) Classical examples indicate that the architectonic designs governing a document's arrangement are generally found in the visual art of the period. Where possible such parallels should be demonstrated. (3) It is also important to be able to show that behind various artistic tendencies there are certain cultural or aesthetic roots for these stylistic traits. Showing that a given technique is indigenous to the cultural mentality is an essential component in any convincing case for the architecture of a piece of literature. Taken together, the internal and external controls suggested here offer at the very minimum as satisfactory a guarantee against scholarly subjectivity as is offered by redaction criticism. For an era in which redaction criticism enjoys a wide popularity, therefore, architecture analysis should present no undue stress on scholarly credibility. Sufficient safeguards are at hand to prevent radical excesses of subjectivity.

The purpose of this study is to try to make sense out of the presence of certain literary patterns uncovered both by past research and by my own work on Luke-Acts. The method will be that of architecture analysis as it is employed in classical scholarship. The argument of the chapters which follow will correspond to the three major emphases of the method to be employed. The next three chapters (2—4) will endeavor to delineate certain key formal patterns of Luke-Acts.[68]   Throughout this section an attempt will be made to show that the architectural patterns are located in the redaction work of the author.[69] The next chapter (5) will focus on the relation of the architectural designs of Luke-Acts to the larger cultural context. Parallels to the Lucan patterns will be sought in the literature and art of the Near East, classical culture, and early Christianity. Our quest will ultimately take us to the "principle of balance" which is so deep-seated in much of Mediterranean culture.[70] The final three chapters (6—8) will explore the functions of the formal patterns in Luke-Acts. A primary task will be to determine, insofar as is possible, their relationship to the theological perspectives of the Lucan writings. This will be done in Chapters Six and Seven with the aid of redaction criticism. Ultimately the question must be faced: why would Luke organize his two volume work around a balanced architectonic scheme? An answer will be sought in Chapter Eight with the aid of genre criticism.[71]

FOOTNOTES

[1]B. H. Streeter, *The Four Gospels* (London: Macmillan, 1924) 548.

[2]Wayne G. Rollins, *The Gospels: Portraits of Christ* (Philadelphia: Westminster, 1963) 97. Rollins says: "Theology and aesthetics are nearly synonymous for this Grecian-Jewish-Christian mind. . . ." (p. 99).

[3]H. F. D. Sparks, "The Semitisms of Acts," *JTS* n.s., 1 (1950) 16-28; Ernst Haenchen, *The Acts of the Apostles* (Philadelphia: Westminster, 1971) 74.

[4]J. M. Creed, *The Gospel according to St. Luke* (London: Macmillan, 1930) lxxvi.

[5]L. Cerfaux, "The Acts of the Apostles," in *Introduction to the New Testament* (ed. A. Robert and A. Feuillet; New York: Desclee, 1965) 366.

[6]Eckhardt Plümacher, *Lukas als hellenistischer Schriftsteller* (Göttingen: Vandenhoeck & Ruprecht, 1972) 51, 63-64, 67-69; Haenchen, *Acts,* 74.

[7]Plümacher, 72-78.

[8]Haenchen, 80.

[9]*The Making of Luke-Acts* (New York: Macmillan, 1927) 221. Cadbury's interest in Lucan style has stretched over many years. Cf., e.g., *The Style and Literary Method of Luke* (Cambridge: Harvard University Press, 1919-20); *JBL,* 44 (1925) 214-27; *JBL,* 45 (1926) 190-209; *JBL,* 48 (1929) 412-25; *JBL,* 52 (1933) 55-65; *JBL,* 82 (1963) 272-78; *NTS,* 3 (1957) 128-32; *Studies in Luke-Acts* (ed. L. E. Keck and J. L. Martyn; Nashville: Abingdon, 1966) 87-102; *Studies in New Testament and Early Christian Literature* (ed. D. E. Aune; Leiden: Brill, 1972) 3-15.

[10]E.g., Matthias Schneckenburger, *Über den Zweck der Apostelgeschichte* (Bern: Christian Fischer, 1841) 52-56.

[11]*Paul: The Apostle of Jesus Christ* (ed. E. Zeller; London: Williams & Norgate, 1875) 6, 81, 87, 95, 96, 98, 104, 145, 150, 165, 174, 191, 196, 198, 202, 227, 229, 231, 237, 240, 250; *The Church History of the First Three Centuries* (London: Williams & Norgate, 1878) 1. 132-36.

[12]*New Testament Studies III: The Acts of the Apostles* (London: Williams & Norgate, 1909) 118-19.

[13]*Ibid.,* ch. 5.

[14](New York: Macmillan, 1927) 216, 218, 223-225, 231-232.

[15]A. J. Mattill, Jr., "Luke as Historian in Criticism since 1840," Ph. D. Thesis, Vanderbilt, 1959, offers the most comprehensive study of the function of this data in the history of research.

[16]*Structure et théologie de Luc 1—2* (Paris: Gabalda, 1957) 32-33. This parallelism has been recognized since the nineteenth century (cf. J. G. Machen, *The Virgin Birth of Christ* [New York: Harper, 1930], 152, n. 49).

[17]"The Chiastic Structure of the Lucan Journey," *Studia Evangelica, II* (ed. F. L. Cross; Berlin: Akademie Verlag, 1964) 195-202; *Type and History in Acts* (London: S.P.C.K., 1964) 138-39.

[18]"The Prefigurement of the Ascension in the Third Gospel," *JTS,* n.s., 6 (1955) 229-33.

[19]"The Lukan Presentation of Jesus' Ministry in Galilee," *Rev Exp* 64 (1967) 485-97.

[20]"Luke's Use of the Birth Stories," in *Studies in Luke-Acts,* 111-30. Cf. also V. E. McEachern, "Dual Witness and Sabbath Motif in Luke," *CJT* 12 (1966) 267-80.

[21]*Die lukanische Geschichtsschreibung als Zeugnis: Gestalt und Gehalt der Kunst des Lukas.* 2 vols. (Zurich: Zwingli-Verlag, 1949). Morgenthaler was indebted to such predecessors as Lyder Brun, "Zur Kompositionstechnik des Lukasevangeliums," *Symbolae Osloenses* 9 (1930) 38-50.

[22]Morgenthaler, 2. 8.

[23]*Ibid.,* 2. 24.

[24]*Type and History in Acts.*

[25]*Ibid.,* x, 34, 61-62.

[26]Cf. the remark of Ernst Haenchen, *The Acts of the Apostles,* 47, about Morgenthaler. Also for one persuaded by Philip Vielhauer's "On the 'Paulinism' of Acts," in *Studies in Luke-Acts,* 33-50 (originally published, 1950-51), Goulder's claim that the patterns of Acts were intended to express Pauline theology is untenable. On their behalf it must be said that Morgenthaler

wrote before the era of redaction criticism began in 1954, and Goulder wrote while he was Rector in sole charge of a parish of nine thousand people in Manchester.

[27]Only of late have we seen the emergence of a concern to locate the Lucan artistry in the context of the artistic conceptions of his times. Cf. W. C. van Unnik, "Éléments artistique dans l'Évangile de Luc," *ETL* 46 (1970) 401-12; Eckhard Plümacher, *Lukas als hellenistischer Schriftsteller.*

[28]*St. Luke: Theologian of Redemptive History* (Philadelphia: Fortress, 1967) ch. 1.

[29]Conzelman's *Die Apostelgeschichte* (Tübingen: J.C.B. Mohr [Paul Siebeck], 1963) 14, lists Morgenthaler's work but is not influenced by it. *The Theology of St. Luke* (New York: Harper and Row, 1960) occasionally refers to individual correspondences (e.g., pp. 64, 81) but they are peripheral to the main thrust of the work.

[30]Haenchen's *Acts of the Apostles* is equally unconcerned with formal patterns.

[31]W. G. Kümmel, "Lukas in der Anklage der heutigen Theologie," *ZNW* 63 (1972) 149-65. Morgenthaler was at least discussed in the earlier survey by C. K. Barrett, *Luke the Historian in Recent Study* (London: Epworth Press, 1960) 36-40. In his discussion of the theological issues raised by the Lucan writings, however, the artistry played no role.

[32]*USQR* 24 (1968) 95-96. A perfect example of the problem to which Keck calls attention is found in Otto Glombitza, "Die Titel διδάσκαλος und ἐπιστάτης für Jesus bei Lukas," *ZNW* 49 (1958) 275-78.

[33]This fact was already pointed out by Martin Dibelius, "Zur Formgeschichte des N.T. (ausserhalb der Evangelien)," *ThRu* n.f., 3 (1931) 207-42. In his discussion of Cadbury (pp. 240-42), Dibelius contends that one should note the literary method of the author of Acts as a methodological first step in the study of the book. Any such effort will have to take account of classical antecedents. Cf. W. C. van Unnik, "First Century A.D. Literary Culture and Early Christian Literature," *Nederlands Theologisch Tijdschrift* 25 (1971) 28-43.

[34]Paul Gaechter, *Das Matthäus Evangelium* (Innsbruck: Tyrolia Verlag, 1963) 17. Beda Rigaux, *The Testimony of St. Matthew* (Chicago: Franciscan Herald, 1968) 22, is sceptical because of the difficulty in proving that such patterns are deliberate.

[35]J. C. Fenton, *Saint Matthew* (Baltimore: Penguin Books, 1963) 15-16.

[36]Gaechter, 15. Rigaux, *Testimony of St. Matthew,* 23, agrees that chiasmus and inclusion point to a Palestinian background for the First Gospel.

[37]Albert Vanhoye, *La structure littéraire de l'Épître aux Hébreux* (Bruges: Desclee de Brouwer, 1963); *A Structured Translation of the Epistle to the Hebrews* (Rome: Pontifical Biblical Institute, 1964).

[38]*The Epistles of John: Structured Greek Text* (Fano: Typis Paulinis, 1966).

[39]There is also a tradition in the history of research on the epistles of Paul, for example, which has been alert to the artistic dimensions of the letters. Cf. Johannes Weiss, *The History of Primitive Christianity* (New York: Erikson, 1937) 1. 400, 409; Rudolf Bultmann, *Der Stil der paulinischen Predigt und die kynisch-stoische Diatribe* (Göttingen: Vandenhoeck & Ruprecht, 1910); Robert Funk, *Language, Hermeneutik, and Word of God* (New York: Harper & Row, 1966) ch. 10.

[40]In this respect Vanhoye and Malatesta function very much as a New Critic would. The so-called New Criticism assumes that a literary work is an organic unity of form and content. The form is not a container for the content but the arrangement and patterning of it. Change the order and you change the meaning. The task of criticism, therefore, is to clarify what the formal patterns are. But in a study of NT writings one cannot assume that the documents are of the nature assumed by New Criticism. Research must not only clarify what the formal patterns are but also demonstrate their relation to the theological perspective of a writing.

[41]In recent years critics have turned to arts outside literature to supplement the vocabulary for the description of prose literature. From painting has come the term "pattern," from music the term "rhythm," and from architectonics the term "architecture." Most recently from linguistics has come a whole new terminology. The result is a highly fluid critical vocabulary. There is simply no consensus in the area of technical terms. Nevertheless, for some time now there has been in some circles of classical study a use of the term "architecture" for certain formal features of

ancient literature. For that widespread approach to the study of ancient literature which is concerned to expose the formal patterns or architecture of the writings, "architecture analysis" seems a useful label. It seems especially appropriate for the gospels if they are folk narrative. Folk narrative's "composition is like that of sculpture and architecture; hence the strict subordination to number and other requirements of symmetry." Axel Olrik, "Epic Laws of Folk Narrative," in *The Study of Folklore* (ed. Alan Dundes; Englewood Cliffs, N.J.; Prentice-Hall, 1965) 137.

[42](Cambridge: Harvard University Press, 1958).

[43]*Ibid.,* 97.

[44](Oxford: Clarendon Press, 1953).

[45](Berkeley: University of California Press, 1930).

[46](Cleveland: Western Reserve University Press, 1966).

[47]By pedimental mode of composition classical scholars refer to a formal arrangement like that in the pediment of a Greek temple. There is a central figure with balanced flanking ones (e.g., ABCB′A′).

[48]*Herodotus: Father of History,* 81-91.

[49]Immerwahr's reservations about Myres' views are unfounded in the main. Herodotus is simply using more than one architectonic principle in the organization of his work. Cf. *Form and Thought,* 12-14.

[50](Ann Arbor: University of Michigan Press, 1962) vii.

[51]*Ibid.,* 1-20.

[52]*Homer and the Heroic Tradition,* 97, 253, 10.

[53]*Herodotus: Father of History,* 85.

[54]*Who Were the Greeks?* 511-25.

[55]*Structural Patterns and Proportions in Vergil's Aeneid,* 15. The reviews of Duckworth's volume are characterized by scepticism or praise depending upon whether the reviewer focuses on the mathematical part of his work or on the patterns. As a representative of the sceptical views, cf. P. F. Hovingh, *Mnemosyne,* Series 4, Vol. 17 (1964) 425-26. As a representative of reviews with a positive attitude towards the patterns, cf. R. B. Lloyd, *American Journal of Philology* 85 (1964) 71-77.

[56]*Homer and the Heroic Tradition,* 98, 252, 255. Whitman says of this complex symmetry: "An audience hence might feel more symmetry than it could possible analyze or describe" (p. 256).

[57]"The Structure of Stichomythis in Attic Tragedy," *Proceedings of the British Academy* 34 (1948) 199.

[58]*Form and Thought in Herodotus,* 15.

[59]*Structural Patterns and Proportions in Vergil's Aeneid,* vii.

[60](Cambridge: Harvard University Press, 1928).

[61]*Ibid.,* 143.

[62](New Haven: Yale University Press, 1944) 19-20.

[63]*Structural Patterns and Proportions in Vergil's Aeneid,* 37.

[64]Robert H. Stein, "What Is Redaktionsgeschichte?" *JBL* 88 (1969) 53.

[65]*Ibid.,* 54. This limited definition of redaction criticism will offend those scholars who see themselves as descendents of H. J. Cadbury. When one observes the practice of redaction criticism, Stein's description seems accurate.

[66]Austin Farrer, *A Study in St. Mark* (Westminster: Dacre, 1951), reflects an approach to the gospels which causes methodologically cautious scholars to shy away from all attempts to determine the architectonic patterns controlling early Christian writings.

[67]Jacques Dupont, *The Sources of Acts* (London: Darton, Longman & Todd, 1964) 49, manifests the type of hostility frequently shown toward an approach like that of "architecture analysis" when he says of Reicke's delineation of the parallels in Acts 1—5: "As to Reicke's imposing symmetrical structures, it seems to us superfluous to discuss them in detail—they will awaken no interest—at least, for the honour of professional scripture scholarship, it is desirable they should not do so."

[68]No attempt will be made to refute other analyses of Lucan architecture that do not offer a direct challenge to the one presented here. This includes the arrangements proposed by J. C. O'Neill, *The Theology of Acts in Its Historical Setting* (2d ed. rev.; London: S.P.C.K., 1970) ch. 2, and by W. C. Robinson, Jr., *Der Weg des Herrn* (Hamburg: Herbert Reich, 1964) 29. Such a task would not only detract from our argument here but is unnecessary since in antiquity double and even triple architectonic design was not uncommon. E.g., Vergil in his *Aeneid* and *Georgics* (G. E. Duckworth, *Structural Patterns and Proportions in Vergil's Aeneid,* 1-19); Horace (R. W.

Carrubba, "The Technique of Double Structure in Horace," *Mnemosyne,* Series 4, Vol. 20 [1967] 68-75); at Qumran (B. Thiering, "The Poetic Forms of the Hodayot," *JSS* 8 [1963] 189-209; "The Acts of the Apostles as Early Christian Art." in *Essays in Honor of Griffithes Wheeler Thatcher* [ed. E. C. B. MacLaurin; Sydney University Press, 1967] 143-44).

[69]At this point I am aware of being caught in a crossfire. On the one hand, opponents of the two source theory will be unhappy because I assume it here. My own estimate of some alternatives may be found in *JBL* 91 (1972) 338-68. Since the alternatives presently available are, in my opinion, even less tenable, and since there still seems to be a consensus favoring the two source theory, it is necessary that one show how his work is related to that point of view. On the other hand, New Testament scholars under the influence of certain currents of modern literary criticism will claim that such source analysis is unnecessary and should be discarded. Since scholars under the influence of redaction criticism demand evidence that something attributed to the author lies in the redaction instead of the tradition, I think that it is still desirable to carry on one's stylistic studies in dialogue with one's source analysis, insofar as the latter is possible. Should the reader think the source analysis included in the following chapters is incorrect or unnecessary, it is hoped that he will not be unduly disheartened but will concentrate on my main line of argument. The source analysis is included for scholars who regard it as necessary and the two source theory to be essentially accurate.

[70]The principle of balance in antiquity finds expression in at least four major ways symbolized in the following patterns: (1) AB:A'B', (2) AB:B'A', (3) ABCA', (4) ABCD:C'B'A'D'. The first involves the recurrence of some element in natural order. The second is an inverted order. The third involves merely the echo in the last member of a series of the first. The fourth involves the recurrence of all or most of the elements in the first series but in no particular order. These recurrences may be of key terms, themes, sounds or forms. There is no agreed upon vocabulary to describe these four expressions of balance. For example, the first is known to biblical scholars as regular parallelism which may be either synonymous or antithetical depending on the content. The second is known by such names as inverted parallelism, chiasmus, and envelope construction. The third is called by some inclusion, by others ring composition, and by still others a bracketing or framing device. The fourth is called the method of counterpoint or *Zweiheitsgesetz.* Since there is no standard vocabulary, I can only beg the reader's indulgence as I try in subsequent chapters to make myself clear with regard to these four expressions of balance.

[71]There are both agreements and divergences between genre and structuralist criticism. On the one hand, both assume that a particular text standing alone is a problem because it lacks meaning. Both view the individual test in terms of a universal type or configuration which is constructed on the basis of an intuitive grouping of texts with common features. It is the particular text's participation in the universal type that gives it a first level of meaning. Both look for the particular text's transformation of the universal type/structure/genre as a further way of saying something about the meaning of the particular. On the other hand, structuralist and genre criticism diverge on at least two points. First, genre criticism seeks those universal types/genres which have a definite function in a specific social and cultural context. A culture would be conscious of such genres or types. Structuralism, however, seems concerned with the unconscious structures that are rooted in the human mind as such. Second, structuralism tends to regard traditional historical approaches such as redaction criticism (diachrony) as antithetical to its own synchronic approach. Genre criticism, however, regards its efforts as complementary to historical methodologies like redaction criticism. So understood, it is genre criticism rather than structuralism which furnishes the perspective for Chapter Eight.

CHAPTER II

Lucan Patterns (1)

The first part of this book has as its aim the presentation of certain key architectural patterns of the Lucan writings.[1] Insofar as possible, within the limits of our knowledge of the author's sources, we will attempt to show that these patterns are located in the redactional activity of the Evangelist rather than in the tradition he received and used.[2] Here no attempt will be made to interpret the meaning of these patterns in Luke-Acts. That task must await Chapters Six, Seven, and Eight.

Gospel—Acts Parallels

Any attempt to determine the architecture of the Lucan literature must begin with its most distinctive feature, the existence of the Acts and the Third Gospel alongside one another.[3] Apparently the authors of Mark, Matthew and John saw no need for a second volume, one containing church traditions, to complement their gospels. In this regard the second and third century apocryphal gospels take their stand with the other three canonical gospels rather than with Luke-Acts. The apocryphal Acts, moreover, show no signs of having felt any necessity for a gospel narrative to precede their apostolic legends. As far as we know, only Luke-Acts in early Christianity reflects the conviction that both the story of Jesus and the story of the apostolic church are incomplete without the other as complement. Hence any attempt at understanding the architecture of the Lucan writings must treat the Gospel-Acts pattern as basic. For this reason, the remarkable correspondences both in content and sequence[4] between the events and persons found in Luke and those in Acts must be regarded as the primary architectonic pattern in Luke-Acts.

In his commentary on Acts published in 1901, R. B. Rackham first called attention to this aspect of the Lucan architecture in a brief paragraph on the method of the author of Acts.[5] Since that time numerous other writers have made observations about the parallels.[6] The list which follows represents a synthesis of typical suggestions put forth over more than half a century, together with my own observations.

LUKE		ACTS
1:1-4 A preface dedicates the book to Theophilus.[7]	1.	1:1-5 A preface dedicates the book to Theophilus.
3:21 Jesus is praying at his baptism.	2.	1:14, 24 The disciples are praying as they await their baptism of the Holy Spirit.
3:22 The Spirit descends after Jesus' prayer and in a physical form.[8]	3.	2:1-13 The Spirit fills the disciples after their prayers with accompanying physical manifestations.
4:16-30 Jesus' ministry opens with a sermon which gives the theme for what follows, fulfillment of prophecy and rejection of Jesus.[9]	4.	2:14-40 The church's ministry opens with a sermon which gives the theme for what follows, fulfillment of prophecy and rejection of Jesus.
4:31—8:56 The theme of fulfillment mentioned in 4:16-30 is illustrated by examples of preaching and healing. Conflicts illustrate the note of rejection.[10]	5.	2:41—12:17 The theme of fulfillment is illustrated by examples of prophesying and wonders. Persecutions illustrate the note of unbelief.

Within this last general section there are several specific correspondences that need to be mentioned.

5:17-26 A lame man is healed by the authority of Jesus.	6.	3:1-10 A lame man is healed by the name of Jesus (cf. 9:32-35).
5:29—6:11 Conflicts with the religious leaders.	7.	4:1—8:3 Conflicts with the religious leaders.
7:1-10 A centurion, well-spoken of by the Jews, sends men to Jesus to ask him to come to his house.[11]	8.	Ch. 10 A centurion, well-spoken of by the whole Jewish nation, sends men to Peter to ask him to come to his house.
7:11-17 A story involving a widow and a resurrection. Jesus says, "Arise" (ἐγέρθητι). And the dead man "sat up" (ἀνεκάθισεν).	9.	9:36-43 A story involving widows and a resurrection. Peter says, "Rise" (ἀνάστηθι). And the woman "sat up" (ἀνεκάθισεν).
7:36-50 A Pharisee criticizes Jesus for being touched by the wrong kind of woman.	10.	11:1-18 The Pharisaic party criticizes Peter for his association with Gentiles.

We may now move on to further parallels between the Third Gospel (Lynn says not to set these.)

10:1-12 The mission of the seventy which foreshadows the Gentile mission of the church.[12]	11.	Chs. 13—20 The missionary journeys of Paul to the Gentiles.
9:51—19:28 Jesus makes a journey to Jerusalem which is a passion journey (9:31; 9:51; 12:50; 13:33; 18:31-33) under divine necessity (13:33) and characterized by the disciples' lack of understanding (9:45; 18:34).[13]	12.	19:21—21:17 Paul makes a last journey to Jerusalem which is a passion journey (20:3; 20:22-24; 20:37-38; 21:4; 21:10-11; 21:13) under divine necessity (20:22; 21:14) and characterized by his friends' lack of understanding (21:4; 21:12-13).

Careful examination reveals seven references to the journey to Jerusalem in both the passion journey of Jesus in the Third Gospel and that of Paul in Acts.

9:51, 53 He set his face to go to Jerusalem.

13:22 He was journeying toward Jerusalem.

13:33 I must go on my way for a prophet cannot perish away from Jerusalem.

17:11 On the way to Jerusalem he was passing between Samaria and Galilee.

18:31 We are going up to Jerusalem.

19:11 He was near to Jerusalem.

19:28 He went on ahead, going up to Jerusalem.

13. 19:21 Paul resolved to go to Jerusalem.

14. 20:22 I am going to Jerusalem.

15. 21:4 They told Paul not to go to Jerusalem.

16. 21:11-12 Agabus told Paul that the Jews at Jerusalem would bind him.

17. 21:13 Paul replied that he was ready to die at Jerusalem.

18. 21:15 We made ready to go to Jerusalem.

19. 21:17 When they had come to Jerusalem.

Not only is Jesus' journey to Jerusalem parallel to that of Paul, but also the events that take place when the two men reach the city, and after, are similar.

19:37 Jesus receives a good reception and the people praise God for the works they have seen.

19:45-48 Jesus goes into the Temple. He has a friendly attitude toward it.

20:27-39 The Sadducees do not believe in the resurrection. The scribes support Jesus.

22:19a At a meal Jesus
λαβὼν ἄρτον εὐχαριστήσας
ἔκλασεν.

22:54 A mob seizes Jesus.

22:63-64 Jesus is slapped by the priest's assistants.[16]

22:26; 23:1; 23:8; 23:13 The four trials of Jesus (Sanhedrin; Pilate; Herod; Pilate).[17]

20. 21:17-20a Paul receives a good reception and God is glorified for the things done among the Gentiles.

21. 21:26 Paul goes into the Temple. He has a friendly attitude toward it.

22. 23:6-9 The Sadducees do not believe in the resurrection. The scribes support Paul.

23. 27:35 Paul has a meal in which he
λαβὼν ἄρτον εὐχαρίστησεν . . .
καὶ κλάσας.[15]

24. 21:30 A mob seizes Paul.

25. 23:2 Paul is slapped at the high priest's command.

26. Chs. 23; 24; 25; 26 The four trials of Paul (Sanhedrin; Felix; Festus; Herod Agrippa).

Some of the details in the trials of Jesus in the Third Gospel and Paul in the Acts correspond.

23:4, 14, 22 Three times Pilate declares Jesus innocent.[15]

23:6-12 Pilate sends Jesus to Herod for questioning.[19]

23:16, 22 Pilate says he will release (ἀπολύσω) Jesus.[20]

27. 23:9; 25:25; 26:31 Three men, Lysias, Festus, and Agrippa, declare Paul innocent.

28. 25:13—26:32 A Herod hears Paul with the permission of Festus.

29. 26:32 Agrippa says: "This man could have been set free" (ἀπολελύσθαι).

23:18 The Jews cry: "Away with this   **30.**   21:36 The Jews cry: "Away with him"
man" (αἶρε τοῦτον).[21]   (αἶρε αὐτόν).

23:47 A centurion has a favorable opinion **31.**   27:3, 43 A centurion has a favorable re-
of Jesus.   lation with Paul.

The parallelism between the sequence of events in the Third Gospel and Acts which we have noted continues to the conclusions of the two volumes.

Ch. 24 Conclusion. The ministry of Jesus **32.**   Ch. 28 Conclusion. The ministry of Paul
concludes on the positive note of the   concludes on the positive note of the
fulfilment of scripture.[22]   fulfilment of scripture.

Are these remarkable correspondences between the content and sequence of the Third Gospel and the Acts due to the Third Evangelist's deliberate arrangement of his material, or are they due to some other cause? Any answer to this question must start from a "methodical comparison" of the finished form of Luke-Acts with the author's sources, "insofar as these are directly available or can be reconstructed."[23] Since the question of the sources of Acts is so unsettled,[24] it must be primarily in an examination of the Evangelist's use of Mark, Q, and L tradition in the Third Gospel that an answer is sought.[25] Only in rare cases will we have sufficient control over the material in Acts to make a judgment about the presence of the author's hand in a distinctive way. With this in mind, let us now take these parallels in the order in which they appear in the preceding list, looking for any indications in Luke's use of his sources that will point to intentional paralleling on his part.

In the case of the first parallel (Luke 1:1-4 par. Acts 1:1-5) there is little difficulty. Both prefaces are from the Evangelist's own hand (Luke 1:3—"it seemed good to *me*"; Acts 1:1—"In the first book . . . *I* have dealt with all that Jesus began to do and teach.") and were assigned to their respective positions by the author of Luke-Acts.

The second and third parallels may be taken together (Luke 3:21-22 par. Acts 1:14, 24; 2:1-13). The correspondence consists of the fact that (1) the chief characters are praying; (2) the coming of the Spirit is after prayer; and (3) the Spirit's coming is accompanied by a physical manifestation of some sort. Luke 3:21-22 is usually taken to be an adaptation of Mark 1:9-11. It is significant that the Lucan modifications of Mark include (a) the reference to Jesus at his baptism at the time when the Spirit descended upon him; (b) the reference to the Spirit's descent in bodily form. Without these modifications of Mark, the correspondence to Acts 1:14, 24; 2:1-13 would not have been possible. The conclusion seems certain. The parallel is due to the hand of Luke.

The fourth parallel consists of the correspondence of Luke 4:16-30 to Acts 2:14-40 in that each speech (1) opens a period of public ministry, and (2) gives the theme for what follows in that ministry, namely, fulfillment of prophecy and rejection of Jesus by many of the Jewish people. The primary literary question in Luke 4:16-30 is whether this pericope is a free adaptation of Mark 6:1-6 or whether it comes from a special source (L).[26] If it is a Lucan rewriting of Mark 6:1-6 (the rejection at Nazareth), then clearly the correspondence to Acts 2:14-40 is due to Luke for the theme of fulfillment (Luke 4:17-21) is peculiar to Luke as is the position of the rejection pericope in the Gospel. Even if the pericope derives from a special source, it is still necessary to see the correspondence to Acts 2:14-40 as reflecting the Lucan hand. It was Luke who then chose the special tradition in preference to Mark 6:1-6 and who placed it at just this point in his gospel so that it would correspond in sequence to Acts 2:14-40. Again the conclusion seems certain. The parallel is due to the Evangelist.

Within the large sections, Luke 4:31—8:56 parallel to Acts 2:41—12:17, it is necessary to note the several specific correspondences. The first, parallel six in the previous list, consists of Luke 5:17-26's correspondence to Acts 3:1-10 in that both involve the healing of a man who cannot walk. It is perhaps significant that though Luke 5:17-26 comes basically from Mark 2:1-12, the evangelist does compose his own introduction to the Marcan tradition, that is Luke 5:17, in which he says "the power of the Lord was with him to heal."[27] This introductory phrase has the effect of emphasizing that the subsequent healing was due to divine power. It is precisely this emphasis that we find in Acts 3:12-26 where in a speech Peter is made to interpret the previous healing miracle. "Why do you stare at us, as though by our own power or piety we had made him walk?" The emphasis is on the divine power in the healing.

The second specific correspondence within Luke 4:31—8:56, parallel seven in the previous list, consists of Luke 5:29—6:11's similarity to Acts 4:1—8:3 in that both are sections involving conflicts with the religious leaders of the Jews. Luke 5:59—6:11 is taken from Mark 2:15—3:6, a series of conflict stories. No specific changes were required in the Marcan material in order to attain the parallel with Acts 4:1—8:3.

The third specific point of similarity, parallel eight in the previous list, consists in Luke 7:1-10's correspondence to Acts 10 in that both tell of a centurion, popular with the Jews, who sends men to a Jew to invite him to his house in order to gain a boon from him. The chief literary question about the pericope, Luke 7:1-10, is its source. Is it a Lucan adaptation of a Q tradition (cf. Matt 8:5-10) or an L tradition perhaps from circles such as that from which John 4:46-54 came?[28] Whatever one's judgment, it is probable that Luke 7:3-5 is a Lucan modification of the tradition he received. Note that in vs. 3 the centurion sends to ask Jesus to come to his house but in vs. 6 (cf. Matt 8:8) tells him that it is not necessary.[29] Moreover, it is precisely in vss. 3-5 that the details for the correspondence with Acts 10 are found.

Luke 7:11-17 which corresponds to Acts 9:36-43, parallel nine in the previous list, is peculiar to Luke's Gospel (L). That such a tradition should occur just here in the sequence and that it would contain such details as a widow, a resurrection, and the near identical words to the one who had died and the similar description of the revived one's response point to the presence of the Lucan hand in creating the parallel.

Parallel ten in the previous list, the last specific correspondence mentioned within the section Luke 4:31—8:56, consists of Luke 7:36-50's similarity to Acts 11:1-18. Pharisees criticize Jesus and Peter for association with the wrong type of people. The chief literary question about Luke 7:36-50 involves the source from which it came. Is it an expanded version of Mark 14:3-9 transposed from its passion narrative setting in Mark to its Galilean context in Luke?[30] Is it tradition peculiar to Luke (L) which has some kinship with the tradition behind John 12:1-8[31] or is it a combination of two traditions?[32] Whatever one's judgment about the source of Luke 7:36-50 it seems probable that its present emphasis, that of Pharisaic criticism of Jesus' permissiveness toward a sinful woman, is due to the Lucan hand (cf. Luke 14:1; 15:1-2; 16:14; 18:9-14).

Parallel eleven consists of the correspondence of Luke 10:1-12 to Acts 13—14, 16—20. The missionary journeys of Paul to the Gentiles parallel the universalistic tendency of the mission of the seventy (or seventy two) in Luke 10. It may very well be that Luke 10:2-12 comes from Q (with vss. 2-3, 8-16 cf. Matt 9:37-38; 10:7-16) and possibly L (vss. 4-7), but there seems little doubt that Luke 10:1 where reference is made to Jesus' sending out the seventy is Luke's own introduction to the Q missionary charge.[33] Hence the correspondence is due to the Evangelist himself.

The lengthy journeys to Jerusalem made by Jesus in Luke 9:51—19:28 and Paul in Acts 19:21—21:17 form parallel number twelve in the previous list. That the journey section in Luke is the Evangelist's own construction is now almost universally accepted.[34] It is also significant that of the seven separate references to the journey to Jerusalem in the travel section of Luke (parallels thirteen through nineteen), 9:51, 53; 13:22; 17:11; 19:11 and 19:28 are all editorial and 13:33 comes from L tradition. Only the reference in Luke 18:31 possibly derives from Mark (10:32) and even that has been recast. Moreover, where his Marcan source had a reference to entering Jerusalem in 11:11, Luke omits it altogether, saying merely: "And he entered the temple" (19:45). It is perhaps of some importance also to note that whereas Paul's letters would lead one to expect the description of his last journey to Jerusalem in Acts to be drawn as a journey to deliver the collection for the saints (cf. Rom 15:25-27, 31), Acts refers to the collection only once and that indirectly, in 24:17. Instead Acts emphasizes the passion aspect of the journey. That the two journeys are intended by the Evangelist to correspond to one another seems beyond doubt.

With parallel twenty of the previous list, Luke 19:37 par. Acts 21:17-20a, we find ourselves in the section of the Gospel and Acts where the heroes have arrived in Jerusalem. This particular parallel consists in the fact that the two passages correspond in (1) the good reception Jesus and Paul are given upon their entry into the city, and (2) the praise addressed to God by various people. Luke 19:28-38 comes from Mark 11:1-10. The Lucan modification of Mark is significant. The Evangelist adds vs. 37 which has χαίροντες and αἰνεῖν τὸν θεὸν φωνῇ μεγάλῃ περὶ πασῶν ὧν εἶδον δυνάμεων.

Luke 19:45-48 which corresponds to Acts 21:26, parallel twenty-one in the previous list, does so on two counts: (1) both Jesus and Paul enter the temple soon after arrival, and (2) both show a friendly attitude toward it. Luke 19:45-48 comes from Mark 11:11, 15-18, but reflects at least two significant modifications of Mark. First, the Third Gospel abbreviates Mark's account. Whereas Mark has two trips of Jesus into the temple separated by the cursing of the fig tree (Mark 11:12-14), Luke has only one trip and the cursing of the fig tree is omitted. This has the effect of taking the note of rejection out of the cleansing and softens its harshness. Second, Jesus is portrayed as teaching continually in the temple. This gives the impression that he is favorably disposed towards it. Here again, therefore, the modifications made by Luke in his source appear significant.

The twenty-second parallel in the previous list, Luke 20:27-39 parallel to Acts 23:6-9, consists of two correspondences: (1) the Sadducees' disbelief in the resurrection, and (2) the scribal support for Jesus and Paul. Among the changes Luke makes in Mark 12:18-27 is the addition of vs. 39 to show the support of the scribes. This appears intentional and may be in the interest of the parallel.

The twenty-third parallel in our list consists of the correspondence of Luke 22:19a to Acts 27:35 in that both speak of a meal at which the chief character "takes bread, gives thanks, and breaks it," in near identical language. The chief literary question with respect to Luke 22:15-20 is whether this account of the last supper comes from an independent passion source or whether it represents a rewritten version of Mark 14:22-25.[35] However one settles the question of Luke's source at this point, a comparison of Luke 22:19a with Mark 14:22 reveals both remarkable similarities and at least one important difference. Mark 14:22 reads: καὶ ἐσθιόντων αὐτῶν λαβὼν ἄρτον εὐλογήσας ἔκλασεν καὶ ἔδωκεν αὐτοῖς καὶ εἶπεν λάβετε τοῦτό ἐστιν τὸ σῶμά μου. Luke 22:19a runs καὶ λαβὼν ἄρτον εὐχαριστήσας ἔκλασεν καὶ ἔδωκεν αὐτοῖς λέγων τοῦτό ἐστιν τὸ σῶμά μου. (Identical words in the same order are underlined.) Note that instead of Mark's εὐλογήσας Luke has εὐχαριστήσας. It is doubtless significant that Acts 27:35 has εὐχαρίστησεν in its reference to Paul's breaking bread. Thus whether Luke was adapting Mark or whether he chose to use a non-Marcan tradition, it appears that he did so at least in part[36] in order to facilitate the parallel with Acts 27:35.

Parallel twenty-four in the previous list consists of the correspondence of Luke 22:54 to Acts 21:30 in that mobs seize both Jesus and Paul. In vs. 54 Luke adds συλλαβόντες to Mark 14:53's statement that they ἀγήγαγον Jesus to the high priest. Matt 26:57 has Jesus seized but his word is κρατήσαντες. Luke's addition may very well be significant since Acts 21:30 uses the cognate ἐπιλαβόμενοι with reference to Paul's seizure.

In Luke 22:63-64 Jesus is slapped by the priest's assistants much like Paul is slapped at the high priest's command in Acts 23:2. No alteration in Mark 14:65 was necessary for this parallel.

The twenty-sixth parallel in the list consists of the four trials of Jesus (Luke 22:26; 23:1; 23:8; 23:13) corresponding to the four trials of Paul (Acts 23; 24; 25; 26). Again, whether the fourfold trial of Jesus is due to Luke's rewriting of Mark so that instead of Mark's three (14:53; 15:1; 15:2) he would have four trials, or whether Luke has here employed an independent source,[37] it seems probable that he did so in order to have both Jesus and Paul go through a fourfold trial process. This judgment is confirmed by the fact that certain details in the process are uniquely Lucan. The threefold declaration of Jesus' innocence by Pilate (Luke 23:4, 14, 22b) is distinctively Lucan (parallel twenty-seven). The trial before Herod in Luke 23:6-12 is peculiar to Luke (parallel twenty-eight). The declaration by Pilate that he will release Jesus (Luke 23:16, 22) is Lucan (parallel twenty-nine). The closest thing to it in Mark is found in 15:9 where Pilate asks: "Do you want me to release for you the King of the Jews?" The cry of the Jews, "Away with this man" (Luke 23:18), is found only in Luke (parallel thirty). The centurion in Luke 23:47 says of Jesus, "Certainly this man was innocent" (parallel thirty-one), whereas in Mark 15:39 he says, "Truly this man was the Son of God." The significance of all of these distinctively Lucan tendencies is that each one was necessary in order to have the narrative of Jesus' trial correspond to some similar Pauline situation in Acts. The entire trial sequence in Luke is shaped, therefore, in order to parallel the trial sequence of Paul in Acts.

The conclusion of the Third Gospel (Luke 24) and the end of Acts (ch. 28) correspond in that each ends on the note of the fulfilment of scripture. In Luke 24 only one of the several traditions could possibly derive from Mark (Luke 24: 1-11, cf. Mark 16:1-8).[38] The appearance on the road to Emmaus (Luke 24:13-32) and the appearance to the eleven in Jerusalem (24:33-49) are found only in Luke. Each of these narratives ends on the same note. Luke 24:32 reads: "Did not our hearts burn within us while he talked to us on the road, while he opened to us the scriptures?" This, of course, refers back to vss. 25-27 and the motif of fulfillment of scripture in the career of Jesus. Luke 24:44-49 contains the same emphasis. The risen Christ says: "These are my words which I spoke to you, while I was still with you, that everything written about me in the law of Moses and the prophets and the psalms must be fulfilled" (24:44). It is highly likely that both vss. 25-27 and vss. 44-49 are Lucan compositions,[39] reflecting a distinctively Lucan point of view (cf. Acts 3:18;[40] 1:4, 8). The end of Luke reflects the hand of the Evangelist in areas necessary to have Luke 24 correspond to Acts 28.

from the preceding examination of the Third Evangelist's use of his sources in the Gospel of Luke it appears that where modifications were necessary to achieve a loose correspondence of content and sequence between persons and events in the Third Gospel and those of the Acts, they were made without hesitation. The conclusion seems irrestible. This architectonic pattern which has Gospel and Acts correspond in content and in sequence at many points is due to deliberate editorial activity by the author of Luke-Acts.

Acts 1-12 and 13-28

If the most basic architectonic pattern in Luke-Acts consists of the remarkable correspondences both in content and sequence between the events and persons found in Luke and those of Acts, the most widely recognized aspect of the Lucan architecture consists of the correspondences between chs. 1—12 and chs. 13—28 of Acts. Called to scholarly attention at least as early as Matthias Schneckenburger's *Uber den Zweck der Apostelgeschichte*,[41] These correspondences became a major plank in the Tübingen school's attack on the historicity of Acts.[42] Often without drawing the same conclusions about Acts' historicity that Baur's followers had drawn, English-speaking scholars have frequently called attention to the same architectural pattern.[43] Only rarely have the correspondences between these two halves of Acts been denied.[44] The correspondences between Acts 1—12 and 13—28 include a loose parallelism of content and sequence along with certain similarities which do not occur in any specific order. We mention first the list of parallels which involve both content and sequence. Again the following list contains a synthesis of representative suggestions made since the early nineteenth century, together with my own observations.

2:1-4 A special manifestation of the Spirit.[45]	**1.**	13:1-3 A special manifestation of the Spirit.
2:14-40 Apostolic preaching results from the special manifestation of the Spirit.[46]	**2.**	13:16-40 Apostolic preaching results from the special manifestation of the Spirit.
3:1-10 A mighty work follows. A man, lame from birth, is healed.[47]	**3.**	14:8-13 A mighty work follows. A man, lame from birth, is healed.
3:12-26 The healing of the lame man is followed by a speech prompted by the response to the healing. It begins, "Men . . . why?"[48]	**4.**	14:15-17 The healing of the lame man is followed by a speech prompted by the response to the healing. It begins, "Men . . . why?"
6:8—8:4 Stephen is stoned to death at the instigation of Jews from Asia and elsewhere after a speech. The result of the persecution is the spread of the preaching in a widening circle.	**5.**	14:19-23 Paul is stoned at the instigation of Jews from Antioch and Iconium after a speech so that he is supposed dead. The result of the persecution is further preaching in a wider context.
Chs. 10—11 Peter has a mission to the Gentiles (cf. 15:7-11). Divine guidance leads Peter in a direction other than that planned by him. In 10:9-16 Peter objects three times but the Spirit guides him through a vision. Peter then has to justify his actions in Jerusalem.[49]	**6.**	Chs. 13—21 Paul has a mission to the Gentiles. Divine guidance leads Paul in a direction other than that planned by him. In 16:6-10 Paul, through a vision, is led to Macedonia. Both in ch. 15 and ch. 21 Paul has to justify his actions in Jerusalem.

Ch. 12 The first half of Acts ends with the imprisonment of Peter (12:4) at an important Jewish feast (12:4). Peter's imprisonment is associated with a Herod (12:5-6, 11); involves escape from the hands of the Jews (12:3-4, 6-11); concludes abruptly with no information about the fate of Peter (12:17); but Acts does make a statement about the success of the Word of God (12:24).[50]

7. Chs. 21—28 The second half of Acts ends with the imprisonments of Paul, beginning at an important Jewish feast (21:16). Paul's imprisonment in Palestine has a loose relation to a Herod (25:13, 23-24); involves escape from death at the hands of the Jews (23:12-35); concludes rather abruptly with no information about the fate of Paul (28:30-31); but Acts does give a statement about the success of the Word of God (28:30-31).

Next we may offer a representative list which gives certain similarities of content and language between Acts 1-12 and 13-28 but which occur in no apparent systematic order.[51]

8:9-24 Peter and John confront a magician, Simon, who draws Peter's curse.[52]

1. 13:6-12 Barnabas and Saul confront a magician, Elymas, who draws Paul's curse.

9:36-43 Peter raises Dorcas from the dead.[53]

2. 20:9-12 Paul raises Eutychus from the dead.

10:25-26 Peter restrains the Gentile Cornelius from worshipping him with the words, "Stand up; I too am a man."[54]

3. 14:13-15 Barnabas and Paul restrain the Gentiles at Lystra from worshipping them with the words, "We also are men, of like nature with you."

12:6-11 Peter is miraculously delivered from prison.[55]

4. 16:24-26 Paul and Silas are miraculously delivered from prison.

8:14-17 The Spirit is given by the laying on of the hands of the Jerusalem apostles.[56]

5. 19:1-6 The Spirit is given by the laying on of the hands of Paul.

6:1-6 The Jerusalem apostles appoint the Seven with prayer and laying on of hands.[57]

6. 14:23 Barnabas and Paul appoint elders with prayer and fasting.

5:34-39 A Pharisee defends the Jerusalem apostles in the Sanhedrin.[58]

7. 23:9 Pharisees defend Paul in the Sanhedrin.

6:13-14 Stephen is accused of acts against the law, the temple, and the customs of Moses.[59]

8. 21:20-21; 25:8 Paul is accused of acts against the law, the temple, and customs of Moses.

1:21-22 The Jerusalem apostles are designated witnesses by the risen Christ.[60]

9. 23:11; 26:16 Paul is designated a witness by the risen Christ.

What shall we say about these similarities between chs. 1—12 and 13—28 of Acts? Are they due to the author of Acts or to some other cause, perhaps either the actual history of the early church or Luke's sources? If they are due to the author of Acts, were they consciously intended or caused by "a tendency to assimilation or to the stereotyping of incidents of which he himself was quite unconscious"?[61]

Would it be possible to argue that the correspondences between the two halves of Acts are due to the fact that the lives of Peter and other Jerusalem Christians on the one hand and Paul on the other actually contained the same kinds of events? Can we say with Rackham, "The parallelism arises out of the facts"?[62] Granted the fact that the Acts of the Apostles does not recount everything which happened in the early church and/or in the lives of Peter and other Jerusalem Christians on the one side and Paul and other Gentile Christian missionaries on the other, we must reckon with the selectivity of the author of Acts. Assuming for the sake of the argument that every incident in Acts is historical, one still has to account for the selection of the materials that are included as well as the relative order of those in the first list and the remarkable verbal similarities throughout both lists. Even if one claims the essential historicity of every incident in Acts, therefore, he still has to recognize the creative efforts of the author. At the few points, moreover, where the evidence of the Pauline epistles gives us some control over the data, there is either epistolary silence about the events of Acts or one gains from the epistles an impression of a different turn of events (cf. e.g., Acts 13: 1-3 with Gal 1—2).[63]

Would it then be possible to argue that the parallels are due to the sources employed by the author of Acts? This might be a plausible line of reasoning if we could assume that behind our Acts is a single source which has been only slightly retouched by the Third Evangelist.[64] Such a view of the sources for Acts, however, has no serious adherents today.[65] If we assume two sources behind Acts, an Acts of Peter and the other Jerusalem Christians on the one side and an Acts of Paul on the other, would it then be possible to attribute the parallels to Luke's sources? Hardly. It would be necessary to posit for both sources a common pattern involving a common principle of selectivity for the events. For the parallels which follow a similar sequence, it would furthermore be necessary to posit two sources which also placed the selected events in the same order. Such an assumption places too great a strain on one's credulity. What is more, no such view of the sources of Acts is held today.[66] At best, if we held that one half of Acts goes back to a single source (e.g., Acts 1—15),[67] then the other half must have been constructed in its present shape by the author of Acts. If we assume multiple sources behind Acts,[68] written or oral or both, again we would find the author's selectivity and arrangement are decisive. It seems impossible, therefore, in light of the present state of source analysis of Acts, to attribute the correspondences between Acts 1—12 and 13—28 to the author's sources.[69]

If by the process of elimination of possibilities it seems certain that the correspondences between the two halves of Acts are due to the author of Acts, is it possible to say whether the parallels are consciously contrived or unconsciously effected? Cadbury, for example, thinks that it "was scarcely intentional repetition"[70] when Luke put such similar speeches into the mouths of Peter and Paul in Acts 2:14-40 and 13:16-41 (parallel 2 in the first list). When we consider not only the similar speeches but also their location in a sequence at just the point that they are, however, it is more difficult to assume unconscious repetition. Also in light of the parallels between the Third Gospel and Acts which were seen to rest on Luke's adaptation of his sources in the Gospel, one feels more inclined to see conscious rather than unconscious paralleling by the author of Acts. Final judgment, however, must await our evaluation of all the evidence to be assembled later both from within Luke-Acts and from the Evangelist's environment. For the time being we may conclude tentatively that the correspondences between Acts 1—12 and 13—28 are consciously contrived, the product of deliberate editorial activity on his sources by Luke.

Luke 9:1-48 and 22:7-23:16

If the primary architectonic pattern in Luke-Acts is the remarkable parallelism both in content and sequence between the events and persons found in Luke and those of Acts, and if the over-all architecture of Acts consists of correspondences between the two main parts of the volume, Jewish Christianity (Acts 1—12) and Gentile Christianity (Acts 13—28), one should not be surprised to find a similar, though not identical, architectonic scheme in the Gospel according to Luke. In the Third Gospel there are significant correspondences between the content of ch. 9 and that of chs. 22—23, that is, between certain events in Galilee and others in Jerusalem. Events mentioned in ch. 9 are either referred to or echoed in chs. 22—23, though not often in the same order. Except for one or two of these correspondences, to my knowledge, they have so far eluded scholarly detection.[71] Seeing the correspondences in parallel columns makes Luke's procedure easier to grasp.

Luke 9:1-48		Luke 22:7—23:16
9:1-6 Jesus sends out the Twelve. Regulations are given for the journey.	1.	22:35-38 There is a recollection by Jesus of the time he sent out the Twelve. The regulations for the journey are mentioned.
9:7-9 Herod hears of Jesus and seeks to see him.	2.	23:6-16 Herod is glad Jesus is sent to him for he had heard about him and was hoping to see some sign.
9:10-17 Jesus speaks of the Kingdom of God in connection with a meal. He blessed, broke, and gave to the disciples to distribute.	3.	22:7-19a (19b-20) Jesus speaks of the Kingdom of God in connection with a meal. He gave thanks, broke, and gave to the disciples.
9:20-22 Peter makes a confession immediately following the meal.	4.	22:31-34 Peter makes a confession immediately following a meal.
9:23-27 If any man would come after me, let him . . . take up his cross daily.	5.	22:28-30 You . . . who have continued with me in my trails.
9:28-36 Jesus is on a mountain with his disciples. As he prays, he has heavenly visitors appear to him and speak of his departure. The disciples are sleepy.	6.	22:39-46 Jesus is on the Mount of Olives with his disciples. As he prays about his death a heavenly visitor appears to him. The disciples are sleeping.
9:37-43a Immediately upon coming down from the mountain Jesus performs a miracle. There is a sharp contrast drawn between Jesus and the disciples.	7.	22:47-53 Immediately after the mountain scene Jesus performs a miracle. There is a sharp contrast drawn between Jesus and his disciples.

9:43*b*-45 The Son of man is to be de-   **8.**   22:21-23 The Son of man goes as it has
livered into the hands of men.   been determined, but woe to the
                                                   man by whom he is betrayed.

9:46-48 There is a dispute over greatness. **9.**   ¨22:24-27 There is a dispute over great-
                                                   ness.

Such correspondences between the climax to the Galilean section of the Third
Gospel and the beginning of the Lucan passion narrative are striking. The
question that must be raised immediately is whether these similarities in
content and language, and occasionally in sequence, are due to the Evangelist
or to some other cause? This can only be answered after an investigation of
Luke's treatment of his sources. Let us then take these correspondences in the
order in which they appear in the preceding list, looking for any indications in
Luke's use of his sources that will point to intentional paralleling on his part.

The first correspondence consists of the similarity between Luke 9:1-6
and 22:35-38 at two points. Both speak of the sending out of the Twelve and
both refer to the regulations for the journey. Though Luke 9:1-6 comes from
Mark 6:7-13 there is a significant modification of Mark found in the
regulations. Mark 6:8 instructs the disciples to take nothing except a staff.
Luke 9:3's instructions say to take nothing at all. The change is significant
because Luke 22:35 implies that the disciples were told to take nothing at all.
Hence the alteration of Mark appears deliberate. Luke 22:35-38 is found only
in Luke and should most likely be classified L tradition.[72] That such tradition
was included in Luke's passion narrative at just this point is surely significant.
The probability is that such inclusion was deliberate and quite possibly in the
interest of the first correspondence.

The second correspondence between Luke 9 and 22—23 consists of the
references to Herod's hearing about Jesus and to his desire to see him found in
both 9:7-9 and 23:6-16. Luke 9:7-9 comes essentially from Mark 6:14-16, but
the Lucan form has a significant modification of Mark. Luke 9:9*b* adds to
Mark that Herod "sought to see him." This appears intended to parallel Luke
23:8 where Luke says that Herod had long desired to see Jesus. Luke 23:6-16,
Christ before Herod, is found only in Luke and is probably L tradition.[73] Why
it was inserted into Luke's passion narrative is in part doubtless due to Luke's
desire for this second correspondence.

The third correspondence between chs. 9 and 22—23 of Luke (9:10-17
par. 22:7-19) may be taken together with the fourth (9:20-22 par. 22:31-34).
The similarity consists of the fact that there is a meal scene in which Jesus does
two things: (1) he speaks of the Kingdon of God, and (2) he blesses, breaks,
and distributes the bread. This is followed by a confession of Peter. Luke 9:10-
17 comes basically from Mark 6:30-44, but there is an important Lucan
addition. In vs. 11 the Third Evangelist adds that Jesus spoke of the Kingdom
of God, obviously necessary for the parallel. Luke 9:20-22 is derived from
Mark 8:27-33. In order to achieve the connection between Peter's confession
in 9:20-22 and the meal at which Jesus speaks of the Kingdom of God, Luke

omits Mark 6:45—8:26, some seventy-four verses.[74] Luke 22:15-19a (19b-20)
is complicated by two major problems. First, there is the textual question. Is
the Lucan text represented by the longer (22:15-20) or shorter (22:15-19a)
version?[75] Second, there is the question of Luke's source for the last supper
tradition. Is 22:15-20 a modification of Mark 14:22-25 or is Luke here relying
on an independent tradition (L)?[76] Regardless of how either or both of these
problems should be settled, the matter of the parallel with Luke 9:10-17 is not
affected. The shorter text as well as the longer one contains all the details
necessary for the parallel. Whether the tradition comes from Mark or from L
the parallel holds. Luke 22:31-34 also presents a problem of source analysis. Is
it an adaptation of Mark 14:26-31 or is it from an independent source (L)?[77] If
it is an adaptation of Mark it is significant that whereas in Mark Peter's
"confession" is set in the context of a journey to the Mount of Olives, Luke
locates it during the meal referred to in 22:15-19a (19b-20). Only at Luke 22:39
do Jesus and his disciples go out to the Mount of Olives. If the tradition comes
from an independent tradition (L), then one has to ask himself why Luke
located the "confession" of Peter during the meal instead of on the way to the
Mount of Olives as in Mark. It would appear that the correspondence the
Evangelist was setting up demanded a confession by Peter in connection with
a meal at which Jesus spoke of the Kingdom of God. The third and fourth
correspondences, therefore, appear to be intentionally contrived by the Third
Evangelist.

   Correspondence number five consists of the similarity of Luke 9:23-27 to
22:28-30, by virtue of the statement, "If any man would come after me, let him
. . . take up his cross daily and follow me," which is echoed in the words, "You
are those who have continued with me in my trials." The correspondence is
furthered by Luke's alteration of Mark 8:34—9:1 so that Luke 9:23 adds
"daily" to cross bearing. This is probably in line with the emphasis of
"continued with me" in 22:28. It is perhaps significant that although 22:28-30
likely echoes the same tradition that is found in a slightly different form in
Matthew 19:28, vs. 28 is only "a connecting verse supplied by Luke,"[78] since
vs. 28 is the essential ingredient for the parallel with 9:23.

   Correspondences six and seven in the previous list may be taken together.
The similarities between 9:28-36, 37-43a on the one hand and 22:39-46, 47-53
on the other are: (1) Jesus is on a mountain with his disciples; (2) as he prays
there appear(s) a heavenly visitor(s); (3) the sleepiness of the disciples; (4) the
performance of a miracle immediately after the mountain scene; and (5) the
sharp contrast drawn between the disciples and Jesus. Luke 9:28-36 adds three
significant facts to Mark's account (9:2-8). Luke says: (1) Jesus was praying;
(2) the conversation between Jesus and the two heavenly figures who appeared
(ὀφθέντες) to him was about his departure; (3) the disciples were sleepy. The
relevance of these additions to the parallel with Luke 22:39-46 is apparent.
Like his Marcan source (9:14-29), Luke follows the mountain scene with a
miracle story (9:37-43a). Luke 22:39-46 probably comes from Mark 14:32-
42.[79] If so, two significant changes in Mark by Luke need to be noted. First,

Luke changes Mark's Gethsemane, 14:32, to the Mount of Olives. Second, he says that a heavenly figure appeared (ὤφθη) to Jesus though Mark relates no such event.[80] Again the importance of these Lucan modifications of Mark is apparent. Luke 22:47-53 also is from Mark (14:43-52),[81] but as so frequently happens elsewhere in Luke, it contains a significant addition to Mark's narrative. Though Mark relates how one of Jesus' disciples cut off the ear of the slave of the high priest, it is left to the Third Evangelist to make the tradition into a miracle story. In 22:51 Luke adds that Jesus "touched his ear and healed him." This was necessary for the parallel. Correspondences six and seven then are clearly due to Luke's intentional adaptation of his sources.

The eighth correspondence in the previous list consists of the similarity of Luke 9:43b-45 to 22:21-23. Luke 9:43b-45 contains no significant alteration of Mark 9:30-32 for our purposes. The same is true of Luke 22:21-23's use of Mark 14:17-21. The two predictions of his coming death by Jesus were already present in Luke's sources in approximately the positions needed.

The ninth and final of this series of correspondences consists of the disputes over greatness in Luke 9:46-48 and 22:24-27. Luke 9:46-48 comes from Mark 9:33-37 and contains no relevant variations. Luke 22:24-27 is another matter. The literary question here is whether 22:24-27 comes from Mark 10:42-45 and has been relocated by Luke at this point in his passion narrative or whether 22:24-27 comes from a special Lucan source (L).[82] Regardless of how one settles the issue, it is clear that the Lucan hand is apparent. If the material comes from Mark, why its position here? If it is L tradition, again we must ask, why does it come at this point in the passion narrative? The probable answer is that it appears in the passion narrative at this point in order to make possible the parallel with 9:46-48.

In almost every case, therefore, where we can trace the Lucan use of sources we have found what appears to be deliberate adaptation of his source material by the Third Evangelist so as to effect the correspondences between Luke 9 and 22-23. Luke's treatment of his sources points to an intentional arrangement of material on his part. Thus, just as the author of Luke-Acts arranged his material so that the Acts would correspond to the Third Gospel and so that the two halves of the Acts would correspond to each other, so he has tied the two major parts of his Gospel together with a similar architectonic scheme.

FOOTNOTES

[1]It is not the intention within this volume to deal with all the patterns of Luke-Acts which express the principle of balance that so influenced the Evangelist. We will treat eleven of the major patterns. Nor does this volume's treatment of these eleven patterns which are expressions of the principle of balance mean to imply that there are not other types of architectural design at work in Luke-Acts. The literature of antiquity would seem to imply that more than one architectural principle should be expected (see ch. 1, n. 68). Since in the ancient world two or three types of architectonic design may be operative in the construction of a literary document at the same time, it is unnecessary in arguing my thesis to attempt to exclude other structural schemes that have been proposed by various scholars.

[2]When a change in his source is made by Luke, how can one say that it was made for this or that reason? In practice what occurs is this. The scholar notes a particular change made by Luke. If he is aware that the effect of this change, be it architectural or theological, is consistent with the effect of changes Luke has made elsewhere, then he makes an inference. The change, he says, reflects a tendency of the Evangelist. If there is a Lucan tendency in a certain direction generally, then one infers it is intentional in this particular case. If one finds that a change serves both an architectural and a theological tendency, then an inference in both directions is in order.

[3]C. K. Barrett, *Luke the Historian in Recent Study,* 55. In my opinion, Acts has the logical priority in the Lucan scheme. Hence the question should be: why did Luke prefix a Gospel to his Acts? Cf. my paper, "The Redaction Critical Quest for Luke the Thologian," in *Jesus and Man's Hope: Proceedings of the Pittsburgh Festival on the Gospels* (2 vols.; Pittsburgh Theological Seminary, 1970) 1. 202 and *passim.*

[4]Only rarely is the sequence violated. Cf. parallels 9, 22, 23, 30.

[5]R. B. Rackham, *The Acts of the Apostles* (London: Methuen, 1901) xlvii.

[6]From among many we may mention F. B. Clogg, *An Introduction to the New Testament* (London: University of London Press, 1954) 247-48; Lucien Cerfaux, "The Acts of the Apostles," in *Introduction to the New Testament,* 332, and *The Four Gospels* (Baltimore: Newman, 1960) 61; Violet Wilkinson, *The Centre of History* (London: Oxford University Press, 1967) 75.

[7]Rackham, *Acts of the Apostles,* xlvii.

[8]Although Helmut Flender, *St. Luke: Theologian of Redemptive History,* 139, claims that Luke draws no parallel between the baptism of Jesus and the Spirit-baptism at Pentecost, such a parallel seems fairly certain. So Rackham, *Acts of the Apostles,* xlvii; G. W. H. Lampe, *The Seal of the Spirit* (London: Longmans, Green & Co., 1951) 44; F. F. Bruce, *Commentary on the Book of Acts* (Grand Rapids: Eerdmans, 1956) 39, n. 29; M. D. Goulder, *Type and History in Acts,* 54; Adrian Hastings, *Prophet and Witness in Jerusalem* (Baltimore: Helicon, 1958) 12.

[9]G. W. H. Lampe, "The Holy Spirit in the Writings of St. Luke," in *Studies in the Gospels: Essays in Memory of R. H. Lightfoot* (ed. D. E. Nineham; Oxford: Basil Blackwell, 1955) 159; Hastings, *Prophet and Witness,* 12.

[10]Goulder, *Type and History in Acts,* 55.

[11]Edward Zeller, *The Acts of the Apostles* (2 vols.; London: Williams & Norgate, 1875-6) 2. 230-31; Maurice Goguel, *The Birth of Christianity* (New York: Macmillan, 1954) 93; A. R. C. Leaney, *A Commentary on the Gospel according to St. Luke* (New York: Harper, 1958) 141; Louis Marin, "Essai d'analyse structurale d'Actes 10:1-11:18," *RSR* 58 (1970) 51.

[12]H. Flender, *St. Luke,* 23. "The number 70 (72) denotes all the nations of the world, seventy in Genesis 10, seventy-two in the LXX. The sending of the Seventy in 10:1ff. prefigures the universal mission to the Gentiles." Cf. also Lampe, "The Holy Spirit in the Writings of St. Luke," 190.

[13]Lampe, "The Holy Spirit in the Writings of St. Luke," 196; J. C. O'Neill, *The Theology of Acts in Its Historical Setting* (London: S.P.C.K., 1961) 63; Flender, *St. Luke,* 131 and 131, n. 3; H. J. Cadbury, The Making of Luke-Acts, 232.

[14]The textual problem, whether the longer or the shorter text, makes no difference in this parallel.

[15]Bo Reicke, "Die Mahlzeit mit Paulus auf den Wellen des Mittelmeers, Acta 27:33-38," *TZ* 4 (1948) 401-10, points out the formal similarities between the last supper in Luke and Paul's meal in Acts 27. He, however, wants to argue for a sacramental interpretation of Acts 27:35. Granting the formal similarities, it would seem that even if this is a genuine historical reference to a sacramental meal observed by Paul on his voyage to Rome its present form which corresponds to Luke 22 must surely be due to the author of Luke-Acts.

[16]Robert Morgenthaler, *Die lukanische Geschichtsschreibung als Zeugnis*, 1. 182-3.

[17]Goulder, *Type and History in Acts*, 40.

[18]Morgenthaler, *Die lukanische Geschichtsschreibung als Zeugnis*, 1. 182-3.

[19]*Ibid.;* also cf. Lampe, "The Holy Spirit in the Writings of St. Luke," 196.

[20]*Ibid.*

[21]*Ibid.* Cf. n. 4.

[22]J. B. Lightfoot, *Saint Paul's Epistle to the Philippians* (London: Macmillan, 1896) 3, n. 2; Paul Schubert, "The Structure and Significance of Luke 24," in *Neutestamentliche Studien für Rudolf Bultmann,* (ed. W. Eltester; Berlin: Alfred Toepelmann, 1954) 165-86.

[23]Hans Conzelmann, *The Theology of St. Luke,* 12.

[24]A point well made by Jacques Dupont, *The Sources of Acts* (London: Darton, Longman & Todd. 1964).

[25]Cf. n. 69 in ch. 1.

[26]G. W. H. Lampe, "The Holy Spirit in the Writings of St. Luke," 171, argues that the pericope is a Lucan re-writing of Mark. Emanuel Hirsch, *Frühgeschichte des Evangeliums, II: Die Vorlagen des Lukas und das Sondergut des Matthäus* (Tübingen: J. C. B. Mohr [Paul Siebeck], 1941) 38-41, thinks 4:16-30 is a combination of Mark and L.

[27]Leaney, *A Commentary on the Gospel according to St. Luke,* 124.

[28]E. Hirsch, *Frühgeschichte des Evangeliums, II.* 88-90, and G. B. Caird, *Saint Luke* (Baltimore: Penguin Books, 1963) 108, both think it is from Q.

[29]Leaney, *A Commentary on the Gospel according to St. Luke,* 141.

[30]So Erich Klostermann, *Das Lukasevangelium* (Tübingen: J. C. B. Mohr þPaul Siebeckῑ, 1919) 454.

[31]So Caird, *Saint Luke,* 25, 115; Hirsch, *Frühgeschichte des Evangeliums, II.* 199-205.

[32]So Leaney, *A Commentary on the Gospel according to St. Luke,* 146.

[33]Rudolf Bultmann, *The History of the Synoptic Tradition* (Oxford: Basil Blackwell, 1963) 334; Caird, *Saint Luke,* 144.

[34]Most recently, cf. W. C. Robinson, Jr., "The Theological Context for Interpreting Luke's Travel Narrative," *JBL* 79 (1960) 20-31; also W. G. Kümmel, *Introduction to the New Testament* (Nashville: Abingdon, 1965) 99-100.

[35]Joachim Jeremias, *The Eucharistic Words of Jesus* (London: SCM, 1966) 99, ascribes the pericope to an independent passion narrative peculiar to Luke. Conzelmann, *Theology of St. Luke, passim,* represents the more usual view that Luke is a rewriting of Mark.

[36]In part it may be an assimilation to εὐχαριστήσας in vs. 17.

[37]As Paul Winter, "The Treatment of His Sources by the Third Evangelist in Luke 21-24," *ST* 8 (1954) 158.

[38]Winter (*ibid.,* 166) thinks it does come from Mark.

[39]Rudolf Bultmann, *The History of the Synoptic Tradition,* 286; W. E. Bundy, *Jesus and the First Three Gospels* (Harvard University Press, 1955) 570, 572.

[40]J. A. T. Robinson, "The Earliest Christology of All?" in *Twelve New Testament Studies* (London: SCM, 1962) 145-146.

[41](Bern: Christian Fischer, 1841). Cf. especially 52-56.

[42]Cf. Edward Zeller, *The Acts of the Apostles* (2 vols.; London: Williams & Norgate, 1875-6).

[43]Rackham, *Acts,* xlvii-xlviii; H. J. Cadbury, *The Making of Luke-Acts,* 232; R. R. Williams, *The Acts of the Apostles* (London: SCM, 1953) 24; F. F. Bruce, *Commentary on the Book of Acts,* 387, n. 13; R. W. Funk, "The Enigma of the Famine Visit," *JBL* 75 (1956) 134.

[44]Most recently by P. H. Menoud, "Le Plan des Actes des Apôtres," *NTS* 1 (1954) 44-51. Menoud argues against the division of Acts into the two halves, chs. 1—12 and 13—28, on two

grounds: (1) chs. 6—7 in their entirety and chs. 8, 9, 11 in part are not concerned with Peter and in ch. 15 Paul is not the chief actor; (2) Luke's major interest in Acts is in the extension the Spirit gives the church by apostolic means, not in the persons of the apostles. Menoud suggests a division of Acts into two parts, chs. 1—15:35 and 15:36—ch. 28. This division, however, is also subject to criticism. (1) Chs. 13—14 are concerned to emphasize the same things that one finds in chs. 16—20 and the chief actor, Paul, is the same in each section. (2) The parallels between chs. 1—12 and chs. 13—28 are not merely between Peter and Paul but rather between various persons and events associated most closely with Jerusalem Christianity and persons and events associated most closely with Gentile Christianity outside Palestine. That Peter is not the actor in chs. 8, 9, 11 is of little consequence. Ch. 15 is necessary in the second half of Acts just as ch. 11 is in the first part. (3) Even if Luke's emphasis in Acts is on the extension of the gospel, it includes a desire to assimilate the actions and words of Jewish Christian missionaries to those of Gentile Christian missionaries. Menoud's arguments, therefore, leave the traditional division of Acts into two parts, chs. 1—12 and 13—28, untouched. Cf. n. 1.

[45]Rackham, *Acts,* xlvii; Funk, *JBL* 75 (1956) 134.

[46]Goulder, *Type and History in Acts,* 83, gives a detailed list of similarities between the two speeches. (1) 2:22-23—13:27-28; (2) 2:24—13:30; (3) 2:25-28—13:35; (4) 2:29—13:36; (5) 2:30-32—13:23, 37.

[47]Rackham, *Acts,* xlviii; Bruce, *Commentary on Acts,* 387, n. 13; Goulder, *Type and History in Acts,* 107.

[48]C. H. Talbert, *Luke and the Gnostics* (Nashville: Abingdon, 1966) 85.

[49]Ernst Haenchen, *Die Apostelgeschichte* (12th ed; Gottingen: Vandenhoeck & Ruprecht, 1959) 425.

[50]Adolf Harnack, *New Testament Studies III: The Acts of the Apostles* 42; C. H. Talbert, "Again: Paul's Visits to Jerusalem," *NovT* 9 (1967) 39-40.

[51]Rackham, *Acts,* xlvii, gives an even fuller list than that given here.

[52]Bruce, *Commentary on Acts,* 387, n. 13; C. S. C. Williams, *The Acts of the Apostles* (New York: Harper, 1957) 156; Talbert, *Luke and the Gnostics,* 86.

[53]Bruce, *Commentary on Acts,* 387, n. 13; Talbert, *Luke and the Gnostics,* 86.

[54]*Ibid.*

[55]*Ibid.*

[56]Rackham, *Acts,* xlviii.

[57]*Ibid.*

[58]*Ibid.*

[59]Talbert, *Luke and the Gnostics,* 86.

[60]Schneckenburger, *Über den Zweck der Apostelgeschichte,* 56.

[61]Cadbury, *The Making of Luke-Acts,* 232.

[62]Rackham, *Acts,* xlix.

[63]This paragraph has followed basically the same line of argument taken in *Luke and the Gnostics,* 87.

[64]Cf. Jacques Depont, *The Sources of Acts,* 17-24, for a summary of the views of Sorof, Gercke, Norden, and Loisy.

[65]Dupont, *Sources,* 24, following Kümmel.

[66]Dupont, *Sources, passim.*

[67]Cf. Dupont, *Sources,* 25-32, for a summary of such views.

[68]As is commonly done today (e.g., Dibelius, Haenchen, Dupont) but without any agreement as to what they are.

[69]This is an expansion of the argument used in *Luke and the Gnostics,* 88.

[70]*The Making of Luke-Acts,* 232.

[71]So far as I know, they were first set forth in published form in my article, "The Lukan Presentation of Jesus' Ministry in Galilee," *RevExp* 64 (1967) 492-95. The material is used here with the permission of the editor.

[72]Paul Winter, "The Treatment of His Sources by the Third Evangelist in Luke 21—24," 159; Heinz Schurmann, *Jesu Abschiedsrede Lk. 22:21-38: III. Teil einer quellen-kritischen Untersuchung des lukanischen Abendmahlsberichtes, Lk. 22:7-38* (Munster: Aschendorffsche Verlagsbuchhandlung, 1956) 116-34.

[73]Winter, "The Treatment of His Sources by the Third Evangelist in Luke 21—24," 166, agrees that it is non-Marcan but does not attribute it to L. This, of course, is because for him L is a connected narrative, a dubious hypothesis from my point of view.

[74]Any number of theories have been advanced to explain Luke's disuse of Mark 6:45—8:26. (1) Luke employed a version of Mark which did not include the passage in question. Bo Reicke, *The Gospel of Luke* (Richmond: John Knox Press, 1964) 34-35. (2) Luke, as an astute historian, saw the section as repetitious and omitted it. R. M. Grant, *A Historical Introduction to the New Testament* (New York: Harper & Row, 1963) 136-37. (3) Luke omitted the section because of considerations of space since papyrus rolls were of limited length. W. F. Arndt, *The Gospel according to St. Luke* (St. Louis: Concordia, 1956) 17-18. (4) Luke did not use the section for theological reasons. For example, Mark 7:1-23 would be of little interest to Gentiles and the story of the Syro-Phoenecian could be taken to show an anti-Gentile bias. G. B. Caird, *Saint Luke,* 128. Our investigation reveals that Luke's architectonic scheme played some part in his omission of this Marcan section; it does not preclude other factors as well.

[75]Among recent advocates of the longer text we may mention Heinz Schürmann, *Der Einsetzungsbericht Lk 22:19-20: II. Teil einer quellenkritischen Untersuchung des lukanischen Abendmahlsberichtes Lk 22:7-38* (Münster: Aschendorffsche Verlagsbuchhandlung, 1955). Schürmann believes 22:15-18 and 22:19-20a were originally two separate traditions but that they were joined in an early written source prior to Luke. A recent advocate of the shorter text is A. Vööbus, "A New Approach to the Problem of the Shorter and Longer Text in Luke," *NTS* 15 (1969) 457-63.

[76]Winter, "The Treatment of His Sources by the Third Evangelist in Luke 21-24," 156, thinks vss. 14-19a are from L, that they are very early, prior to Mark. Schürmann (*ibid.,* 80) also thinks that through 20a is non-Marcan. Vs. 20b, however, is influenced by Mark. On the other side, Conzelmann, *The Theology of St. Luke, passim,* and G. W. H. Lampe, "Luke," in *PCB* 820, think Luke's passion story is taken from Mark.

[77]Winter, "The Treatment of His Sources by the Third Evangelist in Luke 21-24," 159, says L, except for vs. 34 which is from Mark 14:30. Schürmann, *Jesu Abschiedsrede Lk 22:21-38,* 35, thinks Luke 22:33-34 is a Lucan redaction of Mark 14:29-31. On 99-112, he argues that Luke 22:31-32 are a Lucan redaction of a pre-Lucan tradition independent of Mark.

[78]Bultmann, *History of the Synoptic Tradition,* 158; Bundy, *Jesus and the First Three Gospels,* 500.

[79]Winter, however, thinks Luke 22:39-46 are non-Marcan but not L ("The Treatment of His Sources by the Third Evangelist in Luke 21-24," 160-61).

[80]Luke 22:43 is omitted by BAW Øf, the Sinaitic Syriac and other witnesses. It is included by the original hand of Sinaiticus, D Ø, and others. Martin Dibelius, *From Tradition to Gospel* (New York: Scribner's, n.d.) 201-2, n. 1, argues that the verse belongs in Luke's text. If 43-44 were deleted "what remains . . . is quite trite for it has neither the soteriological air of the scene as in Mark or Matthew, nor the legendary air of the full Lucan text. The evangelist Luke could not have written in this way." Flender, *St. Luke,* 54, n. 5, agrees. The necessity of the verse for the parallel argues for its inclusion, even though P[l]ɩ does not contain 22:43-44. See V. Martin and R. Kasser (eds.), *Papyrus Bodmer XIV* (Geneva: Bibliotheque Bodmer, 1961) 134.

[81]Winter, "The Treatment of His Sources by the Third Evangelist in Luke 21-24," 161.

[82]Winter, (*ibid.,* 158) says from L; Schürmann, *Jesu Abschiedsrede Lk 22:21-38,* 63, says from a non-Marcan source.

CHAPTER III

Lucan Patterns (2)

One of the most fascinating aspects of the Lucan style is the Evangelist's practice of employing the same architectonic scheme which governs the arrangement of his whole work in his organization of the smaller subsections of Luke-Acts. Just as there is a parallelism between the Third Gospel and the Acts, for example, so there exist correspondences between Acts 1—12 and 13—28 and between Luke 9 and 22—23. Careful investigation, moreover, reveals that this tendency is to be found in even smaller subsections. We find that one series of persons and events is balanced off against another such series at the beginning of both Luke and Acts. The first part of this chapter will focus on the architecture of Acts 1—5 and Luke 4—8 in that order.

Acts 1:12—4:23 and 4:24—5:42

In Acts 1—5 we find a series of correspondences both in content and in sequence[1] between 1:12—4:23 and 4:24—5:42.[2] The following list should make them clear.

Acts 1:12—4:23		Acts 4:24—5:42
1:12-26 Gathered together, the church is at prayer.	**1.**	4:24-31*a* Gathered together, the church is at prayer.
2:1-13 They were all filled with the Holy Spirit.	**2.**	4:31*b* They were all filled with the Holy Spirit.
2:14-41 Peter preaches.	**3.**	4:31*c* They spoke the word of God with boldness.
2:42-47 The communal life of the church is portrayed.	**4.**	4:32-35 The communal life of the church is portrayed. It is illustrated by examples in 4:36-37 and 5:1-10.
2:43*a* Fear comes upon every soul.	5	5:5*b*, 11 Fear comes upon the whole church and all who heard.
2:43*b* Wonders and signs are done by the apostles.	**6.**	5:12*a* Signs and wonders are done by the apostles.
3:1-11 A lame man is healed by Peter and John.	**7.**	5:13-16 Healings by Peter.
3:12-26 Peter delivers a speech in Solomon's Portico.	**8.**	5:12*b* They are all together in Solomon's Portico.

35

4:1-7 The apostles are arrested by the Sadducees. They are kept in custody until the morrow. Then they are brought before the council.

9. 5:17-28 The apostles are arrested by the Sadducees. They are kept in custody over night. Then they are brought before the council.

4:8-12, 19-20 Peter's defense.

10. 5:30-32 Peter's defense.

4:13-17 The council deliberates.

11. 5:33-39 The council deliberates.

4:18, 21-23 The apostles are released.

12. 5:40-42 The apostles are released.

Are these parallels due to the author of Acts or to some other cause, such as to two very similar series of historical events or to Luke's sources?

Any attempt to answer the question of the influence of the author's sources on the architecture of Acts 1-5 must reckon with the fact that there are at least three basic types of source theories for these chapters. The first is that which argues for one continuous source for the first part of Acts. The classic statement of this position in this century is that of C. C. Torrey,[3] recently revived in the work of Harald Sahlin[5] and accepted in modified form by R. R. Williams.[5] It is Torrey's contention that Acts 1:1—15:35 is a faithful translation of an original Aramaic document which Luke translated into Greek and to which he then added 15:36—28:31. Sahlin has attempted to revive Torrey's view and has joined it with his own version of Proto-Luke so that he sees an Aramaic or Hebrew Proto-Luke running from Luke 1:5—Acts 15, with the exception of interpolations. This Semitic document was then translated into Greek and expanded by the addition of Acts 16—28. Sahlin adds no significant arguments to those of Torrey and has fared no better than Torrey against the critics of such a view of Acts' sources. It will be sufficient, therefore, to limit ourselves to a summary of the arguments marshalled against Torrey's thesis. Such arguments fall into four categories. (1) Linguistic. The second half of Acts has an imposing array of Semitisms. It is incorrect, therefore, to make so sharp a contrast between the first and second halves of Acts as Torrey does.[6] The Semitisms of Acts 1—15, moreover, are uneven. Only the case for 1:1—5:16 and 9:31—11:18 is strong.[7] This questions the unity of the first half of Acts. Also, there is really no difficulty in the Greek that Torrey finds so objectionable. It does not require an Aramaic source to explain it.[8] The quotations from the OT are not from the Hebrew Bible or Targum, as one would expect if Acts 1—15 is a translation from Aramaic. The quotations are from the LXX.[9] The fact that Aramaic specialists cannot agree among themselves as to what is a mistranslation, moreover, does not argue convincingly for Torrey's accuracy.[10] (2) Historical. Whereas in the Gospel Luke had predecessors, it is likely that in Acts he was an innovator. Not only is there a lack of positive evidence for any Acts before the Acts of the Apostles, but there is a difficulty in conceiving of an historical setting for such an Aramaic document in 49 C. E.[11] (3) Literary. Torrey's theory would make Luke nothing more than a faithful translator. The preface, the elaborate dating, and the speeches in Acts seem to point in the opposite direction. Like the Hellenistic historians Luke was a real author and editor.[12] (4) Theological. In ideas, theology, and general outlook, the first and second halves of Acts are a unity.[13]

Such arguments have virtually demolished Torrey's claim, and that of Sahlin, that there is one continuous document behind Acts 1—15.[14] They have not, however, kept some scholars from claiming that an Aramaic source lies behind Acts 1:1—5:16.[15] For example, R. R. Williams claims "to set out those points which command general agreement." In this context he says that "for Acts 1—5:16 an Aramaic source is thought to have been established."[19] In response to this variation of Torrey's theory we may cite two recent studies of the problem of Semitisms in Acts, those of R. A. Martin[17] and Max Wilcox.[18]

On the one hand, Martin's concern is to show that the view that Luke has consciously imitated the LXX does not satisfactorily explain certain Semitic syntactical features, three in particular: the relative frequency of καί and δέ; the relative frequency of various prepositions in relation to the frequency of ἐν; and the relative frequency of separated articles. His conclusions are that (1) the frequency of these Semitic features is greater in Acts 1—15; (2) their frequency is greater in certain parts of chapters 1—15 than in others (1:6-14; 1:15-26; 2:1-4; 4:5-12; 4:23-31; 6:8-15; 7:1-53; 10:26-43; 13:16-41; 15:6-11, he thinks, are within translation Greek frequencies); and (3) there are, therefore, Semitic (Aramaic) sources behind *parts* of Acts 1—15. Martin's conclusions are significant for our purposes because if they are accepted *in toto*, for the sake of argument, they show that multiple sources are necessary to explain the evidence not only for chapters 1—15 but also for Acts 1—5.

Wilcox's aim is to assess the nature, significance, and probable origin of the elements in Acts which have been, or may be, styled Semitisms. As a result of his careful study he can conclude that the so-called Semitisms of Acts are due to at least three factors: (1) Semitic textual traditions of the OT; (2) the influence of the LXX; and (3) hard core Semitisms which likely are surviving vestiges of the originally Semitic origin of the tradition. Though Wilcox thinks oral tradition was most likely the well from which Luke drew, he does grant the possibility of some written source material. In no case, however, does he grant the possibility that one continuous source can be established from the evidence. This reinforces what was asked of Torrey all along. If granted at face value, what can Semitisms and possible mistranslations in the early chapters of Acts prove? Do they prove the tradition was originally in a Semitic form? Do they prove that the Semitic tradition was originally contained in one continuous source? The evidence may conceivably prove the former fact. By no means, however, is it sufficient to demonstrate the latter. If Torrey's theory in any of its forms is accepted as probable we would have to say that the parallels in Acts 1—5 were due to Luke's one continuous source for this section of Acts. Since it is an untenable source theory, however, the question remains open.

The second type of source theory for Acts 1—5 is that which argues for two parallel sources in these chapters. The classic statement of this position was made by Harnack.[19] Harnack claimed that there are two parallel accounts of the same events behind Acts 2—5; Jerusalem Source A which includes 3:1—5:16 and Jerusalem Source B which consists of Acts 2 and

5:17-42. When Luke put Acts 1—5 together he did not "perceive that he was reproducing two traditions concerning the same occurrences . . . ."[20] The parallels, then, are present because of Luke's failure to understand the nature of his sources. Harnack's theory of two parallel sources has been given new life in recent times by Bo Reicke.[21] Reicke argues that Acts 2:42—4:31 and 4:32—5:42 are two parallel traditions which relate the same events. These traditions, he thinks, are very much alike and correspond to one another in most details. Luke repeated these events because he needed narrative material to fill up a relatively long period about which he knew little. If either Harnack or Reicke is correct about Luke's sources for Acts 1—5, then clearly the parallels are due to Luke's sources. Upon close examination, however, it becomes apparent that a whole series of the materials found in Acts 1—5 comes either entirely from Luke himself or from separate traditions that have been recast by him. These materials include the kerygmatic speeches in 2:14-41;[22] 3:12-26;[23] (4:8-12?); 5:30-32; the speech of Gamaliel in 5:34-39;[24] the summaries in 2:42-47; 4:31*b*; 4:32-35; 5:5*b*; 5:11; 5:12*a*; 5:13*b*; 5:14; 5:15-16;[25] and the prayer in 4:24-30.[26] These materials are responsible for ten of the twelve parallels. Only parallels nine and twelve could exist without these materials, that is, only the two arrests, the two appearances before the council, and the subsequent releases of the apostles. It seems almost impossible, then, to speak of two parallel sources of any extent behind Acts 1—5. Hence the parallels do not go back to Luke's sources.

The third type of source theory for the early chapters of Acts is that which sees multiple sources behind these chapters. There are two basic variations on this theme. The first, represented by Etienne Trocme,[27] sees various *written* sources behind the early chapters of Acts as well as a number of oral traditions. For example, there are written sources behind Acts 2, Acts 3—5, Acts 6:1-7, Acts 6:8-15; 7:55—8:3; 9:1-30, and Acts 13:4ff. These have been supplemented by oral traditions and Luke's own contributions. The second, represented by Ernst Haenchen,[28] thinks entirely in terms of *oral* tradition. The author of Acts is dependent on small units of tradition which were originally handed down independently. These independent units of tradition were first joined together by the author of Acts. He organized them dramatically in accord with his didactic purpose. If either of these variations on a multiple source theory for the first part of Acts is accepted as probable, then the parallels must be due to the author of Acts. It is significant that the point of view represented by Haenchen probably has the greatest following at the present time.[29]

If the parallels that we have found between Acts 1:12-4:23 and 4:24—5:42 are not due to the sources employed by the author of Acts, could they be due to Acts' accurate reflection of two series of very similar events? Joachim Jeremias' argument with Harnack[30] could be interpreted along these lines. Claiming that only the double arrest of the apostles and their two appearances before the Sanhedrin justify one's speaking of parallels in Acts 1—5, Jeremias argues that the two narratives represent the two stages of proper Jewish legal process which involved a warning or legal caution before a subsequent arrest and trial. From this point of view, ch. 4 would echo the admonition before witnesses while ch. 5 would refer to the actual trial. The parallels of arrest and appearance before the council, therefore, represent historical events. The other parallels do not exist. In response to Jeremias we may offer two observations. First, even if we grant the historical reconstruction of Jeremias and agree that the events of chs. 4 and 5 are the warning and the subsequent trial of the apostles in line with Jewish law, we cannot deny the existence of the list of parallels given above. The parallels may not prove that doubtlets lie behind the chapters, but the parallels certainly exist. If they do, then how are they to be explained? Second, even if we grant Jeremias' contention and assume that behind Acts 4 and 5 are two stages of Jewish process of law, still we must also acknowledge the contention of both Reicke[31] and Haenchen[32] that Luke's presentation of the events does not correspond exactly to the process Jeremias assumes was followed. For example, according to Jewish law the warning was normally given in private by two witnesses who happened to catch the culprit in his misdeed. This is certainly not the case in Acts 4. If Jeremias' theory is accepted, then Luke has been at work shaping his material in line with his own interests so that both ch. 4 and ch. 5 now sound like trials. It seems almost inevitable, then, that in light of these two observations we must conclude that whatever the original historical situation, the present parallels are a stylistic device due to the author of Acts. If the list of parallels given above is due neither to Luke's sources nor to the historicity of Acts, and if we have found analogous parallels elsewhere where Luke's manipulation of his sources showed them to be due to the Evangelist's conscious intent, then here in Acts 1—5 we are doubtless also confronted with the conscious art of Luke. The parallels of Acts 1—5 are part of the Lucan architecture.

Luke 4:16—7:17 and 7:18—8:56

Luke 4:16—8:56 falls into two parts, 4:16—7:17 and 7:18—8:56, which begin and end in similar ways.[33] For example, Luke 4:16-30 regards Jesus' preaching and healing as fulfillments of Isaianic prophecies. The people take offense. Then there is a reference to God's concern for all men. The same themes are found in Luke 7:18-30, the beginning of the second part. Jesus' healings and preaching are regarded as fulfillments of Isaianic prophecies. "Blessed is he who takes no offense at me." Though the Pharisees and Lawyers reject the purpose of God for themselves, the people and tax collectors respond positively. Thus, the beginnings of the two parts of 4:16—8:56 are similar. The two parts end in similar ways also. Luke 7:1-10 is a healing story in which the emphasis is on the faith of the one who came to Jesus. It is followed by a resurrection story, 7:11-17, in which Jesus raises the widow's son. He says to him: "Young man, I say to you, arise." Luke 8:43-48 is also a healing story whose emphasis is on the faith of the woman who came to Jesus. It is followed by a story in which Jesus raises Jairus' daughter. He says to her: "Child, arise." The endings of the two parts are similar.

Moreover, much of the material between the similar beginnings and endings of the two parts seems to correspond, though not always in order.[34] Seeing the correspondences in parallel columns makes Luke's procedure easier to grasp.

4:31-41 Jesus is in conflict with demons. One cries: "What have you to do with us, Jesus of Nazareth? Have you come to destroy us? I know who you are, the Holy One of God."	1.	8:26-39 Jesus is in conflict with demons. They say: "What have you to do with me, Jesus, Son of the Most High God? I beseech you not to torment me."
5:1-11 Jesus is in a boat with Simon. A nature miracle takes place.		8:22-25 Jesus is in a boat with his disciples. A nature miracle takes place.
5:17-26 While Jesus is in the company of some Pharisees there arises the question of Jesus' forgiving sins. Jesus tells the man: "Man, your sins are forgiven you."	3.	7:36-50 While Jesus eats with a Pharisee the question of forgiveness of sins arises. Jesus tells the woman: "Your sins are forgiven."
5:27—6:5 Jesus and his disciples are shown eating and drinking in contrast to John's disciples who fast often.	4.	7:31-35 John came neither eating nor drinking. The Son of man came eating and drinking.
6:12-16 The Twelve are chosen. This immediately precedes Jesus' teaching within the hearing of the crowds.	5.	8:1-3 Jesus is with the Twelve. This immediately precedes Jesus' teaching the crowds.
6:17-49 Jesus teaches the multitudes. The conclusion concerns "hearing" Jesus' teaching and "doing" it.	6.	8:4-8, 16-21 Jesus teaches the multitudes. The conclusion concerns "hearing" Jesus' teaching and "doing" it.

Are these remarkable correspondences between Luke 4:16-7:17 and 7:18—8:56 due to the Evangelist? An examination of Luke's use of his sources in these chapters will assist us in making a judgment on this matter.

The first thing that must be noted are the Marcan pericopes omitted by Luke in 4:16—8:56. There are six such passages. They are: (1) Mark 1:16-20, the call of the first disciples; (2) Mark 3:20-22, the Pharisees' accusation; (3) Mark 3:23-30, the Beelzebul controversy; (4) Mark 4:26-29, the parable of the seed growing quietly; (5) Mark 4:30-32, the parable of the mustard seed; (6) Mark 4:33-34, Jesus' use of parables. Two of these Marcan passages are in other contexts in Luke. Mark 3:20-22 is probably the source for Luke 11:14-16. Mark 4:30-32 is probably the source for Luke 13:18-19. Not one of these six omissions from Luke 4:16-8:56 would have a place in the correspondences of this section. Their omission from the context is most likely explained as in the interest of the correspondences.

Next we must take the correspondences one by one and examine Luke's use of his sources throughout. The beginnings of the two parts, 4:16-30 and 7:18-30, are similar on three counts: (1) Jesus' preaching and healing are regarded as fulfilments of Isaianic prophecies; (2) people take offense at Jesus; (3) God's concern for all kinds of people. The chief literary question regarding Luke 4:16-30 is whether it comes from a special source (L) or whether it is

Luke's rewriting of Mark 6:1-6.[35] If it is Luke's modification of Mark, then both the emphasis on the fulfillment of the prophecies of Isaiah and the note of God's universal concern are due to Luke as well as the present location at the beginning of Jesus' public ministry rather than after Luke 8:40-56, as it would have been if Luke had followed Mark's order. If Luke 4:16-30 comes from a special source (L), then we have to answer the questions why the Third Evangelist preferred this source to Mark and why he located it at just the point in the Third Gospel that he did. Regardless of how one settles the source question for Luke 4:16-30, therefore, that it corresponds to 7:18-30 is clearly due to the intent of the Evangelist. Luke 7:18-30 comes from Q (cf. Matt 11:1-5). Present in the Q traditions were the emphasis on the fulfillment of Isaiah's prophecies (cf. Luke 7:22 = Matt 11:4-5)[36] and the note of offense at Jesus' actions (cf. Luke 7:23 = Matt 11:6). Luke adds to Q, however, the universalistic note which corresponds to Luke 4:16-30 (cf. 7:29). At this point also, therefore, the Third Evangelist is seen to be at work altering his sources to create the parallel.

The correspondence numbered one in the previous list consists of the similarity of 4:31-41 to 8:26-39 in that both picture Jesus in conflict with demons and both contain similar cries from the demonic world. Luke 4:31-41 comes from Mark 1:21-34. A number of Lucan modifications of Mark seem in the interest of the parallel. (1) In 4:33 Luke adds to Mark 1:23's, ἐν πνεύματι ἀκαθάρτῳ the term δαιμονίου so that vs. 33 reads "the spirit of an unclean demon," doubtless to correspond to 8:27. (2) In 4:33 Luke adds φωνῇ μεγάλῃ to parallel 8:28. (3) In 4:39 Jesus rebukes the fever in words reminiscent of the rebuking of the demon in 4:35. Mark 1:31 merely has Jesus take the woman by the hand and raise her up. Luke, therefore, seems to regard the fever as a demon and its cure as an exorcism. (4) In 4:41a Luke adds to Mark the confession of the exorcized demons: "You are the Son of God." This parallels 8:28. (5) in 4:41b the Third Evangelist adds the significant word used in the two preceding pericopes, ἐπιτιμῶν (cf. vss. 35, 39). This makes the section a unity. It is a unity created by Luke to parallel 8:26-39. In Luke 8:26-39 no changes of Mark 5:1-20 were necessary for the parallel. All the necessary changes were made in Luke 4:31-41.

Correspondence number two in the previous list consists of the fact that both 5:1-11 and 8:22-25 locate Jesus in a boat with his disciples and tell of a nature miracle. Luke 5:1-11 poses the problem of its source. Its similarities with Mark 1:16-20 and with John 21:1-10 raise questions about its development in the evolution of the tradition. It seems highly unlikely that it should be regarded as a Lucan rewriting of Mark. Perhaps it is best to see it as from Luke's special source of tradition (L).[37] If so, then one must ask why Luke chose this story of the call of the first disciples. Was it perhaps because it located Jesus in a boat and involved a nature miracle whereas Mark 1:16-20 did not? Also, one cannot help wondering why he shifted the Marcan order. In Mark the call of the first disciples came before the miracle stories connected with Capernaum (1:16-20 before 1:21-34). In Luke, however, the miracle story complex (4:31-41) comes before the call of the first disciples (5:1-11). Could this possibly indicate that the Evangelist deliberately inverted the order of events to secure the sequence noted above? Luke 8:22-25 comes from Mark 4:35-41. No modifications were necessary for the parallel.

Luke 5:17-26 and 7:36-50 form correspondence number three. The similarity involves the question of Jesus' forgiving sins while in Pharisaic company. Jesus' words of forgiveness in the two cases are nearly indentical. Luke 5:17-26 comes from Mark 2:1-12. A significant modification of Mark by Luke is the Evangelist's addition of ἦσαν καθήμενοι Φαρισαῖοι in 5:17. Luke 7:36-50 possibly is a Lucan rewriting of Mark 14:3-9 but most probably is from Luke's special source of tradition (L).[38] That Luke would include it here was doubtless in the interest of the parallel with 5:17-26.

Luke 5:27—6:5 corresponds to 7:31-35 (number 4 in the previous list). In both there is a contrast between Jesus who eats and drinks and John the Baptist and his disciples who are ascetic. Luke 5:27—6:5 comes from Mark 2:13-28. There are some important modifications of Marcan language in the interest of the parallel. (1) Luke 5:29 adds ἐποίησεν δοχὴν μεγάλην Λευὶς αὐτῷ to heighten the emphasis on Jesus' eating and drinking. (2) Luke 5:30 adds καὶ πίνετε to the ἐσθίετε of Mark 2:16 for the sake of the parallel with Luke 7:34 which has both eating and drinking. (3) Mark 2:18 reads: "Your disciples do not fast." Luke 5:33 changes the wording so that it reads: "Yours eat and drink." This was certainly in the interest of the parallel. (4) Luke 6:1b changes the phrasing of Mark 2:23b from οἱ μαθηταὶ αὐτοῦ ἤρξαντο ὁδὸν ποιεῖν τίλλοντες τοὺς στάχυας to καὶ ἔτιλλον οἱ μαθηταὶ αὐτοῦ καὶ ἤσθιον τοὺς στάχυας ψώχοντες ταῖς χερσίν. The reason seems obvious. Luke 7:31-35 comes from Q (cf. Matt 11:16-19). The Q tradition already contained what was necessary for the parallel. No modifications were necessary.

Correspondences five and six in the previous list may be taken together. Luke 6:12-16, 17-49 consists of a Twelve section followed by a section of Jesus' teaching which is heard by the crowds and which concludes on the note of "hearing" and "doing" Jesus' word. The same series of themes is found in Luke 8:1-3, 4-8, 16-21. While there is no significant alteration to the content of Mark 3:13-19 by Luke 6:12-16, there is a significant change in the order. Whereas Mark places the choice of the Twelve prior to the Beelzebul controversy, Luke locates it just prior to the Sermon on the Plain (6:17-19). By means of this shift of context Luke was able to have his Twelve material followed immediately by a section of Jesus' teaching before the crowds. Luke 6:20-49 comes largely from Q (cf. Matt 5:3, 4, 6, 11, 12, 39-42, 44-48; 7:12; 7:1-5, 16-21, 24-27). The significant modifications come not in the Sermon but in Luke's preceding it with verses 17-19 which belong to the parallel. Luke 6:17-19 is probably a free rewriting of Mark 3:7-12.[39] There are three significant changes. (1) In a change of order Luke places his version of Mark 3:7-12 after rather than before the choice of the Twelve. (2) Whereas Mark 3:8 says that the crowd came to Jesus to be healed because of ἀκούοντες ὅσα ποιεῖ, Luke 6:17 has the crowd come to Jesus ἀκοῦσαι αὐτοῦ καὶ ἰαθῆναι. (3) Luke adds vs. 19 which speaks of all the crowd. All of these changes seem to be in the interest of making Jesus teach in the presence of the crowds, as in 8:4. Though 6:20 might seem to indicate otherwise, the presence of 7:1 establishes this interpretation of 6:17-19. Luke 8:1-3 consists of an editorial introduction (vs. 1) and tradition peculiar to Luke (vss. 2-3).[40] It is significant that the reference to the Twelve is found in the editorial material. Luke 8:4-8, 16-21 comes from Mark 4:1-9, 21-25; 3:31-35. Both the beginning and end of this Lucan section have important alterations of Mark. (1) Luke 8:4 changes Mark 4:1's ὄχλος πλεῖστος to ὄχλου πολλοῦ obviously because Luke 6:17 has ὄχλος πολύς. (2) Luke alters the context of Mark 3:31-35. Instead of the passage of Christ's real brethren coming before the parable of the sower as in Mark, Luke places it at the very end of the section on parables. That Luke 8:19-21 belongs to the section where Jesus teaches the crowds is clear from 8:19. The reason for the shift in context is due to the fact that 8:18-21 ends on the note of hearing and doing the word of God. This is obviously intentional.

The endings of the two parts of Luke 4:16—8:56 are also very similar. Luke 7:1-10, a healing story whose emphasis is on the faith of the one who came to Jesus, is followed by vss. 11-17 in which Jesus raises the widow's son. This climaxes the first part of the Galilean section. Luke 8:43-48 is also a healing story whose emphasis is on the faith of the one who came to Jesus. It is followed by the raising of Jairus' daughter in 8:49-56. This climaxes part two of the Galilean section. Luke 7:1-10 is from Q (cf. Matt 8:5-13). The only significant modification of this Q tradition necessary for the parallel was to follow it with the story of a raising from the dead, 7:11-17, which is peculiar to Luke (L). This linking of traditions was doubtless deliberate. It was probably to parallel Luke 8:43-48 (= Mark 5:25-34) and Luke 8:40-42, 49-56 (= Mark 5:21-24, 35-43) which in following Mark here already had the sequence achieved by joining Q (Luke 7:1-10) and L tradition (7:11-17) in the first part.

Throughout this investigation of the Lucan use of his sources in Luke 4:16—8:56 we have repeatedly found that the correspondences listed at the beginning of our discussion were achieved by omissions, additions, and alterations of the Evangelist's sources. The correspondences between the two parts, 4:16—7:17 and 7:18—8:56, are, therefore, apparently the result of conscious intent on the part of Luke. We have found then that within his overall architectonic scheme the Third Evangelist utilizes a common architectural principle. Just as he balances Gospel and Acts, Jewish Christianity and Gentile Christianity, Galilee and Jerusalem, so he seeks correspondences within the section on Jerusalem Christianity (Acts 1—5) and within Jesus' Galilean ministry (Luke 4—8).

So far our examination of the architecture of Luke-Acts has revealed that the same architectonic pattern which governs the relation of Gospel and Acts also controls the way in which the smaller sections of the two volumes are organized. This conclusion is further reinforced by a careful investigation of the architecture of the beginning of the Third Gospel. This part of our chapter will fall into two sections. The first will take up the birth narratives of Luke 1-2. The second will focus on Luke 3:1—4:15.

Luke 1—2

The first two chapters of Luke fall into two seven-part cycles comparing John and Jesus, joined by 1:39-56.[41] The first cycle is comprised of 1:5-38 and may be broken down as follows.

	John		Jesus
	1:5-7 The parents are introduced. They are Elizabeth and Zechariah.	1.	1:26-27 The parents are introduced. They are Mary and Joseph.
	1:8-11 An angel appears to Zechariah.	2.	1:28 An angel appears to Mary.
	1:12 Zechariah was troubled (ἐταράχθη).	3.	1:29 She was greatly troubled. (διεταράχθη).
	1:13-17 The angel replies "Do not be afraid. A son will be born whose name will be John." A hymn follows which proclaims the son's character and work.	4.	1:30-33 The angel replies: "Do not be afraid. A son will be born whose name will be Jesus." A hymn follows which proclaims the son's character and work.
	1:18 Zechariah utters a question expressing doubt coupled with the reason for his doubt.	5.	1:34 Mary utters a question expressing her amazement coupled with the reason for her wonder.
	1:19-23 The angel's reply to Zechariah.	6.	1:35-37 The angel's reply to Mary.
	1:24-25 Elizabeth's speech relating to God's action.	7.	1:38 Mary's speech relating to God's action.

The second cycle begins with 1:57 and continues through 2:52. It may be broken down as follows.

1:57 Now the time came for Elizabeth to be delivered and she gave birth to a son.	1.	2:1-7 The time came for Mary to be delivered and she gave birth to her first born son.
1:58 And her kinsfolk and neighbors rejoiced when they heard what the Lord had done.	2.	2:8-20 The shepherds rejoiced, glorifying and praising God for all they had seen and heard.
1:65-66 These verses give a description of the reaction (fear) to the events, a mention of the news and of the laying it up in the hearts of those who heard.	3.	2:17-18 These verses give a description of the reaction (wonder) to the event, a mention of the spreading of the news, and of Mary's keeping all this in her heart.
1:59-64 The child is circumcised on the eighth day and named John as the angel had directed.	4.	2:21 The child is circumcised at the end of eight days and named Jesus as the angel had directed.
1:67-79 A prophetic hymn of God's act and John's function.	5.	2:22-38 A prophetic hymn of God's act and Jesus' function.
1:80a The child grew and became strong in spirit.	6.	2:39-40 The child grew and became strong.
1:80b He was in the wilderness until	7.	2:41-52 He went down to Nazareth until . . . .

Thus, it seems that the birth narratives fall into two seven-part cycles comparing John and Jesus, separated by 1:39-56. Is this parallelism of content and sequence[42] due to the Evangelist or to his sources? This question leads us into the complex problem of the sources of Luke 1—2.

There are at least four basic positions as regards the sources of Luke 1—2. The first sees one source behind the first two chapters of the Third Gospel. This source may be either Aramaic/Hebrew or Greek in the form in which it was used by Luke.[43] Scholars who hold to such a one-source theory would of necessity have to refer the parallels to the source. The second basic position asserts that there are two sources behind Luke 1—2.[44] A third type of source theory claims that there are multiple sources behind the first two chapters of Luke.[45] They may all be oral or there may be one document plus several oral legends. For those scholars who hold to two or more sources behind the birth narratives it is inevitable that they attribute the parallels, to some extent at least, to the creative organization of the Evangelist. The fourth basic position regarding the sources of Luke 1—2 sees these two chapters as a free composition by the Third Evangelist on the basis of Old Testament models.[46] Here again, of course, the parallels would be attributed to the creative activity of the Evangelist. None of these theories has widespread acceptance today. Probably the one with the least support is that which sees only a single source behind the birth narratives. This would mean that most scholars would take a position on the sources of Luke 1—2 which would lead to the conclusion that the parallels are the result of Lucan design. This is certainly supported by the numerous instances elsewhere in Luke-Acts where such parallels are due to the Evangelist's conscious intent.

Luke 3—4

At this point our attention must be focused on Luke 3:1—4:15. An investigation of this section yields a cycle comparing John and Jesus in three natural divisions.[47]

John		Jesus
3:1-6 John's person. He is the prophet of the eschaton.	1.	3:21-38 Jesus' person. He is the Son of God.
3:7-17 John's mission. It is eschatological, ethical, and anticipatory.	2.	4:1-13 Jesus' mission. It is the eschatological recapitulation of Adam's decisions.
3:18-20 Summary. The end of John's mission.	3.	4:14-15 Summary. The beginning of Jesus' ministry.

Again the question about the origin of these parallels causes us to undertake an examination of each parallel with a view to determining the Evangelist's use of his sources.

The first parallel involves 3:1-6 and 3:21-38. Luke 3:1-2 has an involved system of dating followed by the statement, "the word of the Lord came to John the son of Zechariah in the wilderness." The style seems to echo the introductions to the Old Testament prophets. This is followed by an extended quotation taken from Isaiah 40:3-5 in vss. 4-6. This quotation designates John as the "voice of one crying in the wilderness" which was to precede God's great eschatological act of deliverance. This form of writing is that which has been called typological.[48] That is, this is the method of writing which describes a person, event, or thing in the New Testament in terms borrowed from the description of its prototypal counterpart in the Old Testament in order to describe its nature. Thereby Luke is saying that John is a prophet, but not just a prophet. He is the eschatological voice in the wilderness. Luke 3:1-6, therefore, answers the question of who John is.

Is this description of the Baptist an expression of Luke's mind, or is it due to his sources?[49] Examination of Luke 3:1-6 reveals that at most only vss. 3 and 4 come from Mark. Vss. 1-2, 5-6 are peculiar to Luke. It is precisely this Lucan matter which gives the passage its typological form. The specific way in which John is presented as eschatological prophet in this pericope, therefore, must be due to the Third Evangelist.

The parallel to Luke 3:1-6 is 3:21-38. This section includes the baptism of Jesus and a lengthy genealogy. The formal link between the baptism narrative and the genealogy seems to be that they both end with designations of Jesus as Son.[50] The genealogy functions to define the Son of 3:22b as Son of Adam. It would seem then that the section, 3:21-38 serves to answer the question as to who Jesus is. Whereas John is the eschatological prophet of Isaiah 40, Jesus, being the supposed son of Joseph, is the Son of God. Is this description of Jesus' person in such a way as to parallel Luke 3:1-6 a reflection of the mind of Luke? The genealogy in 3:23-38 is peculiar to the Third Gospel. Also, it is located not in the birth narratives as Matthew's genealogy is, but precisely at this spot where it can interpret the Son of God motif in the baptism narrative. The hand of Luke is apparent.

The second parallel involves 3:7-17 and 4:1-13. Luke 3:7-17 deals with the Baptist's preaching and teaching. It falls into three sections. Vss. 7-9 characterize John's mission as eschatological. Mention is made of the "wrath to come" and the "fire" which points to the judgment. The expression "even now" of vs. 9 refers to the imminent end. Vss. 10-14 give the specific instructions of John to the multitudes, to the tax collectors, and to the soldiers. They characterize John's mission as ethical in intent. Vss. 15-17 give John's answer to the people's questions about the Christ. They characterize the Baptist's mission as anticipatory. This section, then, functions as a threefold description of John's mission. It is eschatological, ethical, and anticipatory. Can we attribute this description to Luke? Vss. 7-9 are from Q (= Matt 3:7-10). Vss. 10-14 are L tradition. Vss. 16-17 are from Q (= Matt 3:11-12). The major variations from Matthew in the two Q pericopes come on the emphasis on the crowds. Luke 3:7 has ὄχλοις where Matt 3:7 has

Φαρισαίων καὶ Σαδδουκαίων. This is probably because Luke 3:10 (L) has ὄχλοι. Luke 3:15 also is added to give a reference to the crowds. Though the term used is τοῦ λαοῦ, the idea is the same. The introduction of each part of John's mission with the mention of the people makes the three pericopes a unit. The insertion of the L pericope is most likely to make the description of John's mission threefold since the parallel, 4:1-13, has a threefold structure.

The parallel to 3:7-17 is 4:1-13, the temptation narrative. This pericope is formally linked to 3:21-38 by the fact that its two questions about Jesus' Sonship (vss. 3,9) balance the preceding two affirmations of Jesus' Sonship (3:22; 3:38).[51] It is thematically related to what precedes by virture of the fact that its arrangement of the three temptations loosely corresponds to the temptations of Adam in Genesis 3.[52] It thereby reinforces the point made in the preceding genealogy. Son of God for Luke means son of Adam, second Adam. The temptation narrative then functions for Luke as a means of saying that Jesus in his career reversed the decisions of Adam. Can we see the hand of the author in this reading of 4:1-13? The temptation narrative is from Q (= Matt 4:1-11). The order of the temptations in Luke, however, is different from that in Matthew. The second and third temptations of Matthew are reversed in Luke. In Luke, the Devil's challenge to Jesus to throw himself down from the pinnacle of the temple comes last. Is the Lucan order to be explained as a case where Luke follows the original form of Q or as another instance of his modifying his source to fit his theological and/or stylistic intent? That it is due to the Evangelist's intent is made probable by two observations. First, the Lucan order is necessary for the temptations to correspond loosely to those of Adam in Genesis 3. The second Adam motif, moreover, is necessary for Luke's christological emphasis in chs. 3 and 4. Second, in our examination of the relation of the Third Gospel to the Acts we have found the two volumes parallel to each other. Part of that parallelism consists of a visit to Jerusalem and the temple by Jesus which corresponds to a similar visit made by Paul. The visits to the temple in Jerusalem serve to tie the two figures together. As should be clear by the time our investigation of Luke 1:5—4:15 is complete, this part of the Gospel is divided structurally into two parts, 1:5—2:52 and 3:1—4:15. Moreover, both parts end with a journey to the temple in Jerusalem. Luke 2:22-38 and 2:41-50 record two visits of Jesus to the temple in Jerusalem. They conclude the first part of Luke 1:5—4:15. It is unlikely, therefore, in light of the Evangelist's architectonic scheme that the account of the temptations, which virtually concludes the second part of Luke 1:5—4:15, could end other than with a visit to the temple in Jerusalem. It is probable that the order of the temptations is what it is in 4:1-13, in addition to its theological reason, in order to tie the two halves of 1:5—4:15 together.

The third parallel involves 3:18-20 and 4:14-15. Luke 3:18-20 states that while John was preaching Herod took him and shut him up in prison. This brought his ministry to an end. This seems to form a summary statement for this section of Johannine material. Its emphasis is upon the conclusion of the Baptist's ministry. Vs. 18 is editorial. Vss. 19-20 are either L tradition or a free rewriting of Mark 6:17-18. In any case, the arrest of John is given before the baptism of Jesus. Whether this is motivated by Luke's theological desire to separate the Baptist section from the Jesus section so as to distinguish epochs as indicated in Luke 16:16 or not,[53] it is certainly motivated by the stylistic desire to parallel a Johannine summary by a Jesus summary, Luke 4:14-15, composed by the Evangelist.

From the foregoing investigation of Luke 1:5-4:15 it is clear that the beginning of the Third Gospel falls into several cycles of parallels between John the Baptist and Jesus, each apparently due to the conscious intent of the author of Luke-Acts. In this chapter, therefore, we have again found the author of Luke-Acts laboring to organize various parts of his work in terms of patterns which express the principle of balance.[54]

FOOTNOTES

[1]There is only one exception to the regular sequence, namely, number eight.

[2]The correspondences in some form have been widely recognized since Adolf Harnack, *The Acts of the Apostles: Vol. III, New Testament Studies*, ch. 5. Unfortunately it was with Harnack that the correspondences were taken as doublets pointing to Luke's use of sources, after the analogy of Pentateuchal source criticism. Against the use of repetition as a clue to written sources, cf. H. J. Cadbury, "Four Features of Lucan Style," in *Studies in Luke-Acts*, 91.

[3]*The Composition and Date of Acts* (Cambridge: Harvard University Press, 1916).

[4]*Der Messias und das Gottesvolk* (Uppsala: Almqvist & Wiksells Boktryckeri, 1945); *Studien zum dritten Kapitel des Lukasevangeliums* (Uppsala: Lundequistska Bokhandeln, 1949).

[5]*The Acts of the Apostles* (London: SCM, 1953).

[6]J. de Zwaan, "The Use of the Greek Language in Acts," *The Beginnings of Christianity: Part 1, The Acts of the Apostles* (5 vols.; ed. F. J. Foakes Jackson and K. Lake; London: Macmillan, 1922) 2. 45-46; H. F. D. Sparks, "The Semitisms of Acts," *JTS* n. s., 1 (1950) 20.

[7]de Zwann, "The Use of the Greek Language in Acts," 48, 56.

[8]F. C. Burkitt, "Professor Torrey on 'Acts'," *JTS* 20 (1919) 320-29; H. J. Cadbury, "Luke—Translator or Author?" *American Journal of Theology* 24 (1920) 447-53; A. A. Vazakas, "Is Acts 1—15:35 a Literal Translation from an Aramaic Original?" *JBL* 37 (1918) 105-10.

[9]A. W. Argyle, "The Theory of an Aramaic Source in Acts 2:14-40," *JTS* n. s., 4 (1953) 213-14; H. F. D. Sparks, "The Semitisms of Acts," 19. B. M. Metzger, "Scriptural Quotations in Q Material," *Exp T* 65 (1954) 125, argues, however, that Bishop Rabbula's translation into Syriac of Cyril of Alexandria's *De recta fide*, where both Greek and Syriac translations are extant, shows the Syrian bishop often conformed his rendering of the Gospel quotations made by Cyril to the current form of the Syrian vernacular scriptures. This raises some doubts about the premise of Argyle and Sparks.

[10]Matthew Black, *An Aramaic Approach to the Gospels and Acts* (2d ed.; Oxford: Clarendon, 1954) 4, 6-7; D. W. Riddle, "The Logic of Translation Greek," *JBL* 51 (1932) 17-18.

[11]E. J. Goodspeed, "The Origin of Acts," *JBL* 39 (1920) 86-90; Riddle, "The Logic of Translation Greek," 15-16.

[12]H. J. Cadbury, "Luke—Translator or Author?" 455.

[13]H. F. D. Sparks, "The Semitisms of Acts," 21.

[14]J. Dupont, *The Sources of Acts*, 32.

[15]F. F. Bruce, *The Speeches in the Book of Acts* (London: Tyndale, n.d.) 8, for example.

[16]*The Acts of the Apostles*, 21.

[17]"Syntactical Evidence of Aramaic Sources in Acts 1—15." *NTS* 11 (1964) 38-59.

[18]*The Semitisms of Acts* (Oxford: Clarendon, 1965).

[19]*The Acts of the Apostles*, ch. 5.

[20]*Ibid.*, 183.

[21]*Glaube und Leben der Urgemeinde: Bemerkungen zur Apostelgeschichte 1—7* (Zürich: Zwingli-Verlag, 1957).

[22]Richard F. Zehnle, *Peter's Pentecost Discourse* (Nashville: Abingdon, 1971).

[23]*Ibid.*

[24]R. P. C. Hanson, *Acts* (Oxford: Clarendon, 1967) 86. Cf. also J. W. Swain, "Gamaliel's Speech and Caligula's Statue (Acts 5:34-9)," *HTR* 37 (1944) 341-49, who senses the problem.

[25]Cf. H. J. Cadbury, "The Summaries in Acts," *The Beginnings of Christianity*, 5. 392-402.

[26]J. A. T. Robinson, *Twelve New Testament Studies*, 141-42; Max Wilcox, *The Semitisms of Acts*, 69-70.

[27]*Le "Livre des Actes" et l'histoire* (Paris: Presses Universitaires de France, 1957) 154-214.

[28]"Tradition und Komposition in der Apostelgeschichte," *ZTK* 52 (1955) 209, 212.

[29]The case of L. Cerfaux is instructive. Whereas in 1936 Cerfaux's analysis of the sources included a document, reproduced with only slight retouches, behind Acts 2:41—5:40, since 1939 he has ceased to speak of one written source, well delimited, homogeneous, and possessing characteristic traits. Now he thinks it is impossible to delimit any written sources. Cf. Dupont, *The Sources of Acts*, 58-59.

[30]"Untersuchungen zum Quellenproblem der Apostelgeschichte," *ZNW* 36 (1937) 205-13.

[31]*Glaube und Leben der Urgemeinde*, 108, n. 43.

[32]*Die Apostelgeschichte*, 209.

[33]First published in my article. "The Lukan Presentation of Jesus' Ministry in Galilee," *RevExp* 64 (1967) 486-92. The material is used by permission of the editor.

[34]The order runs: a, b, c, d, e, f: f, e, b, a, c, d.

[35]Cf. ch. 2, n. 26.

[36]Joachim Jeremias, *The Parables of Jesus* (New York: Scribner's, 1955) 93.

[37]So Caird, *Saint Luke*, 24-25, 91.

[38]Bundy, *Jesus and the First Three Gospels*, 202-04.

[39]*Ibid.*, 187-88.

[40]W. C. Robinson, Jr., "On Preaching the Word of God (Luke 8: 4-21)," in *Studies in Luke-Acts*, 131-32, thinks that all of 8: 1-3 may be Luke's own composition. If so, it only supports my thesis.

[41]This parallelism has been recognized at least since Gelpke (J. G. Machen, *The Virgin Birth of Christ* [New York: Harper, 1930] 152, n. 49). Among the most recent scholars who have seen the parallels we may mention: (1) Philip Vielhauer, "Das Benedictus des Zacharias (Luk. 1:68-79), *ZTK* 49 (1952) 255; (2) A. S. Geyser, "The Youth of John the Baptist," *NovT* 1 (1956) 72; (3) M. D. Goulder and M. L. Sanderson, "St. Luke's Genesis," *JTS* n. s., 8 (1957) 19; (4) Rene Laurentin, *Structure et théologie de Luc 1-2*, 32-34.

[42]In the second cycle, numbers 2 and 3 are out of order.

[43]From among the most recent adherents of this view we may mention: (1) W. L. Knox, *The Sources of the Synoptic Gospels* (ed. Henry Chadwick; Cambridge University Press, 1957) 2. 40-43; (2) F. W. Goodman, "Sources of the First Two Chapters in Matthew and Luke," *CQR* 162 (1961) 136-43; (3) Paul Gaechter, "Der Verkundigungsbericht Lk 1:26-38," *ZKT* 91 (1969) 322-63; 567-86.

[44]Leaney, *The Gospel according to St. Luke*, 26-27.

[45]Bultmann, *History of the Synoptic Tradition*, 294-301.

[46]Goulder and Sanderson, "St. Luke's Genesis," 12-30.

[47]For a similar arrangement, see Goulder, *Type and History in Acts*, 122.

[48]Cf. G. W. H. Lampe and K. J. Woolcombe, *Essays on Typology* (Naperville: Allenson, 1957) 39-40.

[49]I regard it unnecessary to treat the claim that behind 3:1-20 there is a document containing the Baptist's teaching and owing nothing to Christian editing except the abridgment at its conclusion. So J. C. Todd, "The Logia of the Baptist,' *ExpT* 21 (1910) 173-75; also C. R. Bowen, "John the Baptist in the New Testament," *American Journal of Theology*, 16 (1912) 91. Indeed, I agree with Walter Wink, *John the Baptist in the Gospel Tradition* (Cambridge University Press, 1968) 68-72, in his rejection of a Baptist source behind Luke 1-2.

[50]C. H. Talbert, "An Anti-Gnostic Tendency in Lucan Christology," *NTS* 14 (1969) 268.

[51]*Ibid.*

[52]A. Feuillet, "Le récit Lucanien de la Tentation (Lc. 4:1-13)," *Bib* 40 (1959) 617-31. This is preferable to the claim that Luke's order corresponds to that of Ps 106. So H. Swanston, "The Lukan Temptation Narrative," *JTS*, n.s., 17 (1966) 71.

[53]As Conzelmann, *The Theology of St. Luke*, 18-22 argues.

[54]Let me reiterate. Balance is not the Evangelist's only architectonic concern. It is the one with which this work deals.

CHAPTER IV

Lucan Patterns (3)

In the two previous chapters we have seen a number of examples of Lucan architectonic designs which express the principle of balance. So far none of these designs has represented that type of pattern in which the correspondences occur in inverted order. In this chapter, however, the first two examples of the Lucan architectural method to be examined are patterns in which the elements are balanced in chiastic fashion.

Luke 10:21—18:30

One of the unique features of the Third Gospel's picture of Jesus is the lengthy journey of Jesus to Jerusalem found in Luke 9:51—19:46. This journey has been the subject for numerous studies, one of which has produced results that are relevant for our investigation of the Lucan architecture. M. D. Goulder has argued that much of the journey falls into two parts which loosely correspond to one another both in content and sequence,[1] though the sequence is an inverted one.[2] In other words, the Lucan journey falls into a chiastic pattern. Similar suggestions may also be found in Morgenthaler's work.[3] The list which follows is my own, though it conforms at many points with the contentions of Goulder and Morgenthaler.

Luke 10:21—13:30		*Luke 14:1—18:30*
10:21-24 The Kingdom is revealed to babes. Blessed are the disciples for they see.	1.	18:15-17 The Kingdom must be received as a child, the disciples are told.
10:25-37 Jesus is confronted with the question: "What shall I do to inherit eternal life?" The response to Jesus' answer elicits teaching by Jesus.	2.	18:18-30 Jesus is confronted with the question: "What shall I do to inherit eternal life?" The response to Jesus' answer elicits more teaching from Jesus.
10:38-42 The story of Mary and Martha deemphasizes the importance of good works.	3.	18:9-14 The parable of the Pharisee and the publican deemphasizes the importance of good works.

51

11:1-13 God's willingness to answer prayer.

4. 18:1-8 God's willingness to answer prayer.

11:14-36 A healing followed by a discussion of the signs of the Kingdom of God and a warning about the Last Judgment.

5. 17:11-37 A healing followed by a discussion of the signs of the Kingdom of God and a warning about the Last Judgment.

11:37-54 At a meal Jesus rebukes the Pharisees and lawyers for their sins.

6. 17:1-10 An exhortation to rebuke one's brother when he sins, followed by a parable about a meal.

12:1-48 Three themes are treated in the order: (1) the threat of hell (vss. 1-12), (2) riches (vss. 13-34), (3) faithful stewardship (vss. 35-48).

7. ch. 16 Three themes are treated in the order: (1) unfaithful stewardship (vss. 1-8), (2) riches (vss. 9-15), (3) the threat of hell (vss. 19-31).

12:49—13:9 Four themes are present in the order: (1) transcendence of family loyalties (12:49-53), (2) prudent action taken ahead of time (12:54-59), (3) repentence (13:1-5), (4) the fruitless tree is cut down (13:6-9).

8. 14:25—15:32 Four themes are present in order: (1) transcendence of family loyalties (14:25-27), (2) prudent action taken ahead of time (14:28-33), (3) tasteless salt which is thrown away (14:34-35), (4) repentance (ch. 15).

13:10-17 A woman is healed on the sabbath. Jesus says the Jews treat an ox and ass better than a person.

9. 14:1-6 A man is healed on the sabbath. Jesus says the Jews treat an ox and ass better than a person.

13:18-30 Parables of the Kingdom of God are concluded by the theme of the exclusion of privileged ones from the Messianic banquet and the inclusion of the disadvantaged.

10. 14:7-24 Parables relating to the Kingdom are concluded by the theme of the exclusion from the Messianic banquet of certain privileged people and the inclusion of the disadvantaged.

13:31-33 A prophet cannot perish away from Jerusalem.

11. 13:34-35 O Jerusalem, Jerusalem, killing the prophets and stoning those who are sent to you.

The question must now be raised about the Third Evangelist's role in the construction of these parallels. The answer to such a question is extremely difficult to give for this section owing to the source problems involved. From 9:51 down to 18:15 Luke departs from any use of Mark with the possible exception of Luke 10:25-28 which may come from Mark 12:28-34. This means that only two Marcan passages are with reasonable certainty used by the Third Evangelist in his chiastic journey scheme, namely, Luke 18:15-17 (= Mark 10:13-16) and Luke 18:18-30 (= Mark 10:17-31).[4] This disuse of Mark means that the chiastic journey is built up mainly from Q and L traditions. Q, of course, has always been a somewhat elusive entity. Nowadays it seems almost ghostlike. The strongest argument for a continuous source for Matthew and Luke when they are not using Mark seems to be the fact that passages with the same content in near identical language occur in the same relative order in both Matthew and Luke. Generally speaking, this is true for the traditions usually labelled Q in the Galilean ministry of the Third Gospel. Once one comes to the central section with which we are now concerned, however, the non-Marcan matter in Luke which has parallels in Matthew falls into two categories: (1) that which occurs in the same relative order as its parallel in Matthew, and (2) that which occurs in a relative order different from that in Matthew. If one assumes a continuous source Q which includes both types of material mentioned, then one faces the question of whether Matthew or Luke more adequately reproduces the original order of Q. Reliable scholars stand on both sides of this issue and at present the question is moot.[5] The same kind of question must be faced regarding the more original text of Q.[6] Again the question is moot. Given these uncertainties about Q, a controlled analysis of Luke's use of his sources in the central section of his gospel is virtually impossible. Often the best that can be done is to call attention to possible manipulation of his source material by the Evangelist. These possible indications of the Lucan hand must then be examined by each reader from his own stance on the critical questions relating to the section. With these cautions in mind, let us turn to the parallels in the order listed above and examine them for possible signs of Lucan intent.

The first parallel in the list given above is the correspondence of Luke 10: 21-24 to 18:15-17. In both the Kingdom is accessible only to babes. Luke 10:21-22 (= Matt 11:25-27) is a Q tradition which occurs in the Third Gospel in the same relative order as in the First Gospel. Here it is said that the Kingdom is hidden from the wise and revealed to babes ($\nu\eta\pi\iota o\iota s$). The next verses are also Q material (Luke 10:23-24 = Matt 13:16-17) but do not occur in the same relative order as in Matthew. By joining the two traditions here Luke has in effect said that the disciples are the babes, while the prophets who desired to see and did not are the wise and understanding. The parallel is found in Luke 18:15-17 (= Mark 10: 13-16). It is significant that the Third Evangelist altered Mark's introduction to the pericope from "And they were bringing children ($\pi\alpha\iota\delta\iota\alpha$) to him," to "Now they were bringing even infants ($\beta\rho\epsilon\phi\eta$) to him . . . ." By this change Luke guaranteed that the subsequent $\pi\alpha\iota\delta\iota\alpha$ in vss. 16, 17 would be read as infants rather than as children. This change seems clearly in the interests of the parallel.

Parallel number two in the previous list is the similarity of Luke 10:25-37 to 18:18-30. Both show Jesus confronted with the question, "What shall I do to inherit eternal life?" In both the response to Jesus' answer elicits further teaching from Jesus. Luke 10:25-28 is possibly from Mark 12:28-34.[7] If so, it has been taken out of its Marcan context it the last week in Jerusalem and relocated here in the journey of Jesus to Jerusalem. It serves as an introduction to an L tradition, the parable of the Good Samaritan in 10:29-37. It is possible to see the transposition of the Marcan material as made in the interests of the parallel with Luke 18:18-30 (= Mark 10:17-30) which contained the same question. It is also possible to see the linking of 10:25-28 and 10:29-37 as deliberate since the parallel in 18:18-30 already in its Marcan source found the question about eternal life joined to further teaching by Jesus growing out of Jesus' response to the original question.

Parallel number three, Luke 10:38-42 which corresponds to 18:9-14, would not have been possible had it not been for Luke's use of his special reservoir of material (L) from which both traditions are derived. The fourth parallel in the list above is the correspondence of Luke 11:1-13 to 18:1-8. Both treat the theme of God's willingness to answer prayer. Luke 11:1-13 is comprised of two Q traditions (Luke 11:2-4 = Matt 6:9-13 and Luke 11:9-13 = Matt 7:7-11) which are in different positions in the two gospels, between which is placed an L pericope (11:5-8). The Q material, Luke 11:9-11, is designed as a commentary on the L parable in 11:5-8. It makes the parable speak of God's willingness to answer prayer. This is clearly in the interests of the parallel with the L tradition in Luke 18:1-8 which also treats the theme of God's willingness to answer prayer.

The fifth parallel in our list is the similarity of Luke 11:14-36 to 17:11-37 in that both contain a healing followed by a discussion of the signs of the Kingdom of God and a warning about the last judgment. Luke 11:14-36 is composed of two Q passages (Luke 11:14-23 = Matt 12:11-30 and Luke 11:24-26 = Matt 12:43-45) in the same relative order as in the First Gospel, followed by an L tradition (11:27-28) and two more Q traditions, one in the same relative order as in Matthew (Luke 11:29-32 = Matt 12:38-42) and one in a different order (Luke 11:33-36 = Matt 5:15; 6:22-23). The healing and subsequent discussion of the signs of the Kingdom are present in the first two Q sections in order and the note of judgment is in the third Q section in order. It is, therefore, to the other side of the parallel, Luke 17:11-37, that we must look for signs of Lucan manipulation of sources in the interest of the parallel. This section is composed of two L traditions (17:11-19 and 17:20-21) followed by a Q passage (17:22-37 = Matt 24:26-28, 37-41) in the same relative order as in Matthew. The healing is from L (vss. 11-19), the beginning of the discussion of signs also from L (vss. 20-21), and the continuation of the signs discussion and the warning about judgment from Q (vss. 22-37). It is significant that it was materials with just these three themes that were selected and that they were arranged in exactly the order they were. Definite indications of the Lucan hand at work seem apparent here.

Parallel number six in our list is the correspondence of Luke 11:37-54 to 17:1-10. Both contain a rebuke or an exhortation to rebuke one's brother if he sins which has some relation to a meal. Luke 11:37-54 is essentially from Q (= Matt 23:25-26, 23, 6-7, 27-28, 4, 29-32, 13-14) and is in basically the same relative order as the tradition in Matthew. It is significant that the section is introduced by a Lucan preface: "While he was speaking, a Pharisee asked him to dine with him; so he went in and sat at the table." (vs. 37). This is probably in the interest of the parallel. Luke 17:1-10 is composed of two Q traditions, 17:1-4 (= Matt 18:6-7, 15, 21-22) and 17:6 (= Matt 17:20) which occur in different orders in Matthew, and a parable which is peculiar to Luke (vss. 7-10, L). The exhortation to rebuke one's brother when he sins is found in the Q material (vs. 3) and the meal theme is found in the L parable. Joining the two separate traditions in this way seems an indication of the Lucan hand.

The seventh parallel, Luke 12:1-48 and ch. 16, exists because both sections contain the three themes: (1) the threat of hell, (2) riches, and (3) faithful or unfaithful stewardship. These themes are found in this order in ch. 12 and in inverse order in ch. 16. Luke 12:1-48 is almost entirely Q material: vss. 1-10 = Matt 10:26-33; 12:32; vss. 11-12 = Matt 10:19-20; vss. 22-31 = Matt 6:25-33; vss. 32-34 = Matt 6:19-21, all in an order different from that of Matthew; vss. 39-40 = Matt 24:43-44 and vss. 42-48 = Matt 24:45-51, in the same order as in Matthew. The material that is definitely not from Q is found in vss. 13-21 (L). About vss. 35-38 there is a question. They may be an adaptation of Matt 25:1-13 and therefore Q, or they may be L tradition.[8] The Q material in vss. 1-12 contains the theme of hell and judgment. The Q material in vss. 22-34 serves as an elaboration of the L tradition in vss. 13-21 on the theme of riches. The Q material in vss. 35-48 contains the theme of faithful stewardship. The point at which the Lucan hand is most clearly seen is in the introduction of the L parable of the rich man which sets forth the theme of riches. The Q material by itself (12:22-34) would not have made the clear parallel with ch. 16. With the exception of vss. 13 (= Matt 6:24, Q, in an order different from that in Matthew) and 16-18 (= Matt 11:12-13; 5:18, 32, Q, in an order different from Matthew), ch. 16 is entirely composed of L tradition which contains within its various units the themes necessary for the parallels. Why did the Evangelist select just these L traditions? Why did he include them in the order he did so that the three themes which occur also in ch. 12 are found in reverse order? An answer to these questions points to the deliberate adaptation of his sources by the author of the Gospel.

Parallel number eight consists of Luke 12:49—13:9 and 13:25—ch. 15 which both contain four themes: (1) transcendence of family loyalties, (2) prudent action taken ahead of time, (3) repentance, and (4) the useless quantity which is discarded (a fruitless tree is cut down; tasteless salt is thrown away). In 12:49—13:9 the themes appear in this order. In 13:25—ch. 15 they appear in the order (1), (2), (4), (3). Luke 12:49-53 (= Matt 10:34-36) and 12:54-59 (= Matt 16:2-3; 5:25-26) are Q traditions which have a different order in Matthew. The first contains the theme of transcendence of family loyalties. The second speaks of prudent action taken ahead of time. Luke 13:1-5 which concerns repentance and 13:6-9 which speaks of the fruitless tree which is cut down are both L traditions. It is doubtless important that two of the themes are from L tradition. Luke 14:25-27, 34 (= Matt 10:37-38; 5:13) which concerns transcendence of family loyalties and tasteless salt which is thrown away and 15:3-7 (= Matt 18:12-14) which is part of the material on repentance are from Q and appear in different contexts in Matthew. Luke 14:28-33 which speaks of prudent action is L tradition, as are 15:8-10 and 15:11-32 which complete the repentance material. It is perhaps significant that Luke's ending to the parable of the lost sheep runs: "Just so, I tell you, there will be more joy in heaven over one sinner who repents than over ninety-nine righteous persons who need no repentance" (vs. 7). Matt 18:14 reads: "So it is not the will of my Father who is in heaven that one of these little ones should perish." That Luke 15:7 is so similar to vs. 10 where the emphasis is also on repentance seems to argue that Luke has been active altering Q so that the parable fits into his repentance theme.[9]

With parallel number nine, Luke 14:1-6 and 13:10-17, as with the third parallel, the very existence of the similarity depends entirely upon Luke's special source(s).

The tenth parallel involves Luke 13:18-30 and 14:7-24. Both passages contain parables of the Kingdom which conclude on the theme of the exclusion of certain privileged persons from the Messianic banquet and the inclusion of the disadvantaged. Luke 13:18-30 consists of two collections of Q traditions. 13:18-21 (= Matt 13:31-33) and 13:22-30 (= Matt 7:13-14, 22-23, 8:11-12) which are found in a different order in Matthew. Luke 14:7-24 is composed of an L tradition (vss. 7-14) and a passage from Q (vss. 15-24 = Matt 22:1-10) found in Matthew in another context. It is significant that the Q parable in Luke is prefaced by a Lucan introduction (vs. 15) which makes the parable refer explicitly to exclusion from the Messianic banquet. This may be a conscious attempt to parallel the same theme in Luke 13:22-30.

The final parallel in this section of Luke finds Luke 13:31-33 and 13:34-35 focusing on the theme of Jerusalem's role in killing the prophets. Luke 13:34-35 (= Matt 23:37-39) is a Q tradition which is found in the same relative order in Matthew. Luke 13:31-33 is from Luke's special source (L). Any significance attached to Luke's use of sources here would have to focus on the Evangelist's including this L tradition at just this point.

From the foregoing analysis of the Third Evangelist's use of his sources in the central section of the Gospel it appears that there are certain definite signs that Luke deliberately adapted his materials in order to achieve the chiastic structure suggested in the list at the beginning of this chapter.[10] We have found again, therefore, that it is a characteristic tendency of Lucan architecture to balance one section of his work off against another. What we have seen as a new feature in this part of the chapter, however, has been that such balancing of parts may take place in an inverted order as well as in the normal order or in no regular order at all. It remains for us now to turn to a similar phenomenon in the Acts of the Apostles.

Acts 15:1—21:26

We have seen that the architectonic scheme of Luke-Acts involves a balancing of one series of persons and events off against another, as for example, the journey of Jesus to Jerusalem in Luke is paralleled by Paul's journey in Acts. We have also seen that this tendency to balance corresponding persons and events extends to the practice of using a similar architecture for corresponding sections of the Lucan work, as for example, the two halves of Acts correspond to each other in a way similar to the way the two main sections of Luke correspond. In this light, since the journey of Jesus to Jerusalem in Luke is arranged in a chiastic pattern, it would be in line with the

Lucan stylistic tendency to find Paul's journey which ends in Jerusalem arranged in a similar way. Close examination of Acts 15:1—21:26 reveals that this is exactly what the author of Luke-Acts has done. This section falls into two parts which correspond to one another in an inverted order, that is, they form a chiasmus. The following list should enable this pattern to be seen at a glance.[11]

	Acts 15:1—18:11		*Acts 18:12—21:26*
	15:1-29 Paul and others go to Jerusalem. On the way they report on the Gentile mission and the report is well received. They are welcomed on their arrival to Jerusalem. Jewish Christians raise the issue of the law and circumcision. There is a meeting involving Paul and James over the matter. The decision of James is sent in a letter (abstain from things sacrificed to idols; from unchastity; from what is strangled; and from blood).	1.	21:15-26 Paul and others go to Jerusalem. They are received gladly. Their report on the Gentile mission is well received. The issue of Jewish Christian concern over the law and circumcision is raised. There is a meeting involving Paul and James over the matter. The earlier decision of James which was sent in a letter is echoed (abstain from what has been sacrificed to idols; from blood; from what is strangled; and from unchastity).
	15:30—16:15 Paul returns to the cities where he had earlier preached the gospel. Paul is forbidden by the Holy Spirit to speak in Asia. The Spirit does not allow him to go into Bithynia. A vision calls him to Macedonia.	2.	20:13—21:14 The Ephesian elders sorrow because they well see Paul no more. The Holy Spirit warns against going to Jerusalem. There is a warning of bondage and suffering.
	16:16-40 We hear of an exorcism by Paul; of a riot; of Paul's saving the jailor's life.	3.	19:11—20:12 We hear of Jews who try to imitate Paul's exorcisms; of a riot; of Paul's saving Eutychus' life.
	17:1-15 Synagogue debates.	4.	19:8-10 Synagogue debates.
	17:16-34 The Athenians who are already religious are taught accurately about true religion by Paul.	5.	18:24—19:7 Apollos and twelve disciples who are already on the way to being Christians are taught accurately about true religion by Paul and his helpers.[12]
	18:1-11 Paul argues in the synagogue. Reference is made to the ruler of the synagogue. God promises Paul: "No harm shall befall you in this city."	6.	18:12-23 Paul argues in the synagogue. Reference is made to the ruler of the synagogue. God's promise to Paul that no harm should befall him in Corinth is fulfilled.

Here as elsewhere in our investigation of the architecture of Acts we are confronted with the completely unsettled question of the sources behind Luke's narrative.

If we assume that the "we" sections (16:10-17; 20:5-15; 21:1-18; 27:1—28:16) go back to the diary of an eyewitness,[13] either that of the author of Acts or someone else, it could hardly be said that the parallels which are listed above are due to such a source. Of all the similarities listed above, only

21:4, 11 (part of number 2 in the list above) and 20:7-12 (part of number 3 in the above list) come from material in the "we" sections. The others would have to be due to Luke's selection, arrangement, and adaptation of supplementary material. Hence, assuming a "we" source, the parallels must be due to the author of Acts.

If we assume an itinerary lies behind Acts 15:36—21:16,[14] that is, a report of halting places on the journey, most probably containing brief information on the foundation of new communities and the success of the mission, it is impossible to credit the arrangement of Acts 15—21 to such a source. This is true for the following reasons. (1) Chs. 13—14, which would belong to the itinerary according to Dibelius,[15] do not belong to the chiastic structure described above. Also, if the source is thought to run on through ch. 28, as Trocme thinks,[16] then these chapters are outside the chiasmus too. (2) Acts 15:1-29 does not go back to such an itinerary but it is crucial for the parallels. (3) Acts 16:25-34 (parallel 3); 17:22-31 (parallel 5); 19:14-16 (parallel 3); 20:7-12 (parallel 3); 20:18-35 (parallel 2); are all certainly not parts of any itinerary but are certainly crucial for the chiastic structure described above. Hence, the arrangement must come from the hand of the author of Acts if we assume an itinerary source for these chapters.

If we think in terms of a number of traditions and/or notes plus Luke's own contributions making up Acts 15—21 as Haenchen does,[17] then the chiastic arrangement is inevitably due to the author's selection, shaping, and organization of the material. From the point of view of any one of the three major types of source theories for Acts 15—21, the present arrangement of the text in a chiastic form is due not to the author's sources but to his own hand. It would appear that the architectonic scheme of the author of Luke-Acts demands that a chiastic journey in the Gospel be balanced by a chiastic journey in Acts. The architecture of Luke-Acts, therefore, seems to be built upon a basic stylistic principle, that of balance.

In addition to the architectonic patterns treated up to this point, there are two more examples of the Lucan architecture of a similar nature that are worthy of note: (1) the correspondences between the end of Luke and the beginning of Acts and (2) the correspondences between Luke 9 and Acts 1. These two examples will now be examined in the order in which they are listed here.

Luke 24 and Acts 1

The remarkable similarities between the end of the Gospel according to Luke and the beginning of the Acts of the Apostles[18] have been widely recognized.[19] The following list may be regarded as representative of this scholarly opinion.

Luke 24		*Acts 1*
24:33-34, 36 The risen Christ appears to Simon and then to the eleven apostles.	**1.**	1:3 The risen Christ appeared to the apostles whom he had chosen.
24:36-43 Jesus, now risen, proves that it is he who has appeared to the eleven by offering to be handled and by eating before them.	**2.**	1:3 "To them he presented himself alive after his passion by many proofs...."
24:49 "And behold, I send the promise of my Father upon you; but stay in the city, until you are clothed with power from on high."	**3.**	1:4 "And while staying with them he charged them not to depart from Jerusalem, but to wait for the promise of the Father...."
24:47-48 "... and that repentance and forgiveness of sins should be preached in his name to all nations, beginning from Jerusalem. You are witnesses of these things."	**4.**	1:8b "... and you shall be my witnesses in Jerusalem and in all Judea and Samaria and to the end of the earth."
24:51-52 "... he parted from them. And they returned to Jerusalem...."	**5.**	1:9, 12 "... as they were looking on, he was lifted up, and a cloud took him out of their sight. Then they returned to Jerusalem...."

How does one explain these similarities between the end of Luke and the beginning of Acts? Acts 1:1-2 refers back to the Third Gospel and says that it treated what Jesus did and said "until the day when he was taken up. . . ." From what the author himself says, therefore, the events of Luke 24 and those mentioned in parts of Acts 1 are the same. How then does one explain the two reports of the same series of events? At least five possibilities present themselves. (1) If we assume an interval between the composition of the Gospel and Acts, then it may be that the author gained fresh information during that time. Like a modern scholar, he then used the fresh information which he considered more reliable in his most recent publication.[20] (2) Luke may have been familiar with the two distinct traditions and, following the method so common in the Old Testament, recorded the two as of equal value, without trying to adjudicate between them.[21] (3) The two different accounts of the same series of events may be due to an editorial interpolation into the original text of Luke and/or Acts made in the second century after the Gospel had been separated from its companion volume.[22] (4) The two accounts of the same events may be present because of some theological tendency of the author of Luke-Acts, such as his use of a Raphael typology in Luke 24 and an Elijah typology in Acts 1.[23] (5) The similar accounts may be due to a Lucan stylistic tendency, the use of repetition, and hence a part of the overall architecture of Luke-Acts.[24]

There may very well be two distinct traditions of the ascension behind Luke 24 and Acts 1. This would account for the significant differences between the two passages. The primary question, however, is how one explains their inclusion in Luke-Acts. The least likely alternative is that which posits interpolation in one or both sections.[25] Any explanation which thinks of Luke as a historian in the modern sense whose concern for factual accuracy is uppermost also must be discarded. Nor is it likely that the author of Luke-Acts can be thought of as the type of historian who would include all traditions known to him in order to be fair. This was certainly not the way he treated Mark, for example. In the light of modern study of the Lucan writings, that explanation is most probable which posits the creative hand of the author.[26] Hence, it seems likely that either a theological or a stylistic tendency or both played a role in the inclusion of the two very similar accounts in Luke 24 and Acts 1. This inference is borne out by an examination of each parallel in some detail.

The first parallel involves the similarity of Luke 24:33-34, 36 to Acts 1:3 in that both speak of appearances of the risen Christ to the apostles. Luke 24:34 echoes the same event mentioned in I Cor 15:5, the appearance to Peter. Doubtless this verse, together with its context, vss. 33, 35, is Luke's attempt to link the Emmaus narrative with what follows just as vss. 21-24 serve to link the Emmaus tradition with empty tomb narrative in vss. 1-11. Luke 24:36-42 is an edited passage possibly having at its base a legend of an appearance in Galilee.[27] Neither comes from Luke's Marcan source. Acts 1:3, moreover, is the Evangelist's own summary of events already treated in the Gospel. Hence, it is difficult not to see the first correspondence as due to the hand of Luke.

The second parallel, Luke 24:36-43 and Acts 1:3, consists of their similarity in that the risen Christ offers proof to his disciples of his resurrection. The Gospel passage where Jesus tells the disciples to handle him is roughly similar to John 20:26-29 but nowhere in the New Testament outside of Luke-Acts does the risen Lord prove his resurrection by eating before the disciples. Again, we note that Acts 1:3 is the author's summary. The parallel then is due to Lucan activity.

The third parallel consists of Luke 24:49 and Acts 1:4 in that both refer to Jesus' charge to the apostles to wait in Jerusalem for the coming of the Spirit. Luke 24:44-49 is in its entirety a literary production of Luke,[28] a speech like the speeches in Acts. Acts 1:4 forms the end of the author's summary which begins Acts. This correspondence too is due to Lucan effort.

Parallel number four, Luke 24:47-48 and Acts 1:8b, involves the commission of the apostles as witnesses and the charge to them to go to all peoples. Again, Luke 24:47-48 is part of the speech, vss. 44-49, which is a Lucan construct. Acts 1:8 merely echoes the Third Gospel. This parallel too is due to Luke.

Parallel number five, Luke 24:51-52 and Acts 1:9, 12, consists of the two passages' similarity in referring to both Jesus' ascension and the apostles' return to Jerusalem thereafter. Luke 24:50-53 appears also to be a literary creation in the main.[29] Acts 1:12 which locates the return to Jerusalem after the ascension legend of 1:9-11 is a Lucan transition. This parallel, like the others, then appears to be due to the activity of the author of Luke-Acts.

If the preceding examination of the parallels has given us substantial reason to regard them as due to the creative hand of the author of Luke-Acts, the patterns treated earlier, as evidence of Luke's architectonic scheme in which various parts of his total work have their counterparts so that balance is attained, lead us to conclude that the correspondences between the end of Luke and the beginning of Acts are stylistic tendency of the author and a part of the Lucan architecture. While they may also have theological significance, the parallels most certainly reflect Lucan style.

Luke 9 and Acts 1

The final example of the Lucan architecture which we will examine is one pointed out some years ago by J. G. Davies.[30] Davies' list included some fourteen points at which there were content and/or verbal correspondence between Luke 9:1-34 and Acts 1:1-12. His intent in presenting such a series of links between the two passages was to show that for Luke the transfiguration is a prefiguration of the ascension. While some of the individual suggestions may be discounted, the basic position of Davies seems tenable. Consider but three of the correspondences, for example.

Luke 9		*Acts 1*
9:28-36 The transfiguration story involving (1) Jesus and his disciples going up on a mountain (9:28); (2) a reference to dazzling white raiment (9:29); (3) mention of two men (9:30, 32); (4) these men speak of Jesus' ἔξοδος (9:31); (5) a cloud overshadowed them (9:34-35).	1.	1:9-11 The ascension narrative involving (1) Jesus and his disciples going up on a mountain (1:12); (2) a reference to white robes (1:10); (3) mention of two men (1:10); (4) these men speak of Jesus' going into heaven (1:11); (5) a cloud took him out of their sight (1:9).
9:1-6 The transfiguration is found in the same context with, but following, Jesus' commission to the twelve to preach Kingdom of God. He gave them power and authority.	2.	1:8 Jesus' ascension is preceded by his commission to the apostles to be witnesses. They will be such after they receive power.
9:11-17 A meal tradition is preceded by reference to Jesus' speaking of the Kingdom of God.	3.	1:3-4 Reference is made to Jesus' speaking with the apostles of the Kingdom of God. This is followed by a reference to his eating with them.

An examination of the Evangelist's use of his sources where this can be ascertained is helpful. In the correspondence between the Lucan transfiguration narrative (9:28-36) and the ascension story in Acts 1:9-11, for example, examination of Luke's use of Mark in the transfiguration pericope is instructive. While many of the details which comprise the correspondence are found in Mark 9:2-8 (e.g., the mountain, the cloud, the white robes of Jesus), there are significant alterations of Mark by Luke which seem in the interest of the parallel with Acts 1:9-11. First, in 9:28 Luke uses ἀνέβη instead of

Mark's ἀναφέρει (9:2). Jesus went up rather than Jesus took them up. This is doubtless tied to the ascension motif where Jesus ascends. Second, Luke adds to Mark 9:4's Elijah and Moses his own "two men" (9:30, 32) almost certainly to correspond to the "two men" of Acts 1:10. Third, Luke alters Mark by adding in vs. 31 that these two men spoke of Jesus' departure. The term is ἔξοδος which, in light of Luke's use of εἴσοδος in Acts 13:24, must be a reference to the ascension. With no controls on the sources for Acts 1 it is difficult to say how Luke treated his source material there. All we can say with certainty is that 1:9-11 is peculiar to Luke-Acts.

As regards the second correspondence, that between Luke 9:1-6 and Acts 1:8 because of the references to a commission of Jesus to the apostles for which they either are or will be empowered, it is significant to note that Luke 9:1 adds δύναμιν to Mark 6:7's ἐξουσία probably because Acts 1:8 has δύναμιν and that only by omission of Mark 6:45—8:26 is Luke able to locate the transfiguration and the commission to the Twelve in the same context.[31] Again the source problem for Acts 1 confronts us. The closest thing in New Testament tradition to Acts 1:8 is Matthew 28:18-20 which uses ἐξουσία instead of Acts' δύναμιν and uses it of Jesus rather than of the apostles.

The third correspondence which we have listed between Luke 9 and Acts 1 is the common linking of a meal and Jesus' words about the Kingdom of God found in Luke 9:11-17 and Acts 1:3-4. It is significant that the reference to Jesus' speaking of the Kingdom in Luke 9:11 is peculiar to Luke. It is the Evangelist's alteration of Mark 6:34. Acts 1:3-4 is a summary composed by the author of Luke-Acts. Hence this parallel too ultimately depends upon the hand of Luke.

In this part of Chapter Four, we have examined two additional examples of the Lucan architecture: the correspondences between the end of Luke and the beginning of Acts, and those between Luke 9 and Acts 1. Here we have found again that the author of Luke-Acts so modified his material that he achieved the parallels. These correspondences, moreover, are part of the larger architectonic scheme of Luke-Acts in which one series of persons and events is balanced by another so that the two correspond in some way.

If we reduce the formal patterns about which we have spoken in Chapters Two, Three, and Four to a diagram, it would look something like this.[32]

See diagram facing page.

These formal patterns raise a further question. Is the artistry involved in the composition of Luke-Acts unique to the Lucan literature? Was this a conventional way of writing in antiquity or must one believe that the author of Luke-Acts was a solitary literary genius of his time? It is to this type of question that we turn in the next chapter. Let us now consider these formal patterns of Luke-Acts in the light of evidence from the Lucan milieu.

LUKE

ACTS

1:5-25

1:26-38

1:57-80

2:1-52

3:1-20

3:21-4:15

4:16-7:17

7:18-8:56

Luke 9

Luke 22—23

10:21—13:30 × 14:1—18:30

Luke 9

Luke 24

1:12-4:23

4:24-5:42

Acts 1—12

Acts 13—28

15:1—18:11 × 18:12—21:26

Acts 1

Acts 1

FOOTNOTES

[1]The regular sequence is broken only at correspondences 1 and 2.

[2]"The Chiastic Structure of the Lucan Journey," in *Studia Evangelica* (2 vols., ed. F. L. Cross; Berlin: Akademie Verlag, 1964) 2. 195-202; *Type and History in Acts,* 138-39.

[3]*Die lukanische Geschichtsschreibung als Zeugnis,* 1. 156-57.

[4]That Luke here follows the order of his Marcan source doubtless accounts for the break in the normal order in parallels 1 and 2 in the above list.

[5]Luke's order is the more original; so Rigaux, *The Testimony of St. Matthew,* 119; Vincent Taylor, "The Original Order of Q," in *New Testament Essays* (London: Epworth, 1970) 95-118. Matthew's order is the more original; so Adolf Harnack, *The Sayings of Jesus: Vol. 2, New Testament Studies* (London: Williams & Norgate, 1908) 180.

[6]Matthew is the more original; so Rigaux, *The Testimony of St. Matthew,* 119. Cf. also A. M. Farrer, "On Dispensing with Q," in *Studies in the Gospels* (ed. D. E. Nineham; Oxford: Blackwell, 1955) 65. Harnack (*ibid.,* 115) argues that there is no difference in degree between Matthew and Luke in changes displaying bias in regard to subject matter; Luke, however, does alter style more.

[7]Though Sir John C. Hawkins, "Three Limitations to St. Luke's Use of St. Mark's Gospel," in *Studies in the Synoptic Problem,* 41-45, and Caird, *Saint Luke,* 25, think it comes from L.

[8]E.g., Bultmann, *History of the Synoptic Tradition,* 118, thinks Q, but Leaney, *The Gospel according to St. Luke,* 201, is sceptical.

[9]Jeremias, *The Parables of Jesus,* 29, however, argues that the Lucan setting is more original than Matthew's.

[10]C. F. Evans, "The Central Section of St. Luke's Gospel," in *Studies in the Gospels* (ed. D. E. Nineham; Oxford: Basil Blackwell, 1955) 37-53, argues that Luke 9:51—18:14 has been organized by the Evangelist with a view to presenting it as a Christian Deuteronomy. If one assumes, for the sake of argument, the validity of this view, it poses no challenge to our thesis. Cf. ch. 1, n. 68.

[11]So far as I know, the chiastic construction of this section has eluded scholarly attention. The chiastic arrangement of Acts 13—14 has been recognized by John Bligh, *Galatians* (London: St. Paul Publications, 1969) 7-14.

[12]Cf. Ernst Käsemann, "The Disciples of John the Baptist in Ephesus," in *Essays on New Testament Themes* (London: SCM, 1964) 136-48, for this interpretation of the material.

[13]On the "we-source" in recent discussion, see J. Dupont, *The Sources of Acts,* chs. 5-6.

[14]On the "itinerary source" in recent discussion, see Dupont (*ibid.,* ch. 7) and Kümmel, *Introduction to the New Testament,* 126, 131.

[15]*Studies in the Acts of the Apostles* (ed. H. Greeven; New York: Scribner's, 1956) 197-98.

[16]*Le "Livre des Actes" et l'histoire,* 128-38.

[17]E.g., "The Book of Acts as Source Material for the History of Early Christianity," in *Studies in Luke-Acts,* 260, 272-75.

[18]These correspondences are due only partially to the Lucan appropriation of antiquity's custom of recapitulating an earlier book at the beginning of the next (e.g., Diodorus Siculus, 1.42; 2.1; 3.1; Josephus, *Ant.,* 8.1, 1; 13.1, 1; 14.1, 1; 15.1, 1; Polybius, 2.1; 4.1; 3.1; Dionysius of Halicarnasus, Book 2; Livy, 31.1, 2; 21). On the whole matter of recapitulation, cf. R. Laqueur, "Ephoros," *Hermes* 46 (1911) 161-206. Acts 1:1-5 is indeed a recapitulation but the correspondences go through vs. 12. One may, therefore, say that Luke has expanded a custom of antiquity due to his stylistic tendency.

[19]Morgenthaler, *Die lukanische Geschichtsschreibung als Zeugnis,* 1. 180-82; J. G. Davies, *He Ascended into Heaven* (New York: Association, 1958) 42, 187; Goulder, *Type and History in Acts,* 16-17.

[20]Harnack, *The Acts of the Apostles,* 157.

[21]A possibility mentioned by Davies, *He Ascended into Heaven,* 49.

[22]P. H. Menoud, "Remarques sur les textes de l'ascension dans Luc-Actes," in *Neutestamentliche Studien fur Rudolf Bultmann*, 148-55.

[23]Davies, *He Ascended into Heaven*, 52-56; P. A. van Stempvoort, "Interpretation of the Ascension in Luke and Acts," *NTS* 5 (1958) 30-42.

[24]Goulder, *Type and History in Acts*, 16-17.

[25]One has but to list Menoud's arguments to see their inadequacy. See the remarks of H. Chadwick, *NTS* 2 (1955) 145, and D. P. Fuller, *Easter Faith and History* (Grand Rapids: Eerdmans, 1965) 196.

[26]Cf. Hugh Anderson's remarks, "Broadening Horizons: The Rejection at Nazareth Pericope of Luke 4:16-30 in Light of Recent Critical Trends," *Int* 18 (1964) 259-75.

[27]Bultmann, *History of the Synoptic Tradition*, 286.

[28]*Ibid.*

[29]*Ibid.*

[30]"The Prefigurement of the Ascension in the Third Gospel," *JTS* n. s., 6 (1955) 229-33.

[31]Cf. ch. 2, n. 74. Here is further confirmation for my contention that architectural reasons account for Luke's omission of Mark 6:45—8:26.

[32]Cf. ch. 2, n. 1.

CHAPTER V

The Patterns in the Light
of the Lucan Milieu

Up to this point we have been concerned primarily to show the existence
of certain patterns in the Lucan writings which ultimately are rooted in the
same architectonic principle, that of balance. In this chapter the aim will be
to show that other authors in the Lucan milieu utilized similar architectural
procedures, that such designs can also be found in the visual art of Luke's
time and place, and that this sense of form has its roots in a discernible
Zeitgeist or cultural trait. We will look first of all at the classical world, then
to the Near East where our focus will be primarily on the Israelite-Jewish
tradition, and finally at early Christianity generally. The chapter will close
with a consideration of certain questions that are raised by our survey of the
analogies.

The Classical World

Patterns reflecting the principle of balance abound in classical
literature. Classical scholars have called attention to such patterns in
Homer's *Iliad*[1] and *Odyssey*,[2] in the plays of Aeschylus[3] and Euripides,[4] in
the histories of Herodotus[5] and Thucydides,[6] in the *Odes* of Pindar,[7] in the
works of Catullus,[8] in the *Odes* of Horace,[9] in Vergil's *Aeneid*,[10] *Eclogues*,[11]
and *Georgics*,[12] in the Propertian *Monobiblos*,[13] and in Plutarch's *Parallel
Lives*.[14]

As an illustration of this classical tendency we may focus upon Vergil's
Aeneid because some of its patterns are so very close to what we have seen in
the Lucan writings. The *Aeneid* falls into two halves, the journey of Aeneas
from Troy to Latium (1—6) and Aeneas' adventures after his arrival (7—12).
This twofold structure is mentioned not only in the prooemium (1:1-4, 5-7)
but also indirectly in 7:44-45. It is significant that each book in the first half
of the poem is closely related to the corresponding book of the second half
by means of similarities and contrasts in subject matter.[15] The evidence is
much too extensive to give in full here but presentation of the
correspondences between Books 2 and 8 where the order, as well as the
subject matter, matches beautifully will serve to illustrate the complexity of
the parallels.[16]

Book 2	*Book 8*
Story of Carthage interrupted.	Story of Trojan camp interrupted.
Laocoon killed by two serpents.	Two serpents killed by Hercules.
Greeks destroy.	Greeks help to found.
Trojans suffer from Greeks.	Trojans profit from Greeks.
Helplessness of aged Priam.	Helpfulness of aged Evander.
Luxury of Priam's palace.	Simplicity of Evander's home.
Destruction of Troy.	Picture of later Rome.
Aeneas is center of stage.	Aeneas is center of stage.
Anchises prominent—father of Aeneas.	Evander prominent—father of Pallas.
Venus as goddess appears to Aeneas.	Venus as goddess appears to Aeneas.
Gods against Troy.	Gods for Rome (at Actium).
Ascanius—fire about head, comet.	Augustus—fire about head, comet.
At end, Aeneas carries on his shoulders his father (symbolic of the past).	At end, Aeneas carries on his shoulder the shield (picture of the future).

Not only is the *Aeneid* as a whole organized in such a way that its two halves correspond to one another, but also sections of various books are structured in terms of balance. The simplest form is an ABA' pattern where a section is framed by balancing passages. For example, 2:57-198 (the Simon episode) is preceded and followed by passages concerning Laocoon (2:40-56, 199-227); 7:341-539 (the threefold activity of Allecto) is preceded by Juno's lament and the summoning of Allecto (286-340) and is followed by the dismissal of Allecto (540-600); and 8:184-267 (the story of Cacus) which is framed by rites honoring Hercules (172-183, 268-305). More elaborate patterns, however, occur fairly frequently. For example, there is an ABCDC' B' A' pattern in 1:305-418, and ABCB' A' pattern in 6:56-123, and an ABCDEFGF' E' D' C' B' A' pattern in 4:1-705.[17] Just as in Luke-Acts, therefore, the *Aeneid* is organized both as a whole and in its parts around the principle of balance.

"Literature and the arts belong together as parts of a culture. They manifest in different media the underlying unity of a *Zeitgeist*."[18] The principles of both the literature and the art of Greece are certainly alike. The Greek drama and the Greek temple, for example, are constructed on parallel lines and equally embody the aesthetic ideas of the Greeks.[19] Of this link between art and literature the Greeks themselves were aware. In the ripe archaic period Simonides said: "Painting is silent poetry; poetry is painting that speaks."[20] Later in his *Republic* (605a) Plato called the dramatic poet "the counterpart of the painter." Moreover, in elaborating his theories of art, Plato applied them equally to poetry, painting, and sculpture. In doing so he followed the traditional notion that they were so closely related that they must be treated together in any consideration of their social and ethical uses.[21] Aristotle compared poets and artists several times in the *Poetics*. In fact, the interrelationship between Greek art and literature is so close in the Greek world of antiquity that T. B. L. Webster can say that "our remains of Greek art and literature are fragmentary, and sometimes gaps in the one can be filled by the other."[22] That this same interrelationship was sensed by Roman writers may be shown by the statement of Horace in his *Ars Poetica* (353-355) that "A poem is like a painting."[23]

It is no wonder then that modern scholars have pointed out the links between the architectonic schemes of classical literature and the ordering of classical art. For example, G. E. Duckworth has pointed to the fact that the same structural principles underlie the architecture of the *Aeneid* and the *Ara Pacis* or Augustan altar of peace.[24] He shows that the six friezes of the *Ara Pacis Augustae* are separated into two groups of three each by the two entrances so that there is a Roman half and a Julian-Augustan half which balance each other. In each the historical frieze is framed by legend and symbol. The following diagram shows it clearly:[25]

Roman half—	a.	Legend: Romulus and Remus
	b.	History: Roman magistrates in procession
	c.	Symbol: Roma
Augustan half—	a.	Legend: Aeneas sacrificing
	b.	History: Augustus and imperial family in procession
	c.	Symbol: Italia

Here as in the poetry of Vergil balance and symmetry play an important part. The fact is that the same law of duality arising out of the principle of balance is found in the classical world as widely in art as in literature.[26]

The common use of patterns arising out of the principle of balance in classical literature and art points to a certain facet of the classical mind. The Greek loved symmetry, pattern, and balance. From at least the time of Isocrates,[27] the form of what was said was regarded as more important than what was said.[28] The Greek not only liked his creations to be symmetrical or patterned, he also believed that the universe at large must be so ordered. After all, in the course of a year does not the darkness balance the light, the cold balance the heat?[29] Therefore, Greeks tended to impose pattern where it was not in fact to be found. A most instructive example is to be found in Herodotus.[30] Concerned about the origin of the Nile, Herodotus tells a story he had at third hand. A group of adventurous youths determined to explore the Libyan desert, trying to penetrate farther than had ever been done before. Crossing the desert in a westerly direction they travelled for many days before they were captured by pygmies and taken to their city past which flowed a great river from west to east. Herodotus' informant said the river was the Nile and Herodotus agreed since it was "reasonable." It was reasonable because of natural symmetry. Just as the Danube bisects Europe so the Nile bisects Africa. Since the mouths of the Nile and Danube are opposite one another, and since the Danube rises in the far west, what is more obvious than that the

Nile rises in the west too and so has its source, as well as its mouth, opposite the Danube. Whoever made the earth must have made it properly, that is, in symmetrical form so that its parts balance each other.[31] The principle of balance was believed to be inherent in the nature of reality.

At the beginning of the Christian era, moreover, the Roman educational process tended to reinforce and cultivate the classical perspective just as Greek education had done prior to this time.[32] This was true both of what was read and of how it was read. In what was the equivalent of our secondary schools Vergil was the first Latin poet put into the hands of the young and he served as the foundation of the Latin course. Next to him Horace was most read.[33] Homer's works, of course were the basis of the Greek course. It is precisely in these works that the architectonic skills of the classical world are greatest. A system of education which focused on Homer and Vergil so that they were the only nourishment of the youthful intellect of necessity early developed a sense of form which became second nature for impressionable minds.[34] After completion of this beginning study of poetry, lads and young men were admitted into the rhetorical schools where they studied prose instead of poetical models.[35] Here speech was valued as an artistic product quite apart from its content or significance.[36] The effect of rhetorical dominance of education was that even prose had a poetical quality. An example of this can be seen in the practice of improvisation, which had been popular earlier and was still practiced. The younger Pliny tells of the Assyrian Isaeus who came to Rome before 100 C.E. "He always speaks extempore, and his lectures are as finished as though he had spent a long time over their written composition."[37] Also all literature was written to be read aloud. This was true even of historical works, as the younger Pliny testifies.[38] Reading out loud tends to impress on historical works, as well as other genres, a certain rhetorical character.[39] Thus, both what was read and how it was read would tend to reinforce the aesthetic assumptions of classical man making him highly sensitive to form, pattern, and balance.

At the beginning of the Christian era the Greco-Roman world was possessed of a highly developed sense of form and operated out of an aesthetic which saw the principle of balance as rooted in the nature of reality. The law of duality which is found in the literature and art of the classical world is but a creative expression of the aesthetic assumptions of classical man. In light of the literary, artistic, and aesthetic tendencies of classical civilization, therefore, it is not at all surprising to find a Greek document like Luke-Acts employing the law of duality as its architectonic principle.

Israelite-Jewish Aesthetic

Classical civilization was by no means the only source for the principle of balance in the environment of the author of Luke-Acts. The Near East also reflects a concern with the law of duality in its literary traditions and art. In this section of the chapter our focus will be primarily upon the Israelite-Jewish phase of Near Eastern culture for two major reasons. First, it was through the medium of Israelite-Jewish culture that the Near East most directly influenced early Christianity of which Luke-Acts was a part. Second, though we have ample evidence of the art of the ancient Near East to enable us to make generalizations, it is only of the literature of Israel and Judaism that we have sufficient scholarly study with results relevant for our purposes.

Students of the literature of Israel and Judaism have made it clear that the patterns found in classical literature are by no means peculiar to the writings of Greece and Rome. The principle of balance has been seen controlling the composition of Exod 7:8—10:27,[40] Exod 5—14,[41] 1 Kgs 3—11,[42] 1 Enoch 93; 96:12-17,[43] 1 QS 3:13—4:26,[44] and many of the Qumran *Hodayot*[45] as well as whole books like Ruth,[46] Jonah,[47] Habakkuk,[48] and Micah.[49]

As an illustration of this tendency in the literature of Israel and Judaism we may focus upon the book of Jonah because here in the Near East we find patterns that are very close to those discerned in Luke-Acts. Building upon the work of a number of other scholars,[50] George M. Landes points out that one of the most remarkable features of the book of Jonah is the construction of the narrative into two parts, each roughly parallel to the other.[51]

1:17	The focus shifts to Jonah.	4:1-11	The focus shifts to Jonah.
2:10	Jonah is spared.	4:1	Jonah is angry because Nineveh is spared.
2:1	Jonah prays.	4:2a	Jonah prays.
2:2-6a	He refers back to his distressing situation in the deep.	4:2a	He refers back to his distressing situation in Palestine.
2:6b-7	He asserts God's merciful deliverance.	4:2b	He asserts the mercy of God that leads to deliverance.
2:8	He draws an insight from this deliverance: idolators forsake the one who loves them.	4:2a	He draws an inference from the thought that God may save Nineveh: he must flee to Tarshish.
2:9	Jonah's response to Yahweh: worship with sacrifices and vows.	4:3	Jonah's response to Yahweh: a plea for death.
2:10	Yahweh's response to Jonah: he acts so that the prophet may respond favorably to the divine mission, still to be accomplished.	4:4-11	Yahweh's response to Jonah: he acts so that the prophet may respond favorably to the divine mission, already accomplished.

Moreover, Landes points out that chs. 1 and 2 exhibit several parallel motifs.

1:4	Crisis situation: threatened by destruction by a storm.	2:3	(cf. 1:15) Crisis: threatened drowning in the sea.
1:14	The sailor's response to the crisis: prayer, ultimately to Yahweh.	2:2	Jonah's response to the crisis: prayer to Yahweh.
1:15b	Yahweh's reaction to the sailor's prayer: deliverance from the storm.	1:17; 2:6b	Yahweh's reaction to Jonah's prayer: deliverance from death in the sea.

1:16 The sailors' concluding response to Yahweh's salvation: worship of Yahweh through cultic acts of sacrifice and vows.

2:9 Jonah's concluding response to Yahweh's salvation: worship of Yahweh through praise, culminating in the resolve to perform cultic acts of sacrifice and vow.

As Landes indicates, a similar pattern occurs also in chs. 3 and 4.

3:4 Crisis situation for the Ninevites: threatened destruction of Nineveh.

4:1 Presupposition of 4:1 is a crisis situation for Jonah: Nineveh seems to be saved from destruction.

3:5-8 Response of Ninevites to the crisis: faith in God, acts of contrition and repentance.

4:1-3 Response of Jonah to the crisis: anger, complaint to God, and request for death.

3:10 Response of Yahweh to the Ninevites: He changes his mind about destroying the city.

4:4, 6-11 Response of Yahweh to Jonah: through word and action he tries to get Jonah to change his mind about the destruction of the city.

In addition to Landes' study, R. Pesch[52] has recently shown that the first chapter of Jonah is arranged in a balanced fashion with an inverted order, as may be seen in the following scheme:

A- vss. 4, 5a   The sailors are afraid: the sea rages.
B- vs. 5a, b   The sailors cried to their gods.
 C- vss. 5b, c, 6a   Attempts to save the ship.
  D- vs. 6a, b   Jonah is exhorted to help.
   E- vs. 7a   The sailors ask the cause of their plight.
    F- vs. 7b   The lot fell upon Jonah.
     G- vs. 8   Jonah is asked to explain.
      H- vss. 9, 10a   I fear Yahweh, the creator.
     G'- vs. 10a, b   Jonah is asked to explain.
    F'- vs. 10c   They knew Jonah was fleeing from Yahweh.
   E'- vs. 11   The sailors ask Jonah the remedy to their plight.
  D'- vs. 12   Jonah gives instructions that will help.
 C'- vs. 13   Attempts to save the ship are in vain.
B'- vs. 14   The sailors cry to Yahweh.
A'- vss. 15, 16a   The sea ceased from its raging: the sailors feared Yahweh.

Taking the two studies of Landes and Pesch together, we find that we have a prose work (for the most part) which is divided into two parallel halves, each of which is further divided into two parallel parts. Furthermore, ch. 1 falls into two halves in inverted order around a centerpiece. The similarities with what we have found in Luke-Acts are remarkable.

The art of Israel and Judaism was for the most part a reflection of the dominant foreign influence(s) of the moment.[53] The Hebrews had no artistic tradition of their own. Even when art began to flourish in the reign of Solomon, it was indebted to foreign craftsmen, resources, and techniques.

What was true for Solomon's time remained true throughout the history of Israel and Judaism into the beginnings of the Christian era. This being so, it is significant to note that the principle of balance played a key role in the art of all periods of the two great centers of ancient civilization which framed Palestine in the pre-Hellenistic period, Egypt[54] and Mesopotamia.[55] If we had only the evidence of Mesopotamian, Egyptian, and Greek artistic traditions and we knew that Israelite-Jewish art was influenced by whichever foreign influence was dominant at a given period, we would assume that Israelite-Jewish art too would be controlled in large measure by the principle of balance. It now remains to turn to some of the remains of Israelite-Jewish art from Solomon to the beginnings of the Christian era to see if in fact this is the case.

Solomon's temple which can be reconstructed on the basis of written accounts (1 Kgs 6—8 and to some extent Ezek 41—43) and archeological parallels is the first example. Basically it comes within the category of the long house temple found in various forms in ancient Canaan.[56] From the floor plan, it appears it was built on a line so that each half corresponds to the other. Parrot's reconstruction of a movable laver of Solomon's temple made on the basis of 1 Kgs 7:27-29 and lavers from Larnaka and Enkomi shows a bronze stand decorated with a whole collection of beast and various vegetal or linear motifs arranged in a series of balanced patterns (ABCDC′ B′ A: CDCADA: BDBCDC: ABCDC′ B;A;). [57] Pottery models of local shrines dating from the period of the divided monarchy have been found at Gezer, Tell el Farah near Nablus, and in the Transjordan. All reflect bilateral symmetry in their designs.[58]

From the post-exilic period there are a number of examples that may be cited. First, the frieze in high relief which ran around the entire temple, as cited in Ezek 12:18-19, contained as its major decoration a palm tree between two cherubim each of which had two faces so that the face of the man was toward the palm tree on the one side and the face of a lion on the other. This balanced design is common in the decorative treatment of Persian buildings (e.g., Darius' palace at Persepolis).[59] Second, from the Ptolemaic period we may mention the ruins of the Tobiad Palace at Iraq el Amir which displays all the characteristics of Alexandrine architecture and decoration including balanced animal figures.[50] Third, from the reign of Herod the Great we may mention the triangular tymphanon of a funeral cave known as the Cave of Jehoshaphat. In the center is an acanthus surrounded by tendrils which move out toward the corners. Fruits, leaves, or flowers appear within each of the near-circles formed by the vine tendrils. Each of the four near-circles on the one side is balanced by four on the other. In its general nature, it shows all the characteristics of Hellenistic-Alexandrine art.[61] Also, there is a stone ossuary found near Jerusalem and dating from the first century B.C.E. which has decorations which may be symbolized by the letters ABA′.[62] Finally, one must refer to the golden candelabra from the temple in Jerusalem which appears on the arch of Titus in Rome.[63] The seven branched candelabra seems to be a genuine Jewish creation. At least up to the present, neither in Mesopotamia nor in Egypt nor in any other part of the Near East has a similar lamp form been found.[64] This lamp form, of course, consists of a centerpiece balanced on either side by three pieces. Thus, the remains of Israelite-Jewish art have confirmed what we would have expected from a knowledge of the art of Mesopotamia, Egypt, and Greece. The principle of balance controls much Israelite-Jewish art just as it does much of the artistic expressions of other Mediterranean peoples. The art, as well as the literature, of Israelite-Jewish culture often is organized so that various parts are balanced by other parts.

Having looked briefly at the literature and the art of the ancient Near East as it is focused for us in the literature and art of Israel-Judaism and having found a strong tendency to self-expression in terms of balance, the question naturally arises as to how such literary and artistic style is related to the general mind-set of the Near Eastern peoples. No aesthetic of the Old Testament or of the ancient Near East has yet been written.[65] Nevertheless, certain observations are possible.

In the first place, the very law of duality by which one part is made to correspond to another by being either analogous or contrasting seems deeply rooted in Near Eastern mentality. Regarding Egypt, John A. Wilson has pointed out the correlation between many Egyptian attitudes and the geography of Egypt.[55] A primary aspect of the landscape of Egypt is its symmetry. East bank balances west bank as eastern mountain range balances western mountain range. Corresponding to this is bilateral symmetry in Egyptian art where the best products show a careful counterpoising of parts to secure harmonious balance. Analogies are also found in Egyptian literature with its parallelism of members, and in Egyptian cosmology and theology where each observable phenomenon and each supernatural power had its counterpart. "Probably the most outstanding feature of the Egyptian mentality was the feeling for order and balance which pervades every aspect of its culture."[57] Regarding Mesopotamia, Henri Frankfort has pointed out how Mesopotamian society was entirely adapted to the cyclic succession of the seasons.[68] This involved a counterbalancing of winter harshness and spring relaxation, of the plague of summer and the refreshing rains of autumn. Death was counterbalanced by the recurring miracle of new life. Johannes Pedersen has focused his attention on the psychology of Israel.[69] He contends that whereas we argue by means of conclusions and logical progress, the Israelite's argumentation consisted in showing that one statement associates with another, as belonging to its totality. The Hebrew manner of argumentation was not to persuade by means of abstract reasoning. It rather consisted in assurance and repetition. The *parallelismus membrorum* thereby became his natural manner of expression. He expressed himself twice in a different manner. The result was a totality with a double accent. To argue, he repeated.[70] It would seem then that Israel is a true focus of Near Eastern mentality in this regard. It is part of Near Eastern mentality to think in terms of balance, to argue in terms of balance, to express oneself generally in terms of balance because somehow this symmetry is felt to be rooted in the cosmos itself.

In the second place, there appear to be aesthetic roots in the Near Eastern mind for the practice of organizing a literary piece as a whole and in various ones of its parts in terms of the patterns of balance. Frankfort points out that although it offends our ways of thinking, for the Near Eastern mind the part partakes of the whole.[71] Such participation reduces the significance of distinctions and increases that of every resemblance. Pedersen's observations on Hebrew psychology point in the same direction.[72] Hebrew psychology, he contends, is of such a character that the part is seen as a manifestation of the original totality, the essence of which is diffused throughout the part. Hence, it is likely that an Israelite-Jewish author would have conceived of the whole literary work in terms of the principle of balance first before going on further to organize the various parts of the work along the same lines, thereby infusing them with the character of the whole. Such a procedure certainly seems to make sense in any attempt to understand the manner in which the book of Jonah was constructed, for example.

In the ancient Near East as in classical civilization the principle of balance plays an important role in the self-expression of people both in their literature and in their art. Since early Christianity had roots in and contacts with both the Jewish and the Greco-Roman cultural communities, we would anticipate its reflecting also a preoccupation with the principle of balance in its self-expression.

Early Christianity

Certain early Christian writings other than Luke-Acts have also apparently been organized in terms of the principle of balance. Scholars have argued that the law of duality controls the arrangement of such sources as I Corinthians 8—10,[73] Galatians,[74] Romans 9—11,[75] Philemon,[76] Revelation 1:13—2:18,[77] the Fourth Gospel both as a whole and in its parts,[78] the *Protevangelium Jacobi*,[79] the childhood Gospel of Thomas,[80] some of the apocryphal Acts,[81] and Melito of Sardis' *On the Passover*.[82]

As an illustration of the early Christian use of the principle of balance outside of Luke-Acts we may focus upon the *Protevangelium Jacobi* because its use of the law of duality results in some patterns that have close analogies to some of those found in Luke-Acts. In H. R. Smid's commentary on the apocryphal gospel, this duality is called the method of counterpoint. "The construction may be described as follows: two persons, two events, two stories correspond to one another, because the same theme is treated."[83] Smid gives some thirty-two illustrations of the *Zweiheitsgesetz* in his *Protevangelium Jacobi,* from which we may choose a few examples. The correspondence may occur in very small units, as when in the same verse Joseph's drinking (16:2) is balanced by Mary's drinking, or as when the annuniciation to Anna (4:1) is balanced by the annunciation to Joakim one verse later (4:2). Or the correspondences may involve larger sections, as when Joseph's being afraid of the task assigned to him (9:3) is balanced by Mary's acceptance of the task assigned to her (11:3), or when a wonder outside the cave during the birth of Jesus (18:2) is balanced by a wonder inside the cave (19:2). Sometimes the correspondences are at some distance with little apparent concern for the order of events, as when the presence of a midwife at the birth of Mary (5:2) is balanced by the presence of a midwife at the birth of Jesus (19:2), or as when a voice and an appearance of an angel to Mary (11:1,2) is balanced by an appearance and a voice of an angel to Salome (20:3). Finally, it appears that the first (1:1) and the last (25) parts of the work correspond (an inclusion).

These correspondences are, of course, a bit different from some of the others we have observed. Whereas frequently the correspondences have been found to fall into a set order, either AB:A′ B′ or AB:B′ A′, here they have very little sustained order. In this regard, they are very much like the correspondences of Luke 4—8. Nevertheless, it is the principle of balance that is clearly at work in the selection and formulation of the material in the *Protevangelium Jacobi*.

Turning briefly to the artistic remains of early Christianity, we find ourselves faced with a set of serious problems. First, what is extant of the art of the earliest Christians comes almost entirely from the catacombs. This means that we know very little beyond the funeral art of the earliest church. Frescoes and sarcophal reliefs are the major types of funeral art represented.[84] Second, the earliest of this funeral art comes from a time after Luke-Acts, that is, after 100 C.E. Earlier investigators such as De Rossi, Marucchi, and Wilpert believed that the oldest parts of the cemeteries could be dated from post-apostolic times, that is, near the end of the first Christian century.[85] Of the present generation of scholars, on the other hand, some prefer to set the beginnings of this art in the first half of the second century, others even want to date the earliest catacomb paintings near 200 C.E.[86] Third, Christian art emerged not as a new artistic language but as a perpetuation of the ancient tradition. It was distinguished from late classical art only by its different themes which come in the main from scripture.[87] Thus, what we have of early Christian art is fragmentary, later than 100 C.E., and partakes of the character of Greco-Roman art of its time. Nevertheless, it may be helpful to note some facets of what is available for examination.

From our vantage point it is important to note that in the earliest Christian artistic remains, the classical and pre-classical tradition of heraldic symmetry exerted a considerable influence. For example, Daniel is depicted between two lions and two birds flanking a vase.[88] Or when the Madonna and child are placed between the wise men, they number two or four, one or two on either side of the mother and child. When the Madonna is at one side, however, and the wise men approach, they number the traditional three.[89] Moreover, in the various pictures of the breaking of bread the number of people feasting is always seven. The number of baskets of loaves is seven in all cases except two. In one the number is increased to eight because seven violated the law of symmetry in this painting. In the other the number is twelve partly for the same reason.[90] In fact the physical law of symmetry is rarely violated in catacomb painting. If we find a picture of Moses striking a rock, the scene will be balanced by a scene of the baptism of Jesus.[91] The same balance is found on Christian sarcophagi from the second century. On the long side of one which has the form of a Roman bathtub we find in the center the figure of the good shepherd flanked on either side by vegetation. Beyond the vegetation on the left is a teacher expounding scripture who is flanked by two adult men. Beyond the vegetation on the right is a matron holding a roll of scriptures. Behind her stands a young girl who listens eagerly. Before her stands an orant (i.e., the soul of the girl who died). At either extremity of the sarcophagus is an animal figure facing out. The balance is nearly exact.[92] It would seem legitimate, then, to say that when Christian art emerged in the Greco-Roman world it shared with that culture a concern for balance in its visual self-expression. It is hardly proper to suppose that any earlier Christian art than that extant would have been different. Early Christian art as well as early Christian literature finds balance a congenial architectonic principle within which to express itself.

It is not possible to speak of a unique Christian aesthetic at this early stage of the Christian community's life. Early Christianity was a part of the general Mediterranean culture of the time which, by virtue of both its classical and Near Eastern roots, was characterized by a strong predisposition to balance in all types of self-expression. Early Christianity shared this predisposition and we have seen it come to light both in literature and in art.

Questions Raised by the Survey

(1) One who has immersed himself in the literature referred to within this survey and in the Lucan literature cannot help being struck by the presence of asymmetries in many of the patterns. They are certainly in the *Aeneid*. In the correspondences between Books 1 and 7, for example, three of the eighteen content parallels differ in their order.[93] When Juno laments her lack of power in Book 1, its content parallel in Book 7 in thirteenth in order. Also, the content parallel in Book 7 to the disguised Venus' meeting Aeneas and revealing her identity (item 9, Book 1) is item fourteen in the order of Book 7. The asymmetries are also present in Jonah's patterns.[94] For example, certain disruptions in the order of the two parallel halves of the book are present (cf. 2:10; 4:2b), other verses have no counterpart in the opposite section (cf. 1:9-15a, 16; 4:5, 8cd-11), and there are differences in the length of balanced sections (cf. 1:6b as over against 3:6b-8; 1:1-9 as over against 4:2-3). The asymmetries are there in Luke-Acts too. In the correspondences between John and Jesus in the birth narratives, for example, there is a disruption in the order of the cycle in Luke 1:57—2:52. Although there is a content correspondence between John's being circumcised on the eighth day and named as the angel

had directed and Jesus' being circumcized at the end of eight days and named as the angel had directed, 1:59-64 is the third theme of 1:57-80 while 2:21 is the fourth item in the order of 2:1-52. In the correspondences between the Third Gospel and the Acts, moreover, there is a significant difference in the length of Luke 10:1-12, the mission of the seventy which foreshadows the Gentile mission of the church, and Acts 13—20, the missionary journeys of Paul to the Gentiles. One cannot help wondering why, if an author really intended to construct his work around certain patterns expressive of the principle of balance, the patterns are sometimes marred by asymmetrical elements?

One does not need to look far for an answer. Imperfections of form are the rule in antiquity. Though the symmetry is often near perfect, it is no surprise to find asymmetrical elements amid the most elaborate architectonic schemes. The classical mind seems adverse to perfect symmetry. Zoilus of Amphipolis (4th century B.C.E.), whose name is proverbial for criticism of Homer, filled nine books with such criticisms. Among them was his attack on "the perfect symmetry with which Odysseus, in his contest with the Cicones, lost exactly six men from each of his ships."[95] The rhetoricians say to the credit of Demosthenes that his antitheses were not painfully exact throughout.[96] Horace (65 B.C.E.—8 B.C.E.) in his *Ars Poetica* (347—351) said that in large scale works of art one can well afford to be neglectful in small matters, provided that the whole conception stands out boldly.[97] Longinus, *On the Sublime*, (either 1st century B.C.E. or 1st century C.E.) has a similar position. In 33:1 it is said. "Now I am well aware that the greatest natures are least immaculate. Perfect precision runs the risk of triviality, whereas in great writing as in great wealth there must needs be something overlooked."[98] Also in Demetrius, *On Style*, 5:250 (50—100 C.E.) there is a condemnation of too perfect a balance. It would seem that while symmetry is dominant in Greek and Roman literature from the arrangement of a whole to the organization of the parts, it was considered poor form to have a too perfect symmetry. There must be asymmetrical elements present. For the classical mind "pure form is never beautifull; it is neither natural nor living. It is the infinite minute variations within the law of form which gives beauty both to nature and to the greatest art."[99]

The ancient Near Eastern man seems as adverse to perfect symmetry as classical man. Relevant to this observation is the statement of John A. Wilson that the ancient Egyptian "had a strong sense of symmetry and balance, but he had little sense of incongruity: he was perfectly willing to balance off incompatibles."[100] More to the point, however, are the words of George Adam Smith.

> In every form of Oriental art we trace the influence of what may be called Symmetrophobia: an instinctive aversion to absolute symmetry, which if it knows no better, will express itself in arbitrary and even violent disturbances of the style or pattern of the work.

Every visitor to the East knows how this tendency operates, and sometimes grotesquely, in weaving and architecture. But its opportunities are more frequent, and can be worked out more gracefully, in the art of poetry, particularly when that art is wedded to music.[101]

Our survey of analogies has shown that symmetrophobia is at work in the composition of Israelite-Jewish prose as well. Given the aversion to perfect symmetry in both classical and Near Eastern cultures, it is no surprise to find imperfections in the patterns of the early Christian writings of our survey and of Luke-Acts. They are to be expected in the midst of the most perfect symmetry.

(2) It would seem that any author who produced such a complex work, organized as a whole and in its parts around the law of duality, must have consciously contrived to get such a result. Would not such an author have had to have some kind of ground plan from which to work? Several strands of evidence from the classical world indicate that authors did in fact work from a preliminary sketch. In his *Poetics* (17:5-8) Aristotle give the advice that the "stories, whether they are traditional or whether you made them up yourself, should first be sketched in outline and then expanded by putting in episodes." Vergil apparently followed this guidance. The Donatus-Suetonius *Life* (23), written between 106-113 C.E., says that Vergil worked from a preliminary sketch, a prose outline, which he subsequently turned into verse. A similar procedure seems to be suggested for the writer of history in Lucian's *How To Write History*, 48. According to his letters (9:36), Pliny followed such a procedure. Furthermore, just as a Vergil, following Aristotle's dictates, would first make a prose outline and work from that to his finished product, so the classical artist used a preliminary sketch.[102] This explains how such complex balanced form could be attained. The pattern was a reasoned conclusion before the artist began. Though we have no explicit statement from the ancient Near East along these lines, insofar as I know, it is difficult to think that the practices there differed substantially. The complexity of the patterns demanded some preliminary plan from which an author could work.

(3) Is it likely that so complex an arrangement of a literary work would have been perceived by the readers/hearers of the document? This is an exceedingly difficult question to answer. There are at least four possibilities: (a) the architectonic scheme was the secret of the author; (b) a few besides the author may have been conscious of the pattern but only after considerable reflection; (c) the pattern was immediately felt by most readers/hearers but was not consciously perceived by anyone until after reflection; (d) the pattern was generally recognized at the conscious level at the time of reading. In attempting to indicate a preference from among these four possibilities we must take account of two facts. On the one hand, a great artist always puts into a work more than is ordinarily realized. This would seem to argue that Vergil, for example, never intended his architectonic application of the principle of

balance to be consciously grasped by his readers/hearers.[103] On the other hand, we must consider the heightened sensitivity to form which characterized man in antiquity. In a world sensitive to form, moreover, the law of duality was a conventional way of shaping one's expression. It was a type of literary and artistic design that people expected. This would seem to argue that though Vergil never intended his readers to grasp his architectonic scheme, they may very well have done so. The way out of the dilemma posed by these two facts lies in the recognition that an author's use of a clear-cut pattern such as the principle of balance could be expected to touch a reader/hearer first of all at the level of what Kenneth Burke calls the "muscular imagination." What Burke means by this is that the rhythm embodied in the form of a writing is closely allied with the rhythm of "bodily" processes. The contraction and relaxation of the heart, alternation of the feet in walking, breathing in and breathing out, up and down, back and forth, in and out, are the kinds of motor experiences "tapped" by rhythm.

> The rhythm of a page, in setting up a corresponding rhythm in the body, creates marked degrees of expectancy, or acquiescence. A rhythm is a promise which the poet makes to the reader—and in proportion as the reader comes to rely upon this promise, he falls into a state of general surrender which makes him more likely to accept without resistance the rest of the poet's material. In becoming receptive to so much, he becomes receptive to still more. . . .[104]

Burke's point is that in all rhythmic experiences one's muscular imagination is touched.

Consider the light this sheds on our understanding of Luke-Acts. The reader/hearer would have been confronted at the very first in Luke's preface (1:1-4) with a balanced unit in which a threefold protasis is balanced by a threefold apodosis.[105] Using Burke's categories, the arrangement of the preface would tap the reader's "muscular imagination" from his first contact with the Gospel and would lead him to expect more of the same. The birth narratives of Luke 1—2 with their balancing of John and Jesus that is unmistakeable even to the uninitiated would both satisfy the expectancy created by the rhythmic promise of the preface and create further expectation. This expectation would be intensified by confrontation with the Benedictus (1:68-79) which as a whole and in its parts is organized according to a balanced concentric symmetry.[106] For a person conditioned by his culture to expect such patterns, these instances of balance at the very beginning of the Third Gospel would be enough to set up a rhythm and to create an expectancy in the reader for more. In becoming receptive this far, he would become receptive to still more. He would *feel* with the author in this rhythm. As Robert L. Scranton has incisively put it:

Apart from their meanings, words may appeal to the sense of motion in their rhythmic arrangement . . . . Such rhythms may be apparent in single lines or through *larger sections* of a composition and may vary in a number of ways from simple alternating rise and fall of stress to *complex patterns* of varied character or speed.[107] (Italics mine)

Afterwards in a reflective moment the pattern could become a conscious intellectual perception, though it need not become such. If the pattern did become a conscious perception then the reader would be enabled to see the section as a whole. Of the alternatives, then, it seems more probable that the architectonic patterns would have been immediately sensed or felt but not consciously and rationally perceived until after reflection.

(3) What relation did such architectonic patterns expressive of the principle of balance have to the meaning of an ancient piece of literature? There are signs that such structural procedure was originally mnemonic and functional.[108] For example, in the *Odyssey* 11: 170—203, Odysseus asks the shade of his mother five questions and she answers precisely in reverse order. Pattern and repetition are certainly significant aids to the memory. Such a purpose is superseded, however, in the *Iliad* when the principle of balance becomes the structural basis for a fifteen-thousand-line poem. Here it is an artistic principle with primarily an aesthetic function. Homer seems to be playing with abstract form for its own sake.[109] There are times, however, when pattern functions neither as a mnemonic device nor as an abstract architectonic principle. It is related frequently to the meaning an author seeks to convey. This may be illustrated from the classical world by Vergil's *Aeneid*. Vergil's hero is the pious Aeneas whose *pietas* is an achievement. The battle between *pietas* and impious rebellion had to be fought out inside the hero as well as between the hero and his impious opponents. This can be seen depicted in the plan of the whole poem: the first six books depicting the inner struggle for *pietas;* the last six books showing the triumph of *pietas* over the impious. The former is the basis and the prototype for the latter.[110] The same fact may be illustrated from the Near East by the book of Jonah. For example, the parallels between chs. 1 and 2 point up the fact that when faced with similar perils, there is no significant difference between the pagans and Jonah with respect to their supplicating Yahweh, the deliverance they receive from him, and the response they make to their Savior. The correspondences between chs. 3 and 4 are contrasts. In his refusal to repent and change his mind about the destruction of the Ninevites Jonah's attitude is in striking contrast to that of the Ninevites.[111] To summarize: in the Mediterranean world an architectural pattern could function as (a) an assist to the memory of the readers/hearers, that is, a mnemonic device; (b) an assist to the meaning of the whole or of a section; or (c) an abstract architectonic principle, a convention, used solely for aesthetic purposes. Frequently the patterns of a piece of literature functioned in more than one of these ways. Sometimes all three functions are found in the same document.[112]

What functions do these Lucan patterns serve? Is there a relation between pattern and meaning in Luke-Acts? It is to this question that we turn in the final three chapters.

FOOTNOTES

[1]Cedric H. Whitman, *Homer and the Heroic Tradition.* G. S. Kirk, *The Songs of Homer* (Cambridge: Cambridge University Press, 1962), 261-67, is critical of Whitman. Kirk is mainly concerned to minimize this type of architectural evidence as an argument for the unity of the *Iliad* and the *Odyssey.* There is simply too much evidence for this type of design, however, for it to be rejected out of hand. For earlier statements of positions similar to that of Whitman, cf. J. T. Shepherd, *The Pattern of the Iliad* (London: Methuen, 1922); C. M. Bowra, *Tradition and Design in the Iliad* (Oxford: Clarendon, 1930); J. L. Myres, "The Last Book of the Iliad," *JHS* 52 (1932) 264-96; "The Structure of the Iliad, Illustrated by the Speeches," *Ibid.,* 74 (1954) 122-41; S. E. Bassett, *The Poetry of Homer* (Berkeley: University of California Press, 1938).

[2]Whitman, *Homer and the Heroic Tradition,* 285-309; J. L. Myres, "The Pattern of the Odyssey," *JHS* 72 (1952) 1-19.

[3]George Thomson, "Notes on *Prometheus Vinctus,*" *Classical Quarterly* 23 (1929) 155-63; John Myres, "The Structure of Stichomythis in Attic Tragedy," *Proceedings of the British Academy* 34 (1948) 199-231.

[4]T. V. Buttrey, "Accident and Design in Euripides' *Medea,*" *American Journal of Philology* 79 (1958) 1-17.

[5]John L. Myres, *Herodotus: Father of History* (Oxford: Clarendon, 1953) 81-91. Tilman Krischer, "Herodots Pooimion," *Hermes* 93 (1965) 195-67, points out the balanced beginning of Herodotus. This is important because Luke also begins with a balanced prologue.

[6]J. L. Myres, *Who Were the Greeks?* (Berkeley: University of California Press, 1930) 605, n. 112.

[7]Gilbert Norwood, *Pindar* (Berkeley: University of California Press, 1945) 72; R. W. B. Burton, *Pindar's Pythian Odes* (Oxford: Oxford University Press, 1962).

[8]Clyde Murley, "The Structure and Proportion of Catullus 64," *Transactions of the American Philological Association* 68 (1937) 308; Niall Rudd, "Colonia and Her Bridge: A Note on the Structure of Catullus 17," *ibid.* 90 (1959) 238-42; Joseph Wohlberg, "The Structure of the Laodamia Simile in Catullus 68b," *Classical Philology* 50 (1955) 46; C. W. Mendell, "The Influence of the Epyllion on the *Aeneid,*" *Yale Classical Studies* 12 (1951) 212-18.

[9]G. E. Duckworth, *Structural Patterns and Proportions in Vergil's Aeneid* (Ann Arbor: University of Michigan Press, 1962) 14; "The *Aeneid* as a Trilogy," *Transactions of the American Philological Association* 88 (1957) 3-4; "*Animae Dimidium Meae:* Two Poets of Rome," *ibid.* 87 (1956) 301; R. W. Carubba, "The Technique of Double Structure in Horace," *Mnemosyne,* Series 4, Vol. 20 (1967) 68-75.

[10]G. E. Duckworth, *Structural Patterns and Proportions in Vergil's Aeneid;* R. S. Conway, *The Vergilian Age,* ch. 9, especially 139-41; B. Fenik, "Parallelism of Theme and Imagery in *Aeneid* II and IV," *American Journal of Philology* 80 (1959) 2; H. L. Tracy, "The Pattern of Vergil's *Aeneid* I-VI:1," *The Phoenix* 4 (1950) 7; Brooks Otis, *Virgil: A Study in Civilized Poetry* (Oxford: Clarendon, 1964), Appendix 9; W. A. Camps, "A Note on the Structure of the *Aeneid,*" *Classical Quarterly,* n.s. 4 (1954) 214-15; "A Second Note on the *Aeneid,*" *ibid.* 9 (1959) 53-56.

[11]Brooks Otis, *Virgil,* 128-30, 216; Duckworth, "The Architecture of the *Aeneid,*" *American Journal of Philology* 75 (1954) 3.

[12]Otis, *Virgil,* 151; Duckworth, "Vergil's *Georgics* and the *Laudes Galli,*" *American Journal of Philology* 80 (1959) 230; D. L. Drew, "The Structure of Vergil's *Georgics,*" *ibid.* 50 (1929) 242-54; Gilbert Norwood, "Vergil, *Georgics* 4," *The Classical Journal* 36 (1940-41) 354.

[13]O. Skutsch, "The Structure of the Propertian *Monobiblos,*" *Classical philology* 58 (1963) 238-39; E. Courtney, "The Structure of Propertius Book I and Some Textual Consequences," *The Phoenix* 22 (1968) 251.

[14]J. F. Carney, "Plutarch's Style in the Marius," *JHS* 80 (1960) 24-31.

[15]G. E. Duckworth, *Structural Patterns and Proportions in Vergil's Aeneid*, ch. 1. One should note that here, as elsewhere, the correspondences do not necessarily involve exact verbal identity.

[16]Duckworth, *Structural Patterns and Proportions in Vergil's Aeneid*, 9. The material is used in accordance with the general directives of the University Presses.

[17]Duckworth, *Structural Patterns and Proportions in Vergil's Aeneid*, ch. 2.

[18]Joseph T. Shipley (ed.), *Dictionary of World Literature* (New York: Philosophical Library, 1943) 51.

[19]Percy Gardner, *The Principles of Greek Art* (New York: Macmillan, 1926) 7.

[20]Cited in Plutarch, *De gloria Atheniensium*, 3.

[21]C. M. Bowra, *The Greek Experience* (New York: Mentor Books, 1959) 155.

[22]*The Interplay of Greek Art and Literature* (London: H. K. Lewis, 1949) 2.

[23]This is very much like the eighteenth century critics who compared the disordered structuring of the *Faerie Queen* and the architecture of a Gothic cathedral.

[24]Duckworth, *Structural Patterns and Proportions in Vergil's Aeneid*, 15.

[25]On the *Ara Pacis*, see Jocelyn M. C. Toynbee, "The *Ara Pacis* Reconsidered and Historical Art in Roman Italy," *Proceedings of the British Academy* 39 (1953) 67-96.

[26]For our purposes it will be instructive if we note a number of examples of art objects of all types from a time near the beginning of the Christian era which possessed a balanced structure such as we have noted in classical literature: in simplest form either AB:A'B' or AB:B'A' or ABCA. (1) The entrance portico of the temple of Baalbek, which was begun in the reign of Augustus and was finished by the time of Nero, possesses the same balanced symmetry that is found in earlier Greek temples. D. S. Robertson, *A Handbook of Greek and Roman Architecture* (2d ed.; Cambridge: Cambridge University Press, 1959) fig. 97, p. 226. (2) Two Roman coins of 35—36 C.E. have on them images of the temples of Apollo and Divus Augustus. In each case the temple's image falls into a balanced structure: ABCDC'B'A. O. L. Richmond, "The Temples of Apollo and Divus Augustus on Roman Coins," in *Essays and Studies Presented to William Ridgeway* (ed. E. C. Quiggin; Cambridge: Cambridge University Press, 1913) 198-212. (3) A number of victories and a shield on a limestone relief found in Rome and dating from 100-50 B.C.E. are arranged in heraldic symmetry. T. B. L. Webster, *Hellenistic Art* (London: Methuen, 1967) fig. 45, p. 166. (4) The glass-paste mosaic facade of a nymphaeum installed in one wall of the internal courtyeard of the house of Neptune and Amphitrite at Herculaneum, dated first century C.E., follows the principle of balance. J. M. C. Toynbee, *The Art of the Romans* (New York: Frederick A. Praeger, 1965) Plate 85. (5) The arch of Trajan at Benevento (114 C.E.) follows the arch of Titus, erected at Rome some twenty years earlier, right down to the details of the ornamentation. The two sides of the arch correspond to each other. Heinz Kahler, *Rome and Her Empire* (London: Methuen, 1963) 24-25. (6) On a Roman sarcophagus, dated probably first century C.E. and not later than early second century, we find on the long sides both a top and a bottom decoration, each symmetrically arranged. Jocelyn Toynbee, "A Roman Sarcophagus at Pawlowsk and Its Fellows," *JRS* 17 (1927) 14-27, Plate 2; cf. also Plate 3 for a similar sarcophagus dated 132—34 C.E. (7) Many pagan lamps coming from the Hellenistic and Roman periods are decorated so that one side corresponds to the other. J. C. Wampler, *Tell En-Nasbeh* (Berkeley: The Palestine Institute of Pacific School of Religion and the American Schools of Oriental Research, 1947) 2. 56-66, and Plates 72, 73; M. S. Schloessinger, "Five Lamps with Fish Reliefs from Israel and Other Mediterranean Countries," *IEJ* 1 (1950-51) 84-95, and Plate 22. (8) Bowls and jugs with their elaborate decorations are found to have the same balanced or symmetrical design that is found in architecture, mosaics, arches, sarcophagi and lamps. Donald Atkinson, "A Hoard of Samian Ware from Pompeii," *JRS* 4 (1914) 27-64, and Plates 2-16; T. D. Pryce, "Roman Decorated Red-Glazed Ware of the Late First Century B.C. and the Early First Century A.D.," *JRS* 32 (1942) 14-26, especially 21, 23. (9) A diadem, a cult object used in the worship of the Great Mother goddess, dated in the late Hellenistic Roman period, has Cybele at the center, her hands holding the paws of a lion on either side of the goddess. Also on either side of the goddess are seven other gods and goddesses balancing one another. Rudolf Jonas, "A Diadem of the Cult

of Kybele from the Neapolis Region (Samaria)," *PEQ* 94 (1962) 118-28, and Plates 27, 28. (10) Whether it is a terra cotta plaque from the first century B.C.E. or the first century C.E. or a soldier's helmet found at Pompeii, there is a heraldic arrangement of figures on each. G. M. A. Richter, "Was Roman Art of the First Centuries B.C. and A.D. Classicizing?" *JRS* 48 (1958) 10-15, and Plate 5, fig. 17; also A. Maiuri, *Pompeii* (Paris: F. Nathan 1952) fig. 45. (11) The wall paintings of P. Fannius Synistor's villa at Boscoreale, dating from the third quarter of the first century B.C.E., of the House of the Vetti at Pompeii, of the Villa Farnesina just outside Rome from the late first century B.C.E., and of the house of Spurius Maesor at Pompeii (dated late Augustus or Tiberius) follow the principle of balance in their composition. T. B. L. Webster, *Hellenistic Art*, Plate 38, p. 137; Pierre Devambez, *Greek Painting* (New York: Viking, 1962) fig. 176; Michael Grant, *The World of Rome* (Cleveland: World, 1960) fig. 17, p. 254; also Grant, fig. 19, p. 256.

These examples show that in art as well as in literature a certain asymmetry is found. They also show that just as the outline of a Greek temple is repeated in its cornice and in smaller forms so the patterns of balance which govern the overall form of other works of art in the classical period appear frequently in their parts. This is the artistic counterpart to the literary phenomenon in which the architectonic patterns of the whole work are also the patterns of many of its parts.

²⁷ *Panegyricus* 9-10.

²⁸ D. R. Stuart, *Epochs of Greek and Roman Biography* (Berkeley: University of California Press, 1928) 103-04.

²⁹ H. D. F. Kitto, *The Greeks* (rev. ed.; Baltimore: Penguin Books, 1957) 186-87.

³⁰ *The Histories* 2: 32-35.

³¹ Kitto, *The Greeks*, 187-88.

³² Cf. P. Gardner, *The Principles of Greek Art*, 266.

³³ Ludwig Friedlander, *Roman Life and Manners Under the Early Empire* (4 vols.; New York: Barnes & Noble, 1909) 3. 4.

³⁴ Friedländer, *Roman Life*, 3. 8-9.

³⁵ Friedländer, *Roman Life*, 3. 11.

³⁶ George Kennedy, *The Art of Persuasion in Greece* (Princeton: Princeton University Press, 1963) 22.

³⁷ Cited by Friedländer, *Roman Life*, 3. 79.

³⁸ Epistle 7:17; 9:27.

³⁹ J. F. D'Alton, *Roman Literary Theory and Criticism* (London: Longmans, Green & Co., 1931) 523-24.

⁴⁰ D. J. McCarthy, "Moses' Dealings with Pharoah: Ex 7: 8—10:27," *CBQ* 27 (1965) 336-47.

⁴¹ D. J. McCarthy, "Plagues and Sea of Reeds: Exodus 5—14," *JBL* 85 (1966) 137-58.

⁴² Bezalel Porten, "The Structure and Theme of the Solomon Narrative (I Kings 3—11)," *HUCA* 38 (1967) 93-128.

⁴³ Jacob Licht, "Time and Eschatology in Apocalyptic Literature and in Qumran," *JJS* 16 (1965) 177-82.

⁴⁴ Jacob Licht, "An Analysis of the Treatise of the Two Spirits in DSD," in *Scripta Hierosolymitana, Vol. 4:X Aspects of the Dead Sea Scrolls* (ed. C. Rabin and Y. Yadin; 2d ed.; Jerusalem: Magnes, 1965) 88-100.

⁴⁵ Barbara Thiering, "The Poetic Forms of the Hodayot," *JSS* 8 (1963) 189-209; also "The Acts of the Apostles as Early Christian Art," in *Essays in Honor of Griffithes Wheeler Thatcher* (ed. E. C. B. MacLaurin; Sydney: Sydney University Press, 1967) 143-44.

⁴⁶ Stephen Bertman, "Symmetrical Design in the Book of Ruth," *JBL* 84 (1965) 165-68.

⁴⁷ Georges M. Landes, "The Kerygma of the Book of Jonah," *Int* 21 (1967) 3-31; R. Pesch, "Zur konzentrischen Struktur von Jona 1," *Bib* 47 (1966) 577-81.

⁴⁸ H. H. Walker and N. W. Lund, "The Literary Structure of the Book of Habakkuk," *JBL* 53 (1934) 355-70.

⁴⁹ John T. Willis, "The Structure of the Book of Micah," *SEA* 34 (1969) 5-42; cf. also "The Structure of Micah 3—5 and the Function of Micah 5:9-14 in the Book," *ZAW* 81 (1969) 191-214.

[50]"The Kerygma of the Book of Jonah," *Int* 21 (1967) 16. Landes' main debt is to the unpublished doctoral dissertation of Phyllis Trible, "Studies in the Book of Jonah," Columbia University, 1963 (see p. 5, n. 11).

[51]"The Kerygma of the Book of Jonah," 16, 26. The material is used with the permission of *Interpretation.*

[52]"Zur konzentrischen Struktur von Jona 1," *Bib* 47 (1966) 577-81.

[53]G. A. Barrois, "Art," *IDB* 1. 237-239.

[54]Several representative examples are useful. (1) The geese in a painting on stucco from a tomb near Medun, dated about 2900 B.C.E., Dynasty 4, are so arranged so that they follow the pattern AB:B′A′. Hermann Ranke, *The Art of Ancient Egypt* (Vienna: Phaidon, 1936) Plate 244. (2) From the 12th Dynasty (1840—1792 B.C.E.) there is a decorative inscription of Amenemhat 3d, from the temple of the crocodile-headed god Sobek at Crocodilopolis in the Faiyum, in the middle of which, between two standards depicting the god Sobek, is the royal title of Amenemhat 3d. Further designs balance each other on either side. Here writing and figures combine in a symmetrical composition. Irmgard Woldering, *The Art of Egypt* (New York: Crown, 1963) fig. 30, p. 105. (3) From about 1170 B.C.E. we have a lateral relief on the sarcophagus of Ramses 2nd, Dynasty 20, in which the goddess Isis is flanked by animal figures in heraldic fashion. Ranke, *Art of Ancient Egypt,* Page 240. (4) From around 653 B.C.E. there is a gray granite altar of Atlanersa from Gebel Barkal temple of Amon. On all four sides the detail is organized in heraldic fashion. William S. Smith, *Ancient Egypt As Represented in the Museum of Fine Arts, Boston* (4th ed.; Boston: Beacon Press, 1961) fig. 104, p. 168. (5) The layout of the Horus Temple at Edfu, dating from the Ptolemaic period (237—147 B.C.E.), follows that of the New Kingdom temples without adopting any Greek or Roman influence. The temple is symmetrically arranged, one half reproducing the other with only minor variations. Ranke, *Art of Ancient Egypt,* Plates 23-24. This is characteristic of Egyptian architectural design in which there is a strong symmetry around a longitudinal axis. Elements on either side of the axis are exactly identical to each other, although balanced elements that are not symmetrical are permitted in restricted amounts and in areas of secondary importance. The same layout and facade patterns are also found at the temple of Trajan at Philae, dated 98—117 C.E. Alexander Badawy, *Ancient Egyptian Architectural Design* (Berkeley: University of California Press, 1965) 26, 160-61. It is generally acknowledged that Egyptian works of art resemble one another over a period of several thousand years, the same principles governing the late as well as the early. We are safe, then, in concluding that the principle of balance controlled much Egyptian art down into the Christian era.

[55]Representative examples of Mesopotamian art reflecting the principle of balance are not hard to find. (1) Numerous cylinder seals from the Protoliterate Period (3500—3000 B.C.E.) contain heraldic groups of animals and one has two groups of animals attacked by beasts of prey face in different directions so that there is a play of antithetical correspondences. Henri Frankfort, *The Art and Architecture of the Ancient Orient* (Baltimore: Penguin Books, 1955) fig. 7E, p. 16; fig. 7C, p. 16; Plate 8A. The same patterns are also found controlling the carvings on the side of a stone trough which was probably used to water a temple flock. Frankfort, Plate 3C. (2) In the Early Dynastic Period (3000—2340 B.C.E.) the seal impressions continue to reflect a heraldic pattern. Frankfort, fig. 14A, p. 37; fig. 14B, p. 37. Also a copper relief from the temple at Al'Ubaid shows in the center a lion-headed eagle gripping with either claw two flanking stags. Frankfort, Plate 27A. (3) In the Akkadian Period (2340—2180 B.C.E.) the seal impressions continue to reflect the principle of balance. Frankfort, ch. 3. (4) The same is true when we investigate the beginnings of Assyrian art (1350—1000 B.C.E.). Frankfort, fig. 24A, p. 68); Plates 76A, B, C, D. Cf. E. L. B. Terrence, *The Art of the Ancient Near East in Boston* (Boston: The Museum of Fine Arts, 1962) Plate 16. (5) In the late Assyrian period (1000—612 B.C.E.), besides the balanced designs of the cylinder seals (Frankfort, Plate 119A, B; Terrence, Plate 28), a most interesting example presents itself. The city of Khorsabad, founded by Sargon II and dedicated in 706 B.C.E. shortly before the ruler's death, has been laid out in a symmetrical pattern. It is clear that the planners aimed at regularity and balance so that each side of the square city wall should have two gates for the lie of the land does not permit an equal flow of traffic in all directions. A regular plan, an abstract symmetry with balanced sides, was aimed at. Frankfort, pp. 75-76.

(6) The same concern for balance can also be found on a golden bowl from Ras Shamra (Frankfort, fig. 68, p. 149), controlling the design of certain reliefs from Carchemish and Sakjegeuzi (Frankfort, fig. 88A, B, p. 182; fig. 89, p. 183), and ivory inlays from the period 850-650 B.C.E. (Frankfort, Plate 168A, B, D), as well as a seventh century bowl (Frankfort, fig. 97, p. 198). Persian art shows a continuity at the point of balance. George Perrot and Charles Chipiez, *History of Art in Persia* (London: Chapman & Hall, 1892) fig. 221, p. 456; fig. 223, p. 456; fig. 224, p. 456; Maximilian Cohen, "Jewish Art at the Time of the Second Temple," in *Jewish Art,* ed. C. Roth, 120.

56Benedict S. Isserlin, "Israelite Art During the Period of the Monarchy," in *Jewish Art,* ed. C. Roth, 84.

57Andre Parrot, *The Temple of Jerusalem* (London: SCM, 1957) fig. 12, p. 48.

58Isserlin, "Israelite Art During the Period of the Monarchy," fig. 27 (c. 90); fig. 28 (cols. 89-90); fig. 29 (cols. 91-92).

59Maximilian Cohen, "Jewish Art at the Time of the Second Temple," 120.

60Cohen, "Jewish Art at the Time of the Second Temple," 125; cf. 45 (cols. 123-24).

61Cohen, "Jewish Art at the Time of the Second Temple," fig. 55 (cols. 145-46).

62Cohen, "Jewish Art at the Time of the Second Temple," fig. 57 (cols. 147-48).

63Cohen, "Jewish Art at the Time of the Second Temple," fig. 44 (cols. 121-22). *Jewish Symbols in the Greco-Roman Period* by E. R. Goodenough furnishes numerous examples of the role of the principle of balance in Jewish art at the beginning of our era. Cf. especially figs. 625, 810, 817, and 995 in Vol. 3 (New York: Pantheon, 1953), and fig. 12 in Vol. 11 (New York: Pantheon, 1964).

64Guido Schoenberger, A Review of *A History of Jewish Art* by Franz Landsberger, *Historia Judaica* 8 (1946) 194.

65Gerhard von Rad, *Old Testament Theology* (2 Vols.; Edinburgh: Oliver & Boyd, 1962) 1. 364, n. 18.

66"Egypt," in *The Intellectual Adventure of Ancient Man* (Chicago: University of Chicago Press, 1946) 41-42.

67William A. Ward, *The Spirit of Ancient Egypt* (Beirut: Khayats, 1965) 4.

68*Kingship and the Gods* (Chicago: University of Chicago Press, 1948) 3-5.

69*Israel: Its Life and Culture, 1-2* (London: Oxford University Press, 1926).

70*Ibid.,* 115, 123.

71*Kingship and the Gods,* vii.

72*Israel, 1-2,* 110.

73J. Dupont, "Le problème de la structure littéraire de l'Épître aux Romains," *RB* 62 (1955) 372, n. 2; J. J. Collins, "The 'ABA' Pattern and the Text of Paul," in *Studiorum Paulinorum Congressus Internationalis Catholicus* (Rome: Pontifical Biblical Institute, 1963) 2. 582.

74John Bligh, *Galatians in Greek* (Detroit: University of Detroit Press, 1966).

75Collins, "The 'ABA' Pattern and the Text of Paul," 577; A. Feuillet, "La citation d'Habacuc 2:4 et les huit premiers chapitres de l'Épître aux Romains," *NTS* 6 (1959) 71.

76John Forbes, *The Symmetrical Structure of Scripture* (Edinburgh: T. & T. Clark, 1854) 40; N. W. Lund, *Chiasmus in the New Testament* (Chapel Hill: University of North Carolina Press, 1942) 219.

77Austin Farrer, *St. Matthew and St. Mark* (Westminister: Dacre, 1954) 165-66.

78David Deeks, "The Structure of the Fourth Gospel," *NTS* 15 (1968) 107-28; Charles H. Talbert, "Artistry and Theology: An Analysis of the Architecture of John 1:19—5:47," *CBQ* 32 (1970) 341-66; N. W. Lund, "The Influence of Chiasmus upon the Structure of the Gospels," *ATR* 13 (1931) 41-46; M. E. Boismard, *Le prologue de Saint Jean* (Paris: Cerf, 1953) 107.

79H. R. Smid, *Protoevangelium Jacobi* (Assen: Van Gorcum, 1965).

80Martin Blumenthal, *Formen und Motive in den apokryphen Apostelgeschichte* (Leipzig: J. C. Hinrichs'sche Buchhandlung, 1933).

81Blumenthal, *Formen und Motive in den apokryphen Apostelgeschichte.*

[82]J. Smith Sibinga, "Melito of Sardis: The Artist and His Text," *VC* 24 (1970) 99. F. D. McCloy, "The Sense of Artistic Form in the Mentality of the Greek Fathers," *Studia Patristica* 9 (1966) 69-74, speaks of the Fathers' sense for balanced form and claims that 1 Clem 20 views all order as part of the cosmic balance.

[83]*Protevangelium Jacobi,* 172.

[84]Ludwig Hertling and Englebert Kirschbaum, *The Roman Catacombs and Their Martyrs* (Milwaukee: Bruce, 1956) 161-62.

[85]Hertling and Kirschbaum, *The Roman Catacombs,* 165.

[86]Cf. Andre Grabar, *The Beginnings of Christian Art* (London: Thames and Hudson, 1967) 82.

[87]Grabar, *Beginnings of Christian Art,* 2; cf. also Walter Lowrie, *Art in the Early Church* (rev. ed; New York: Harper, 1965) 3.

[88]Lowrie, *Art in the Early Church,* 7, 40; Plate 4a.

[89]Clark D. Lamberton, *Themes from St. John's Gospel in Early Roman Catacomb Painting* (Princeton: Princeton University Press, n.d.) 23, n. 24.

[90]Lamberton,*Themes from St. John's Gospel in Early Roman Catacomb Painting,* 79-80.

[91]Lamberton, *Themes from St. John's Gospel in Early Roman Catacomb Painting,* 67; Goodenough, *Jewish Symbols,* Vol. 3, fig. 2, gives a picture from the Catacomb of Domitilla in which Christ raising Lazarus is balanced by Moses striking the rock.

[92]Lowrie, *Art in the Early Church,* Plate 24b; also p. 76.

[93]Duckworth, *Structural Patterns and Proportions in Vergil's Aeneid,* 7-8. The substance of the material in the section on *Questions* comes from my article in *CBQ* 32 (1970) 360-66, and is used by permission.

[94]Landes, "The Kerygma of the Book of Jonah," 17-18.

[95]J. E. Sandys, *A History of Classical Scholarship* (3d ed.; Cambridge: Cambridge University Press, 1921) 109.

[96]F. Blass, A. Debrunner, R. W. Funk, *A Greek Grammar of the New Testament* (Chicago: University of Chicago Press, 1961) 260.

[97]Cf. H. L. Tracy, "The Pattern of Vergil's *Aeneid* I-VI, 1," *The Phoenix* 4 (1950) 7.

[98](LCL; New York: G. P. Putnam's Sons, 1927) 218-19.

[99]S. E. Bassett, *The Poetry of Homer,* 141.

[100]*The Intellectual Adventure of Ancient Man,* 42.

[101]*The Early Poetry of Israel* (London: H. Frowde, 1912) 17-18.

[102]P. E. Corbett, "Preliminary Sketch in Greek Vase-Painting," *JHS* 85 (1965) 16-28.

[103]Duckworth, *Structural Patterns and Proportions in Vergil's Aeneid,* 37.

[104]*Counter-Statement* (2d ed.; Los Altos, Calif.: Hermes, 1953) 140-41.

[105]Friedrich Blass, *Philology of the Gospels* (Amsterdam: B. R. Gruner, 1969) 10.

[106]A. Vanhoye, "Structure du 'Benedictus'," *NTS* 12 (1966) 382-89.

[107]Robert L. Scranton, *Aesthetic Aspects of Ancient Art* (Chicago: University of Chicago Press, 1964) 21.

[108]Shepherd, *The Pattern of the Iliad,* 12.

[109]Whitman, *Homer and the Heroic Tradition,* 98.

[110]Otis, *Virgil,* 223.

[111]Landes, "The Kerygma of the Book of Jonah," 26-29.

[112]Talbert, "Artistry and Theology: An Analysis of the Architecture of John 1:19—5:47," 365-66.

CHAPTER VI

Lucan Heilsgeschichte and the Patterns of Luke-Acts

Up to this point we have been concerned with two basic questions: (1) what are the major architectural patterns expressive of the principle of balance in Luke-Acts? (2) are there similar patterns elsewhere in the Lucan milieu? In the final chapters of this book we turn to a third question. How are the Lucan architectural patterns set forth in Chapters Two, Three, and Four related to meaning? This question will be dealt with in two stages. First, Chapters Six and Seven will attempt to show which patterns are explicitly related to Lucan *theology,* how they are related, and which patterns exist primarily for aesthetic ends. In these two chapters redaction criticism makes its contribution to architecture analysis. Second, Chapter Eight will focus upon the question of the *genre* of Luke-Acts and the relationships among the Evangelist's theological needs, his choice of genre, and his employment of the principle of balance in an architectonic plan. In this final chapter genre criticism makes its contribution to architecture analysis.

Chapter Six will treat five sets of correspondences: those between the Gospel and the Acts, between Acts 1—12 and Acts 13—28, between Acts 1:12—4:23 and 4:24—5:42, those in Luke 1:5—ch. 2, and those in Luke 3:1—4:15. My contention is that the function of these five patterns in Luke-Acts can be grasped if they are viewed in the context of the Lucan understanding of *Heilsgeschichte.* In order to enter into the Lucan mind at this point, however, it is necessary to concern ourselves with three separate themes in Luke-Acts: (1) the Lucan appropriation of the popular image of the philosopher in the Hellenistic world at the beginning of the Christian era; (2) the Lucan appropriation of the Early Catholic "decadence theory" of Christian origins; (3) and the Lucan view of the relationship between John and Jesus. Let us begin with the first of these.

The Popular Image of the Philosopher

The popular image of the philosopher in the Hellenistic world at the beginning of the Christian era was highly fluid, but it frequently contained all or most of the following elements: (1) the philosopher was pictured as a wandering preacher whose journeys were sometimes the result of a divine command; (2) the philosophy he expounded was a way of living rather than an explanation of life; (3) his philosophy was learned by imitation of his life-style as much or more than by remembering his precepts, a learning procedure he consciously cultivated; and (4) in the controversy over the true and the false philosopher, succession lists often functioned to designate where th "living voice" could be found, that is, where the way of life was lived   well as expounded. It is now our task to explain and document this image.

We may begin with a sketch of the philosophic image in the Greco-Roman world. (1) The philosophic missionary was a widespread phenomenon in the ancient world. In his *Discourses* Dio Chrysostom (40—120 C.E.) provides us with primary source material from an itinerant philosophic preacher. It was at Apollo's temple at Delphi that Dio received an oracle which instructed him to carry on his work " 'until thou comest,' said he, 'to the uttermost parts of the earth' (ἕως ἄν, ἔφη, ἐπὶ τὸ ὕστατον ἀπέλθῃς τῆς γῆς)."[1] So he muses: "Should I not follow his (Odysseus') example if God so bade?"[2] He proceeded to roam everywhere experiencing all manner of sufferings such as storm and shipwreck, but achieving in the meantime a reputation as a philosopher because of his moral advice and his message of ideal kingship. So prestigeous was the philosophic image in antiquity that most itinerant preachers tried to appropriate it. For example, when Philostratus wanted to rehabilitate Appollonius of Tyana he cast him in the image of a wandering philosophic preacher accompanied by disciples.[3]

(2) At the beginning of the Christian era philosophy was "a guide to life more than an explanation of life."[4] As Seneca (4 B.C.E.—65 C.E.) put it, living well is the gift of philosophy.[5] In his letters which come probably from the period 63—65 C.E. Seneca says that philosophy

> moulds and constructs the soul; it orders our life, guides our conduct, shows us what we should do and what we should leave undone; it sits at the helm and directs our course as we waver amid uncertainties. Without it, no one can live fearlessly or in peace of mind. Countless things that happen every hour call for advice; and such advice is to be sought in philosophy.[6]

(3) At the beginning of the Christian era there was a new emphasis on the personality of the teacher in philosophic instruction.[7] For example, the history of Stoicism in the period from Nero to Marcus Aurelius "is the history not of a development of doctrine, but of a series of teachers who inspired admiration and discipleship by their example and their personality as well as by their arguments and their eloquence."[8] Roots of this mentality can be found already in the fourth century B.C.E. in Xenophon's defense of Socrates. Socrates, he says, benefited his companions both by example and by precept.[9] His very manner of life was a means of instruction.

> Socrates was so useful in all circumstances and in all ways, that any observer gifted with ordinary perception can see that nothing was more useful than the companionship of Socrates, and time spent with him in any place and in any circumstances. The very recollection of him in absence brought no small good to his constant companions and followers; for even in his light moods they gained no less from his society than when he was serious.[10]

Seneca advises that one should find someone whose life can teach him the lessons of philosophy. One should "choose a master whose life, conversation, and soul-expressing face have satisfied you; picture him always to yourself as your protector and pattern. For we must indeed have someone according to whom we may regulate our characters. . . ."[11] The way to wisdom is long if one follows precepts but short if one follows patterns (*exempla*).[12]

> Cleanthes could not have been the express image of Zeno, if he had merely heard his lectures; he also shared his life, saw into his hidden purposes, and watched him to see whether he lived according to his own rules. Plato, Aristotle, and the whole throng of sages who were destined to go each his different way, derived more benefit from the character than from the words of Socrates. It was not the classroom of Epicurus, but living together under the same roof, that made great men of Metrodorus, Hermarchus, and Polyaenus.[13]

Such examples may be chosen from the living[14] or from among the dead.[15] In either case, however, they must be men who teach us by their lives, who tell us what to do and prove it by their practice. They must be men whom one can admire more when they are seen than when they are heard.[16]

For Dio Chrysostom also the philosopher's word alone, unaccompanied by the act, is invalid and untrustworthy.[17] So too, to be a disciple means to imitate a teacher's acts and words (τὰ ἔργα καὶ τοὺς λόγους) so as to become like the teacher. "That is precisely, it seems, what the pupil does—by imitating his teacher and paying heed to him he tries to acquire his art."[18] In Quintilian (35—100 C.E.), who is attempting to bring the orator under the philosopher's image, the same mentality is found. One should not, he says, restrict one's study to the precepts of philosophy alone. Rather it is important to know both the noble sayings and deeds that have been handed down from ancient times.[19] Finally, we note that in Philostratus' *Life of Apollonius of Tyana* where Apollonius is cast into the image of a wandering philosopher, it is said that his disciples not only heard but also imitated him.[20]

(4) The authority of philosophic doctrine in antiquity was very closely connected with the theme of a succession of teachers from the master, teachers whose great task was to transmit faithfully the doctrine of the school. A whole literature on these successions (διαδοχαί) grew up in the Hellenistic world. Sotion of Alexandria, between 200 and 170 B.C.E., produced his work entitled Διαδοχή or Διαδοχαί.[21] Heraclides of Lembus, about 181—146 B.C.E., brought out his Διαδοχή in six books.[22] Two citizens of Rhodes, Sosicrates and Antisthenes, in the second century B.C.E. wrote works on the

successions of the philosophers.[23] Cicero traces a succession from Plato of those who inherited his "system and authority." Of several of these successors he says that they "were assiduous defenders of the doctrine they had received from their predecessors.[24] Near the time of Shammai and Hillel, Suidas traced the fourteen stage succession in the Epicurean school which lasted from 271—44 B.C.E.[25] In his *Natural History* Pliny (23—79 C.E.) expresses his astonishment over the survival of magic through so long a period in spite of the fact that "treatises are wanting, and besides there is no line of distinguished or continuous succession to keep alive their memory."[26] The implication is, of course, that a line of succession was the normal thing among such teachers. Plutarch refers to such a succession of Stoic teachers in Babylon.[27] Clement of Alexandria also gives a brief sketch of the successions of the Greek philosophers.[28] The fullest discussion of the successions is found in Diogenes Laertius' *Lives of Eminent Philosophers* early in the third century C.E.[29] In speaking of one Metrodorus, an eminent disciple of Epicurus, Laertius says that from his first acquaintance with Epicurus he never left him except for once for six months when he visited his native place.[30]

Consider this concern with succession in the context of several facts. First, philosophy since Socrates was regarded as not merely technical knowledge but rather as a mode of life thought to have been discovered by the founder of the philosophical school.[31] It is to be expected, therefore, that the later Stoics would look back to the founders of their school, Zeno and Chrysippus, to provide themselves with the authentic doctrine. Second, it was believed that the school's founder had lived his doctrine as well as expounded it. It is to be expected, therefore, that perpetuation of this mode of life was not only by teaching as he had taught but also by living as he had lived.[32] Within this context, the philosophical succession lists function to point to those who had "lived" a doctrine as the locus of the true teaching. This was the importance of a living succession. It was a school's comment on where the true tradition was to be found.[33]

We find in Judaism near the beginning of the Christian era a very similar cluster of ideas. (1) Though we hear of Jewish itinerants from a number of different types of sources, it is not until the fourth century that one finds a true Hellenistic type of wandering preacher in Rabbi Abbahu.[34] On the other aspects of the image, however, the evidence is clear-cut. (2) It takes no argument to establish what everyone knows, namely, that Judaism's concern for the Law was a concern for it as a guide for life. The Law functioned in Judaism to create the righteous man very much like philosophy did in the Greco-Roman world to create the wise man or sage.

(3) In Hellenistic Judaism we find the same concern with example alongside precept that we found in the Greco-Roman philosophical schools. When the Ep Arist 127 says that it is safer "to hear" about the provisions of the Torah from a wise man than "to read" them, we are meeting the conviction that the written precept needs the living example of the sage to enable one to reach the desired goal of life.[35] Moreover, in Philo the concept of the "living law" functions in very much the same way. In *On Abraham* 1:3-5, Philo speaks

of the patriarchs as men who have lived good and blameless lives and "whose virtues stand permanently recorded in the most holy scriptures . . . for the instruction of the reader and as an inducement to him to aspire to the same; for in these men we have laws endowed with life and reason(οἱ γὰρ ἔμψυχοι καὶ λογικοὶ νόμοι ἄνδρες ἐκεῖνοι γεγόνασιν)."[36] Also in *Moses* 1:162, Philo portrays the lawgiver as an embodiment of the law, that is, as a living law. Moses was "the reasonable and living impersonation of law (νόμος ἔμψυχος)."[37]

The Pharisaic-Rabbinic stream of Judaism also reflects this mentality. In Pharisaism-Rabbinism the pupil not only learned his teacher's words but also his way of life. That is, a rabbi taught by means of what he did as well as by what he said.[38] A pupil could say that he "saw" his teacher do thus and so[39] as well as that he "heard" him teach a certain way.[40] Pupils paid careful attention to a rabbi's actions to the point of deducing *Halachah* from them. For example, to justify the claim that men may eat haphazardly outside the *Sukkah*, the Mishnah relates the narrative of the contrasting behavior of Rabbis Johannan ben Zakkai and Gamaliel on the one side and Rabbi Zadok on the other.[41] In another case, in answer to the question, where should one shake the *Lulab*?, the Mishnah cites Rabbi Akiba as saying: "I once watched Rabban Gamaliel and Rabban Joshua, and while all the people were shaking their *Lulabs*, they shook them only at 'Save now, we beseech thee, O Lord.' "[42] Such observation of a rabbi's life went so far as a pupil's intrusion into his teacher's most intimate moments. Asked why he carried his observations so far, Akiba responded: "It is a matter of Torah, and I require to learn."[43] Aware that their disciples scrutinized their every action, the rabbis paid careful attention to their behavior lest it be misconstrued by their disciples. When in another rabbi's sphere of jurisdiction and confronted by an interpretation that was unacceptable, the rabbi might turn his face away to indicate his disapproval. Even this act would become the basis for a ruling based on his authority but arrived at by implication by his disciples.[44] Once Rabbi Ishmael said to Rabbi Eleazar regarding his actions in saying the *Shema* : "I had to act thus, lest the disciples should see and fix the *Halachah* so for future generations."[45] This idea of the teacher as pattern and the pupil as imitator was not created by the rabbis or Hellenistic Jews. It came to them from the Hellenistic world and its image of the philosopher as example.[46]

(4) The Jews also utilized the Hellenistic succession principle. Eusebius says that in the second century B.C.E., Eupolemos, a Jew, set forth the idea of a succession of prophets from Moses.[47] In the first century C.E. Josephus is aware of a prophetic succession.[48] At the beginning of Pirke Aboth the rabbis set out what is perhaps the best known succession list in antiquity. "The Pharisees also—in order to be respectable and respected—wanted to establish their pedigree of spiritual ancestry. They traced what might be called a professorial succession for their school just as the Platonists did for theirs."[49] To receive the Torah from someone, however, was not merely a matter of learning precepts but also of perpetuating a style of life. Hence when we hear

of the succession of the Law from Moses through various teachers, the succession points to the people the Pharisees believed lived as well as remembered the tradition.

The early Christians could hardly escape the influence of the philosophic image on their ways of thinking. Two examples, one taken from the end of the second century and one from near 100 C.E., should suffice at this point. In Irenaeus we find the widespread concern for a teacher's actions as well as his words as instruction for disciples (Christians). Irenaeus' appeal to Polycarp, for example, is both to precept and example.[50] He refers to the Epistle of Polycarp written to the Philippians "from which those who choose to do so ... can learn the character of his faith, and the preaching of the truth."[51] He refers also to Polycarp's behavior, citing an incident in which he reacted to Marcion in a certain way. Furthermore, Irenaeus indicates that Polycarp himself appealed to the example of John, the disciple of the Lord, who rushed out of the bath house when he became aware of Cerinthus' presence. Perhaps it is this concern with the example of the teacher as a mode of instruction that causes Irenaeus to include a reference to his having seen Polycarp. From Irenaeus' point of view, therefore, Polycarp passes on the apostolic tradition by both precept and life.

This close association of precept and example in the passing on of the apostolic tradition is linked with the concept of succession in Irenaeus. Irenaeus' concern with "that tradition which is derived from the Apostles, and which is safeguarded in the churches through the succession of presbyters"[52] is well known. He believed that the apostolic tradition and faith had come down to his day through the successions of bishops. What is not so often recognized is that this succession concerns both example and precept. Two passages make this clear. In *Against Heresies* 3:3:3, Irenaeus is giving an episcopal list which ends: "In this order, and by this succession, the ecclesiastical tradition from the apostles, and the preaching of the truth, have come down to us."[53] Within this context Irenaeus speaks of Clement as bishop of Rome. "This man, as he had seen the blessed apostles, and had been conversant with them, might be said to have the preaching of the apostles still echoing in his *ears*, and their traditions before his *eyes*."[54] What Clement saw is as much a part of the apostolic faith as what he heard. The point is made even more precisely in *Against Heresies* 4:26:2-5 where he is discussing the marks of the true presbyter. A true presbyter is one who holds the doctrine of the apostles and who displays sound speech and blameless conduct. Such men are the locus of true tradition.

Where, therefore, the gifts of the Lord have been placed, there it behooves us to learn the truth, namely, from those who possess that succession of the church which is from the apostles, and among whom exists that which is sound and blameless in conduct, as well as that which is unadulterated and incorrupt in speech.[55]

With such a concern for teachers who live what they teach, Irenaeus' view of Christian faith can only be a way of life. Of the four aspects of the image of the philosopher in the ancient world, therefore, only the first is missing in Irenaeus' picture of the ideal presbyter. Historical circumstances most likely ruled out any possibility for an itinerant ministry. It was usually from the travelling preachers that heresy was introduced into the church. A ministry tied to a specific geographical locale was the almost inevitable result.

In the Pastoral Epistles we find a clear-cut succession of tradition and teachers, with Paul as the first link in the chain. To Paul has been entrusted the "glorious gospel of the blessed God" (1 Tim 1:11; 2 Tim 1:12). Paul, moreover, has publicly (2 Tim 2:2) entrusted the gospel to Timothy (2 Tim 1:13-14; 1 Tim 6:20). Now Timothy is exhorted to pass it on to faithful men who will be able to teach others (2 Tim 2:2). In this chain we are able to see the transition from the itinerant minister, symbolized by Paul, Timothy and Titus, to the minister tied to a specific locale, the elders-bishops. Within this succession teaching is done by example as well as by precept. Paul instructs Timothy: "I am writing these instructions to you so that, if I am delayed, you may know how one ought to behave in the household of God . . ." (1 Tim 3:14-15). He can also say, however: "Now you have observed my teaching, my conduct, my aim in life, my faith, my patience, my love, my steadfastness, my persecutions, my sufferings. . . . But as for you, continue in what you have learned . . . knowing from whom you learned it" (2 Tim 3:10-11, 14). Timothy is not only to "preach the word, . . . convince, rebuke, and exhort . . ." (2 Tim 4:2), but also to "set the believers an example in speech and conduct, in love, in faith, in purity" (1 Tim 4:12; cf. 6:11). Titus also is exhorted not only to "teach what benefits sound doctrine" (Tit 2:1) but also to "show yourself in all respects a model of good deeds . . ." (2:7). The faithful men who are appointed to serve as elders and to whom the tradition is entrusted must be men who not only "hold firm to the sure word as taught" (Tit 1:9) but also are "blameless . . . a lover of goodness, master of himself, upright, holy, and self-controlled . . ." (1:7-8). The aim of the true tradition is "love that issues from a pure heart" (1 Tim 1:5) and "good deeds" (Tit 3:8; 3:14). It is difficult, therefore, to avoid the conclusion that the picture of the apostolic figure with his pupils in succession from him is shaped significantly by the image of the philosopher in the Hellenistic world, whether it be a direct or an indirect influence.[56] Various early Christian as well as certain Jewish streams of thought and life were most definitely influenced by the philosophic model in antiquity.[57]

Among those streams of early Christian life and thought that felt the influence of the Hellenistic·image of the philosopher is that represented by Luke-Acts. In Luke-Acts both Jesus and the apostles are depicted as itinerant preachers.[58] The travel section of the Third Gospel (9:51—19:46) is universally recognized as a Lucan distinctive. It does not, however, exhaust Luke's concern to present Jesus as always "on the move." From the beginning of his ministry in Galilee the Lucan Jesus is pictured as in the midst of one journey after another (cf. 4:16, 31, 44; 5:12; 6:12, 17; 7:1, 11; 8:1, 26, 40; 9:10, 28).[59]

Moreover, in Acts Paul is depicted as the ideal wandering preacher. The picture of Paul found there is that of a purposeful traveler whose itinerary is altered by nothing less than the intervention of God. It is not only Paul, however, who is portrayed as a traveling preacher in Acts. The words of the risen Jesus in Acts 1:8 ("You shall be my witnesses in Jerusalem and in all Judea and Samaria and to the end of the earth") are the oracle which controls the paths of the early Christians in Acts. From Acts 8:1 the missionary efforts spread beyond Jerusalem, carried by wandering preachers, some of whom are named, some are not (cf. 8:4, 5, 26; ch. 10; 11:19-26, etc.).

Just as in the Pastoral Epistles, we find in Luke-Acts a succession motif. Of course, there is at least one significant difference. In the Pastorals Paul is the first link in the chain.[60] In Luke-Acts Jesus is the beginning of the tradition and the twelve apostles are the primary bearers of it. The total chain runs from Jesus to the Twelve to Paul to the Ephesian elders.[61] The Twelve are chosen in Galilee at the beginning of Jesus' public ministry and, like the eminent disciple of Epicurus, never leave him except for once, during which brief interval Luke recounts nothing in Jesus' career. The apostles, like Plato's successors, inherit Jesus' system and authority, being fully instructed and empowered. Accordingly they control the extension of the gospel from Jerusalem. When the emphasis shifts from the original Twelve to Paul, it is only after Paul's "ordination" to apostleship by a church approved by Jerusalem.[62] The succession then follows from Paul to the Ephesian elders, who being fully instructed, are to guard the flock of God. As Luke sees it, there is a succession from Jesus to the Twelve to Paul to the Ephesian elders. The Christians have a "professorial succession" for their "school" just as the Platonists and Pharisees do for theirs. As a result of the succession motif in Luke-Acts, one is left with a consciousness of a certain pattern in the web of relationships among those in the chain of succession. The Evangelist aims to portray a *unity* among the four links in the chain and a *subordination* of each link to the one or ones preceding it. Hence the unity of faith from Jesus to the elders is due to the elders' subordination to Paul who in turn is subordinate to Jerusalem whose apostles were with Jesus from the baptism of John until the day when he was taken up into heaven.

Within this chain of succession we find a Lucan concern with the *imitatio magistri* motif. It is clear-cut in the farewell speech of Paul to the Ephesian elders in Acts 20:17-35. The elders who are to take care of the flock after Paul's departure are men to whom Paul has declared "the whole counsel of God" (20:27). To them Paul did not shrink from declaring "anything that was profitable" (20:20). They are also, however, men who know how Paul lived (20:18-19) and to whom Paul's example is known (20:33-35). In this speech it is obvious that Paul's example is crucial. It is the content of Paul's behavior rather than the content of his precepts that is spelled out.

The *imitatio magistri* motif is also evident in the Lucan treatment of the relationship between Jesus and his disciples after his death. On the one hand, it seems that Luke wants to ground the disciples' acts in the deeds of Jesus. No example is clearer than that supplied by the parallelism between the death of

Jesus and that of Stephen.[63] Both are tried before the council (Luke 22:66-71; Acts 6:12-15). Both die a martyr's death. Two utterances of Jesus are echoed in the words of Stephen. Acts 7:59, "Lord Jesus, receive my spirit," echoes Luke 23:46, "Father, into thy hands I commit my spirit" (L). Acts 7:60, "Lord, do not hold this sin against them," echoes Luke 23:34, "Father forgive them; for they know not what they do" (L). At the death of each there is a "Son of man saying." Luke 22:69, "But from now on the Son of man shall be seated at the right hand of the power of God," is paralleled by Acts 7:56, "Behold, I see the heavens opened, and the Son of man standing at the right hand of God." This is remarkable since Acts 7:56 is the only occurence of the title "Son of man" outside the Gospels and on any lips except those of Jesus. Finally, the martyrdom of each has evangelistic effects. Luke 23:39-43, L tradition, indicates how the innocent death of Jesus leads to the conversion of thief. After acknowledging the innocence of Jesus (23:41), the thief says, "Jesus, remember me when you come in your kingly power." Jesus replies, "Truly, I say to you, today you shall be with me in Paradise." Acts 8:1-4 reports that the martyrdom of Stephen led to the spread of the gospel (cf. 11:19-26). It would seem, therefore, that the author of Luke-Acts deliberately paralleled the martyr deaths of Jesus and Stephen. In Luke-Acts such parallelism is frequently used by the author to emphasize unity. The design of Luke, then, is to accent the unity between the martyr death of Jesus and the first or typical martyr death in the church. Luke describes the death of Jesus as a martyrdom in order to give a basis for Christian suffering-martyrdom. The parallelism gives dominical authority for the martyr deaths of Christians.

On the other hand, it seems that Luke wants to ground the disciples' teaching in the instruction of Jesus. No example is clearer than that supplied by the parallelism between the church's interpretation of scripture and that of Jesus.[64] Close examination of the Lucan literature reveals that the interpretation of Scripture made by Jesus in Luke and that of the church in Acts are paralleled. This parallelism may be seen in the following sketch.

Luke: Jesus as Interpreter		*Acts: The Church as Interpreter*
John is the one who prepared the way as Mal. 3:1 foretold (7:27).	1.	The accurate exposition of Scripture sees John as only a forerunner (18:24-28).
My person is the fulfillment of the Old Testament hopes (4:16-30; 20:17).	2.	The man Jesus is the fulfillment of the Old Testmanet hopes (3:22-26; 4:11; 10:43; 13:23; 17:2-3; 28:23).
My sufferings, death, resurrection, and exaltation are a fulfillment of the Old Testament (9:22, 44; 17:25; 13:33; 24:7; 18:31-34; 22:37; 24:25-27, 32; 24:44-49).	3.	Jesus' sufferings, death, resurrection, and ascension were a fulfillment of the Old Testament (2:25-28, 31; 3:24-25, 17-18; 8:30-35; 13:27-39; 17:2-3, 11; 26:22-23).
The Old Testament promised the Holy Spirit (24:49; Acts 1:4).	4.	The coming of the Holy Spirit is the fulfillment of the Old Testament (2:16-21).

The Old Testament points to the rejection of the Christ by the Jews (20:17-18).	5. The rejection of Jesus by the Jewish people is a fulfillment of the Old Testament (13:40-41, 27; 28:25-27).
The Old Testament foretold a mission to the Gentiles (24:47; possibly 4:25-27).	6. The Old Testament is fulfilled in the church's mission to the Gentiles (13:47 and possibly 14:26; 15:15-18; 26:22-23).
The Old Testament teaches a general resurrection of the dead (20:37).	7. The Old Testament teaches a general resurrection of the dead (24:14-15; 26:6-8).

When we reflect upon these seven points of Christian exegesis, we become aware of the fact that they present seven aspects of a Christian picture of salvation-history running from the Baptist to the general resurrection. This salvation-history was foretold by the Old Testament. It is, therefore, a predetermined plan of God which has largely been fulfilled in these last times. It is as though Luke were trying to say that the church's interpretation of Scripture is nothing more than an extension in time of Jesus' interpretation of the Old Testament. That this is precisely what Luke intends may be gleaned from Luke 24:25-27, 44-49, where the risen Christ interprets Scripture for the disciples and opens their minds to understand its meaning. In both the apostolic church's deeds and words, therefore, the Evangelist would have us see not only a unity with but also a subordination to what Jesus "began to do and teach" (Acts 1:1). The apostolic church learns from Jesus as the Ephesian elders learn from Paul by means of *imitatio magistri*.

It is within such a context, I think, that we may come to understand the function of the correspondences between the career of Jesus in Luke and the events in the life of the church in Acts on the one hand and the correspondences between the two halves of Acts, in part at least, on the other. Of course, these architectural patterns need not necessarily have a meaning-function to perform. They could very well serve only aesthetic ends as such patterns often did in antiquity. In the context of the Lucan appropriation of the Hellenistic image of the philosopher who as a wandering preacher taught a way of life to his pupils by example even more than by precept and often had the truth of his tradition guaranteed by a succession list, the patterns seem to serve more than merely aesthetic ends. We find in Luke-Acts an architectural pattern of correspondences between the career of Jesus and the life of the apostolic church. We know that in the Lucan milieu that stream of thought which furnished him his controlling image for thinking about Jesus and the disciples emphasized the value and necessity of choosing a master who embodied his teachings and making him one's pattern to imitate. We find that the Evangelist definitely wanted to portray the deeds and teachings of Jesus as the pattern for the acts and instructions of the apostolic church. It is, therefore, near impossible to avoid the conclusion that these correspondences between Jesus and the church serve the same *imitatio magistri* motif. In terms of the philosophic image, Jesus is the master who is the source of the Christian way of life. The apostolic church is composed of his pupils who have truly learned his way inasmuch as their subordination to him as teacher results in a unity of life and doctrine. The tradition of Jesus is passed on to posterity through the life and teaching of the apostolic church.

We find in the two halves of Acts correspondences between the life and teaching of the Jerusalem church and Paul. We know that in the Lucan milieu that stream of thought which furnished him his controlling image for thinking about the relation of Jesus and the disciples emphasized in its succession motif that the passing on of tradition meant not only transmitting precepts but also perpetuating a style of life. We find that the farewell speech of Paul in Acts 20 definitely considers the example of Paul as well as his teachings to be part of the elders' equipment to deal with heresy. It is, therefore, near impossible to avoid the conclusion that these correspondences between Paul and Jerusalem serve the same succession mentality. In terms of the philosophic image, the "living voice" is found in Pauline tradition because he embodies the same life and speech which are found in Jerusalem (i.e., the eyewitnesses). The tradition of Jesus which found embodiment in the eyewitnesses of Jerusalem has also found embodiment in Paul. This means that when the Ephesian elders look to Paul as their pattern and imitate him, they are a "living voice." To indicate correspondences between Paul and Jerusalem, therefore, serves both to legitimate Paul and the line of succession from Paul.

It would seem that these two architectural patterns of the Lucan literature do function in the service of meaning. Both the correspondences between the career of Jesus in the Third Gospel and the life of the apostolic church in Acts on the one side and the correspondences between Paul and Jerusalem in Acts on the other contribute to the overall Lucan appropriation of the Hellenistic image of the philosopher in order to describe the relationships between Jesus and his disciples and between various Christian leaders.

The Early Catholic "Decadence Theory"

While this explanation enables us to see something of the function of these two sets of correspondences in the theological task of Luke-Acts, ours is only a partial vision at this point. Certain questions clamor for attention. First, how is it that Luke can conceive of the apostolic church as such a perfect embodiment of the way of life which began with Jesus? Did he really believe that the church was so flawless a pupil of the master? Second, if Luke conceives of the first and second links in the chain of succession (i.e., the Twelve and Paul) as such ideal transmitters of the tradition, does he believe that the subsequent links will be ideal too? Does he really believe that the kind of unity evident between Paul and Jerusalem will be continued in successive links of the chain?[65] Such questions as these, which arise out of our study so far, can be dealt with satisfactorily only if we understand Luke's use of the "decadence theory" of Early Catholicism with its idealization of the apostolic

16324

age. Let us, therefore, examine this aspect of Early Catholic thought and Luke's appropriation of it.

The spirit of Roman imperial times was essentially backward looking.[66] The remote past was idealized and history became an instrument of propaganda. This idealization of the past and the estimate of it as a guide for the future accompanied the feeling that Greco-Roman man had fallen from a high estate which he had once enjoyed. Hence he began to look backward on a more glorious past and to regard the achievements of the past as classical paradigms.[67] By the third Christian generation a variation of this same spirit had begun to permeate the outlook of the Christian community on its past and present. It became a basic conviction of Early Catholicism that schism and heresy had been unknown in the earliest days of Christianity, that is, when the apostles were alive.[68] They had arisen only after the apostolic age had come to an end. The post-apostolic age, therefore, was a decadent time, a time that had fallen from a high estate. Two poles of thought were held together in this Early Catholic conception. On the one hand, there was the idealization of the apostolic age. On the other, there was a belief in the subsequent decadence of the Christian community. These two poles of thought are found in Tertullian. He argued: (1) the Lord's apostles constitute the church's authority; and (2) since truth precedes its copy, Christian truth precedes error.[69] Taken together these two tenets express the Early Catholic idealization of the apostolic times and despair with what followed. The view is stated explicitly by Hegesippus. Eusebius reports that Hegesippus

> explaining the events of these times, adds that until then the Church remained a pure and uncorrupted virgin, for those who attempted to corrupt the healthful rule of the Saviour's preaching, if they existed at all, lurked in obscure darkness. But when the sacred band of the Apostles and the generation of those to whom it had been vouchsafed to hear with their own ears the divine wisdom had reached the several ends of their lives, then the federation of godless error took its beginning through the deceit of false teachers who, seeing that none of the Apostles still remained, barefacedly tried against the preaching of the truth the counter-proclamation of "knowledge falsely so-called."[70]

In another place Eusebius says that Hegesippus reported that at the early period "they called the church virgin, for it had not yet been corrupted by vain messages. . . ."[71] In the Shepherd of Hermas we hear of the apostles who "always agreed with one another and were at peace with one another. . . ."[72] This, of course, is set in the context of contrasting behavior in Hermas' own time.

Within the New Testament, 2 Peter reflects the Early Catholic point of view.[73] In form 2 Peter is a farewell speech which (1) describes the situation of the apostle who foresees his departure (1:13-15), (2) foretells the problems which will arise after his demise, that is, the emergence of heresy (2:1-22), and appeals to apostolic example and tradition as the safeguard against error

(1:16-18; 1:20-21; 3:2). The author of 2 Peter relied upon the testament form because this offered him a way to maintain two of his pet convictions, both the freedom of the apostolic age from heresy and the apostle's authority against error. For the author of 2 Peter, the apostolic age is free from heresy and schism, which arise after the departure of the apostle. Jude 17-18 also appears to reflect the same view.

Perhaps as early an example of the decadence view of Early Catholicism as we know about outside the canon is found in 1 Clement (95—96 C.E.).[74] In 1 Clem 1:2—2:8 the author draws a picture of the Corinthian community, prior to the present uprising, as the ideal community. In this passage we find a picture of the apostolic age as the ideal time of allegiance to the apostles and things apostolic. The apostles foresee the emergence of heresy and schism after their departure, however. Here again we hear the two-pronged assertion of the ideal past and the decaying present.

There are a number of indications that Acts reflects the same Early Catholic mentality. On the one hand, it seems certain that the Evangelist intended to idealize the apostolic age. (1) In the first chapters of Acts we are given an "ideal picture of the peace and order of the earliest period"[75] of the church in Jerusalem (cf. 2:42-47; 4:32-37). It is a picture that does not fit with what we know from Paul's epistles (cf. Gal 2:4-5). Moreover, the story itself contains hints of contradictory tendencies in the church (cf. 5:1-11; 6:1-6). Luke apparently conceived his picture of the Jerusalem church in a spirit of harmonistic idealizing. (2) In the picture we are given of Pauline Christianity, moreover, there is no hint of the Gentile controversies that we hear about, for example, in 1 and 2 Corinthians. Why this portrait of Paul's churches? "Part of its purpose was to picture the unanimity of the early Church; and the writer seems to have selected some incidents, omitted others, and changed others in order to serve this purpose."[76] Pauline as well as Jerusalem Christianity is idealized. (3) The relations between the two wings of the church are also smoothed over. One need only mention the relations of Peter and Paul on the one side and the relations of Paul and Barnabas on the other. In Acts 10—11, 15, Peter is portrayed as the initiator of the Gentile mission and the supporter of Paul in Jerusalem. One would hardly get this impression from Galatians. In Acts 15:36-41 Paul and Barnabas separate, but not because of doctrinal differences as one might imply from Galatians. Their division is over personal matters involving relatives. Luke does not allow for basic theological differences between the two, Paul and Jerusalem.[77] It is within the context of this idealization of the apostolic age that several of Luke's sets of correspondences may be understood to play a contributing role. The correspondences between Jesus' career in the Third Gospel and the church's life in Acts are in line with the Evangelist's conviction that in the apostolic age the church was in a religious "state of nature," uncorrupted by heresy and schism. The church in the apostolic age was a perfect pupil of the master teacher, embodying in her life as in her words the life of Jesus. Furthermore, it would seem that the correspondences between the two cycles in Acts 1—5 may serve the role of intensifying, through repetition, the idealization of the Jerusalem church. Finally, in line with the author's desire to avoid serious disagreements between the two wings of the church, it seems likely that the Paul-Jerusalem correspondences should be understood as one more part of Luke's attempt to paint a picture of the apostolic church in ideal terms, free from schism and heresy.

W. C. van Unnik has recently contended that Luke does not picture the apostolic age as free from heresy and schism.[78] He first appeals to such evidence as the Jewish claims that Jesus was not the Messiah (4:18; 5:28; 6:8-14; 17:5-9; 18:12-17, etc.), the conflicts between Christians and magicians (8:13-24; 13:4-12) and other pagans (16:19-39; 19:23-41), and the conflict between the Hebrews and the Hellenists (6:1-6). The problem with van Unnik's argument at this point is his assumed definition of heresy and schism. From the Early Catholic point of view both heresy and schism implied (a) that the subjects of the action were Christians, and (b) that they were acting or teaching in a way contrary to the apostles. For a Christian to be anti-apostolic was to be guilty of heresy or schism. Most of the examples van Unnik points to are examples of non-Christian opposition to the gospel. Where the examples include Christians, as for example in the conflict between the Hebrews and the Hellenists, the problem is resolved by apostolic authority. Conflicts existed in the apostolic age, according to Luke, but heresy and schism did not. Van Unnik then argues that the lack of overt concern with heresy in Acts does not necessarily imply that Luke idealized the apostolic age. What must we say, however, when it becomes apparent that Luke himself is very much involved in a struggle with heresy? Moreover, the farewell speech of Paul to the Ephesian elders in Acts 20:17-35 explicitly says that heresy and schism will arise *after* the apostle's departure (cf. vss. 29-30).[79] Luke-Acts, therefore, shares not only in the tendency to idealize the apostolic age but also in the conviction that it was after the apostles' departure that heresy and schism arose. His generation, the Third Evangelist believes, participates in post-apostolic decadence.

If Luke believed that the post-apostolic church had fallen from the high estate of the apostolic age, then although he conceived of the first and second links of his chain of succession, the Twelve and Paul, as ideal pupils of the master and transmitters of the tradition, he did not necessarily regard subsequent links in this way. From Acts 20:17-35 it is clear that the Evangelist's desire is that the Ephesian elders perpetuate the Pauline example and teaching into their era. They were to extend into their age the apostolic ideal they had learned from Paul. Luke, however, did not let the matter rest there with his intentions. He set up a twofold norm by which the behavior and doctrine of the elders could be tested to see if they truly perpetuated their master's way.

In the first place, Luke did not employ a succession list as was customarily done in the ancient world. Instead he constructed a succession narrative in which the actions of the apostles are described and their teaching recorded. This narrative of apostolic word and deed, when read publicly in church as it was doubtless intended to be, would form a public criterion of what was apostolic. Only that elder whose life and teaching did not deviate from this canon of truth could be regarded as a legitimate pupil of the apostles. In the second place, the Third Evangelist prefixed to his Acts a Gospel, a practice unknown elsewhere in early Christianity.[80] By placing a narrative of Jesus' words and deeds before his narrative of the apostles and by making the events in the two narratives correspond, Luke set up a further norm. This norm was one by which even the apostles were judged. It was the norm of what Jesus "began to do and teach." The apostles bear authority because they embody the way of Jesus. Hence, those elders who embody the way of Jesus as it was perpetuated by the apostles are men to whom the Christians of Luke's generation should listen and from whom they should learn.

As a result of Luke's construction of this twofold norm, both the Gospel and the Acts function as judges or criteria of the legitimacy of the elders in succession from Paul. This means that for the Evangelist the apostolic age is set apart from all subsequent Christian history and becomes its norm. The correspondences between Jesus and the apostolic church do not, any more than those between Paul and Jerusalem, imply that the Evangelist believed that henceforth the same type of succession could be expected. It appears rather that Luke did not expect the ideal to be perpetuated effortlessly and, therefore, set up certain norms by which a teacher could be judged.

It is, therefore, within the framework of the Lucan appropriation of the popular image of the philosopher in the Hellenistic world and his utilization of the Early Catholic concept of an ideal apostolic age followed by the emergence of heresy that three sets of Lucan correspondences can be seen in alliance with meaning. The correspondences between the Gospel and Acts, between Jerusalem and Paul, and those in Acts 1—5, all function in one way or other to support the Lucan perspective on *Heilsgeschichte*. It now remains for us to examine two more sets of correspondences, those between John and Jesus in Luke 1—2 and in Luke 3—4, to see how they are linked with the Evangelist's theology.

The Relation between John and Jesus

Hans Conzelmann's understanding of the relation between John and Jesus in Luke-Acts still occupies the dominant position in exegetical circles in spite of its obvious problems.[81] It is Conzelmann's thesis that the Third Evangelist has separated John and Jesus geographically and theologically in order to develop a three-phased understanding of salvation-history: the Law and the Prophets, Jesus, and the Church. His arguments for such a separation of John and Jesus into two distinct phases within salvation history include: (1) John's ministry is over before Jesus is even baptized, so that Luke makes no mention of the Baptist in connection with the baptism; (2) Luke 16:16 says that the Law and the Prophets are climaxed with John, while from then onwards the Kingdom of God has been preached; (3) Luke omits John's role as Elijah which was found in the pre-Lucan tradition, a contention made possible in part by Conzelmann's omitting Luke 1—2 from consideration. Conzelmann's thesis regarding the separation of John and Jesus into distinct phases of salvation history has come under sharp attack from H. H. Oliver, William C. Robinson, Jr., Helmut Flender, and S. G. Wilson.[82] They respond: (1) Luke's telling of John's imprisonment before recounting Jesus' ministry is found in part in Mark 1:14; moreover, the Evangelist's tying up the loose ends of the story of John before going on to that about Jesus is characteristic of Lucan style; (2) Luke 16:16 does not yield a threefold periodization of history since the text speaks only of two periods; moreover, not only do Luke's sources not show the Baptist preaching the Kingdom of God but also Luke 16:17 shows that for Luke the Law carries over into the new period after John; (3) the birth narratives are integral to Luke-Acts and must be taken into account; moreover, Luke 1:17, 76, apply the Malachi prophecy with all its Elijah overtones to John.

In light of such criticisms, it is possible to say that Conzelmann's description of the Lucan periodization of history has retained its convincing power in the scholarly world in spite of the deficiencies of his arguments for the distinction between the first two phases, the Law and the Prophets and Jesus. Indeed, we have seen earlier in this chapter that the author of Luke-Acts certainly did see salvation-history unfolding in distinct phases: Jesus and the church, with the latter distinguished into apostolic and post-apostolic ages. Certain architectural patterns, moreover, played a role in Luke's divisions within salvation history. This raises a question of the possibility at this point that the correspondences between John and Jesus in Luke 1—2 and 3—4 may play a role in Luke's thought and can, thereby, assist in the debate over the Lucan understanding of John and Jesus.

The correspondences between John and Jesus in Luke 1—2 and 3—4 are tied up with two Lucan emphases: on the one hand, Jesus' exaltation over John and John's subordination to Jesus, and on the other, the unity of these two men in salvation history. On the one hand, there is the motif of John's subordination to Jesus. In all of the discussion of the patterns of the first two chapters of Luke nothing was said concerning the passage which dealt with Mary's visit to Elizabeth. Now it must be asked: what is the place and function of this block of material, 1:39-56, which lies between the two seven point cycles of chapters 1—2 comparing Jesus and John? The answer to this question seems to be contained in three elements found therein. First, the story is based upon the assumption that Mary and Elizabeth are blood relatives (1:36). This fact endows Jesus from his mother's side with any advantage of Aaronic descent that John could boast of, making him, as a descendent of both David (3:31) and of Aaron, the inevitable choice among those through whom the hoped for deliverance might come.[83] Secondly, within the story, the speech of Elizabeth in vss. 42-45 emphasizes the subordinate place of her son and thereby herself in the presence of Mary and the yet unborn Lord Jesus. Finally, the typological method of writing is used here in portraying the incident. The ancients commonly stated the conviction that a relationship between two people was not incidental or coincidental by projecting it back into their antecedents by means of a story form.[84] This was done in the Old Testament, for example, in Gen 25:22-26 in the story of the birth of Jacob and Esau. Here the idea is that the movement of the unborn babe foreshadows the future lot of the child.[85] Luke 1:41 has been written in such a way as to portray John the Baptist's movements in the womb so as to echo the Genesis story. In reading the Old Testament passage of the movement of Rebecca's children in the womb, attention should be called to the fact that the movement is followed by an explanation of the phenomenon given in the words of God,

> the one shall be stronger than the other, the elder shall serve the younger. (Gen 25:23)

To a Christian steeped in the Old Testament this allusion would testify that in God's purpose the elder, the son of Elizabeth, was really the lesser and the servant of the younger, the son of Mary. From these facts there should be no doubt but that this section, 1:39-56, was placed here between the two cycles comparing Jesus and John in the birth narrative in order to emphasize the exaltation of Jesus over John, the subordination of John to Jesus.

This same motif is found in 3:1—4:15 where 3:1-6 presents John as the prophet whose function is to "prepare the way of the Lord" (3:4). His mission in 3:15-17 is also described as anticipatory, looking towards the one who would "baptize with the Holy Spirit and with fire" (3:16). Finally, the fact that whereas John's summary statement indicates the end of his ministry (3:18-20) while Jesus' summary statement indicates that he is only beginning serves to show that John must decrease while Jesus must increase. The literary patterns of Luke 1:5—4:15, therefore, reveal a marked tendency to accentuate the exaltation of the son of Mary over the Baptist.

On the other hand, there is the motif of unity between John and Jesus. If Luke had wished to say nothing more than that John was subordinate to Jesus or even primarily that, why did he arrange his Baptist material into three cycles which relate John with Jesus so closely that their early lives seem so very similar and so that pains had to be taken to emphasize Jesus' superior position in relation to John? Luke's careful and orderly arrangements warn one to look further for yet another message regarding the Baptist and Jesus. What does he have to tell us?

Here it will be necessary to remember other examples of correspondences which we have found related to meaning. Take the Gospel-Acts parallels, for instance. We have seen that the Evangelist definitely intended his readers to see the church in a position subordinate to her Lord. At the same time, however, the correspondences spoke of a unity between the Master and his apostolic age pupils. The same themes were found to be characteristic of the correspondences between Jerusalem and Paul in Acts. While the author of Acts clearly regarded Paul as subordinate to the Twelve, he also regarded the two apostolic links in his chain of tradition to be one in deed and word. With this in mind we may see why the Evangelist parallels the Baptist and Jesus so carefully. It is part of Luke's unity-motif. It is an attempt to tie the lives of John and Jesus together just as the author wants to tie together Christ and the church. There is continuity between John and Jesus at the same time that John is subordinate to Jesus.

As a result of our findings concerning the links between the correspondences of Luke 1—2 and Luke 3—4 and the Lucan theology taken together with evidence uncovered earlier in this chapter, a certain picture of the history of salvation as Luke understands it begins to emerge. As the author of Luke-Acts portrays it, salvation-history runs from the faithful among the Jewish people, symbolized by John the Baptist and the circles from which he comes, to Jesus, and from Jesus to the Twelve, then through Paul to the Ephesian elders, symbolizing the authentic Gentile church of the post-apostolic age. From the Baptist to the elders there is a certain continuity that holds the entire process together as one history. At the same time, however, there is a principle of subordination that runs throughout the Lucan salvation-history. John is subordinate to Jesus as the one who prepares the way for the Lord is to the Lord when he comes. The apostolic church, including Paul who is subordinate to the Twelve, is subordinate to Jesus as an ideal pupil is related to his master. The post-apostolic age, finally, is subordinated to the apostolic age as a pupil must be to his teacher. The following diagram expresses Luke's understanding concisely.

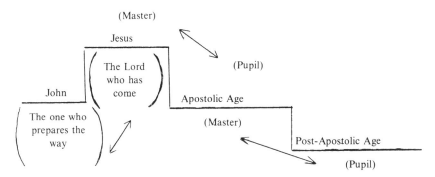

In spite of the deficiency of his arguments concerning the relationship between John and Jesus, therefore, part of Conzelmann's conclusion is basically correct. The author of Luke-Acts does construct a salvation-history in stages: the Law and the Prophets, Jesus, the church. To be entirely accurate, however, it is necessary to recognize that Luke makes a distinction in the third stage of salvation-history so that the apostolic age must be separated from the post-apostolic church. For Luke this distinction is so radical that it may very well be necessary to speak of a four phase salvation-history if we are adequately to express the Lucan intention. Moreover, the Lucan emphasis seems to be on the continuity between the various stages rather than their separateness as Conzelmann contends.

At this point we are able to say that least five of the eleven patterns noted in Chapter Two, Three, and Four have some connection with the Lucan understanding of *Heilsgeschichte*. Architecture, in these instances at least, is in alliance with meaning. What can be said of the other six patterns? To this question we turn in the next chapter.

FOOTNOTES

[1] Discourse 13:9 (LCL).

[2] Discourse 13:10 (LCL).

[3] Walter Lewis Liefeld, "The Wandering Preacher as a Social Figure in the Roman Empire," unpublished Ph.D. thesis, Columbia University, 1967, p. 81.

[4] M. L. Clarke, *The Roman Mind* (Cambridge: Harvard University Press, 1960) 72.

[5] Epistle 110:1.

[6] Epistle 16:3 (LCL).

[7] Clarke, *The Roman Mind*, 124.

[8] *Ibid.*

[9] *Memorabilia* 1:3:1; 4:3:18; 4:4:25.

[10] *Memorabilia* 4:1:1 (LCL).

[11] Epistle 11:9-10 (LCL).

[12] Epistle 6:5.

[13] Epistle 6:5-6. Used in accordance with the general directives of the University Presses.

[14] Epistle 52:8-9.

[15] Epistle 25:6.

[16] Epistle 52:8-9.

[17] Discourse 70:6.

[18] Discourse 55:4-5 (LCL).

[19] *The Institutio Oratoria* 12:29-30.

[20] *Life* 5:21.

[21] See R. D. Hicks' Introduction in Diogenes Laertius' *Lives of Eminent Philosophers* (LCL; Cambridge: Harvard University Press, 1950) 1. xxiv; C. H. Turner, "Apostolic Succession," in *Essays on the Early History of the Church and the Ministry* (ed. H. B. Swete; London: Macmillan, 1918) 198. The substance of some of the material which follows appeared originally in *Jesus and Man's Hope*, 1. 198-200, and is used by permission.

[22] *Ibid.*

[23] *Ibid.*

[24] *Academica* 1:34-35 (LCL).

[25] Elias Bickermann, "La chaine de la tradition Pharisienne," *RB* 59 (1952) 49.

[26] 30:4 (LCL).

[27] *De exilo*, c. 14 (cited by Turner, "Apostolic Succession," 198. In the "Appendix" to his essay Turner gives additional references to succession terminology used of philosophical schools and teachers.).

[28] *Miscellanies* 1:14.

[29] See especially 1:13-15; 2:47; 10:16-17.

[30] 10:22.

[31] Bickermann, "La chaine de la tradition Pharisienne," 49.

[32] Cf. Epicurus' last will as it is recorded in Diogenes Laertius, *Lives of Eminent Philosophers* 10:16-17.

[33] Bickermann, 50; apparently accepted by W. D. Davies, "Reflections on Tradition: The Aboth Revisited," in *History and Interpretation*, ed. W. R. Farmer *et al*, 141.

[34] Liefeld, "The Wandering Preacher as a Social Figure in the Roman Empire," 131-32.

[35] David Daube, *The New Testament and Rabbinic Judaism* (London: Athlone, 1956) 87.

[36] (LCL).

[37] (LCL).

[38] Birger Gerhardsson, *Tradition and Transmission in Early Christianity* (Lund: C. W. K. Gleerup, 1964) 45, n. 110.

[39] E.g., b. Ber. 24a, b; b. Ber. 38b; b. Ber. 39b.

[40] E.g., Mishnah, *Erubin* 2:6; Mishnah, *Orlah* 2:5.

[41] Mishnah, *Sukkah* 2:5.

[42] Mishnah, *Sukkah* 3:9.

[43] b. Ber. 62a (Soncino ed.).

[44]b. Erub. 93b.

[45]b. Ber. 11a (Soncino ed.).

[46]Gerhardsson, *Tradition and Transmission in Early Christianity*, 17.

[47]*Praeparatio Evangelica* 9:30.

[48]*Against Apion* 1:8.

[49]Davies, "Reflections on Tradition," 141; D. Georgi, "The Records of Jesus in the Light of Ancient Accounts of Revered Men," *Proceedings of the Society of Biblical Literature*)1972) 2. 529.

[50]*Against Heresies* 3:3:4.

[51](Ante-Nicene Fathers).

[52]*Against Heresies* 3:2:2 (Ante-Nicene Fathers).

[53](Ante-Nicene Fathers).

[54](Ante-Nicene Fathers).

[55](Ante-Nicene Fathers).

[56]Walter Schmithals, *The Office of Apostle in the Early Church* (Nashville: Abingdon, 1969) 287-88, wrongly asserts that the origin of the succession idea of the Catholic Church is to be sought in Judaism rather than the prototypes of the ancient philosophical schools.

[57]Clement of Alexandria, *Strom* 50:7, says that Valentinus claimed to have derived his views from Theodas or Theudas, a pupil of Paul. Ptolemaeus' *Letter to Flora* (in Epiphanius, *Pan* 33:3-7) speaks of "the apostolic tradition which we too have received by succession." Such references as these indicate that Gnosticism as well as orthodoxy appealed to the succession principle.

[58]Cf. W. L. Knox, *Some Hellenistic Elements in Primitive Christianity* (London: British Academy, 1944) 13.

[59]E. E. Ellis, *The Gospel of Luke* (Camden, N. J.: Nelson, 1966) 125.

[60]Hans Conzelmann, "Luke's Place in the Development of Early Christianity," in *Studies in Luke-Acts,* ed. Keck and Martyn, 308 and 315, n. 101.

[61]Cf. *Luke and the Gnostics*, ch. 3, "The Succession of Tradition," and "The Redaction Critical Quest for Luke the Theologian," in *Jesus and Man's Hope*, 1. 200. The succession from Jesus to the Twelve to Paul is also found in the Epistle of the Apostles 31.

[62]B. S. Easton, "The Purpose of Acts," in *Early Christianity* (ed. F. C. Grant; Greenwich, Conn.: Seabury Press, 1954) 59.

[63]For what follows, see *Luke and the Gnostics*, 76. Used by permission.

[64]For what follows, see *Luke and the Gnostics*, 33-34. Used by permission.

[65]It is in misunderstanding Luke at this point that Ernst Käsemann's entire estimate of Lucan theology is led astray. Cf. especially his "Ministry and Community in the New Testament," in *Essays on New Testament Themes* (London: SCM, 1964) 63-94.

[66]B. E. Perry, *The Ancient Romances* (Berkeley: University of California Press, 1967) 6. Cf. Livy, 1:1:5.

[67]Moses Hadas, *Hellenistic Culture* (New York: Columbia University Press, 1959) 115-17.

[68]Cf. Käsemann, "An Apology for Primitive Christian Eschatology," in *Essays on New Testament Themes*, 170; "The Disciples of John the Baptist in Ephesus," *ibid.*, 145.

[69]*The Prescription against Heretics* 6; 20; 21-29; 30; 32; 35.

[70]*The Ecclesiastical History* 3:32:7-8 (LCL). Used in accordance with the general directives of the University Presses.

[71]*Ibid.* 4:22:4 (LCL).

[72]Vision 3:5:1.

[73]Cf. my article, "II Peter and the Delay of the Parousia," *VC* 20 (1966) 137-45, for what follows.

[74]Kirsopp Lake, "Paul's Controversies," in *The Beginnings of Christianity*, 5. 223.

[75]Hans von Campenhausen, "Tradition and Succession in the Second Century," in *Ecclesiastical Authority and Spiritual Power* (London: Black, 1969) 153.

[76]F. J. Foakes-Jackson and K. Lake, "The Disciples in Jerusalem" in *Beginnings of Christianity*, 1. 311. Cf. also F. F. Bruce, *PCB*, 937-38.

[77]Cf. John Knox, *Chapters in a Life of Paul* (Nashville: Abingdon, 1950) 72, n. 8.

[78]"Die Apostelgeschichte und die Haeresien," *ZNW* 58 (1967) 240-46.

[79]Georg Gunther Blum, *Tradition und Sukzession* (Berlin: Lutherisches Verlagshaus, 1963) 39, says that in Acts 20: 17-35 the "decadence theory" of the Catholic Epistles and Hegesippus has its first roots.

[80]See my article, "The Redaction Critical Quest for Luke the Theologian," in *Jesus and Man's Hope*, 1. 203-4.

[81]*The Theology of St. Luke*, 18-27.

[82]Oliver, "The Lucan Birth Stories and the Purpose of Luke-Acts," *NTS* 10 (1963-64) 202-26; Robinson, *The Way of the Lord: A Study of History and Eschatology in the Gospel of Luke* (A doctoral dissertation submitted to the Theological Faculty of the Univeristy of Basel, Privately published, c. 1962); Flender, *St. Luke*; Wilson, "Lukan Eschatology," *NTS* 15 (1970) 330-47.

[83]Carl H. Kraeling, *John the Baptist* (New York: Scribner's, 1951) 126.

[84]*Ibid.*, 126-27.

[85]J. M. Creed, *The Gospel according to St. Luke*, 21.

CHAPTER VII

The Patterns
and Lucan Christology

This chapter has as its objective the presentation of the meaning-function of three more sets of correspondences in the Lucan theological perspective: namely, the correspondences between Luke 9 and 22—23, those between Luke 9 and Acts 1, and those between Luke 24 and Acts 1. My contention is that the meaning-function of these three patterns can be understood if they are seen within the context of one facet of the Lucan picture of Jesus. It is to the task of supplying evidence for this assertion that we now turn.

It is clear that there is no one Christology in the writings of the New Testament.[1] For example, whereas passages such as Rom 1:3-4,[2] Acts 2:36, and 13:33[3] reflect an exaltation or adoptionist point of view, other passages such as 1 Tim 3:16 and John 1:1-18 reflect an epiphany or incarnation christology.[4] Recent scholarship has been reasonably successful in making clear the worlds of thought within which these christologies are formed and in clarifying the kinds of questions each is trying to answer.[5] These types are by no means the total christological output of the New Testament period, however. For example, yet another type of attempt to express the significance of Jesus is found in Luke-Acts. It will be the purpose of the following pages to describe at least a major facet of this Lucan christology[6] and to seek an answer to the question why this manner of speaking of Jesus is used.

Before going on we must consider two methodological questions. First, how can one find the Lucan christology? An answer to this question is linked to our understanding of Luke's audience. When Luke-Acts was read aloud[7] in the worship of the early church,[8] its readers and hearers did not sit with copies of Luke's sources before them so that they could compare what they heard with Mark and Q.[9] Even if they had possessed such source materials, they would not have been concerned with such comparisons. They read and listened to Luke's story of Jesus as a whole. It was the total impression of Jesus which they gained from Luke-Acts that was significant. The source of this total impression would be the overall pattern of the Lucan picture of Christ. Consequently, if an author wanted to be understood, he would write with this in mind. It would be through the overall pattern of Jesus' career that he would seek to convey his christology. Hence, any examination of the Lucan christology must begin where Luke and his audience began, with the overall pattern of the Lucan picture of Christ.

A second methodological question is: how can one be sure that the total impression he receives from the Lucan story of Jesus is really a reflection of the Lucan mind? An answer to this question is linked to our understanding of the situation of the modern scholar. The scholar knows Luke's sources. He has them before him. By a careful comparison of Luke-Acts with its sources one can determine how Luke used his material, what tendencies are present in this usage, and thereby infer something of the Lucan mind.[10] By means of his knowledge of the Lucan use of sources the scholar can know that the Lucan framework is the Evangelist's construction. He is able to see that the overall picture of Jesus is a theological rather than a strictly historical entity.

Any attempt to speak of the christology of Luke-Acts must take into account both the situation of Luke's audience and that of the modern scholar.[11] One must search out the overall pattern of Luke's picture of Jesus as it can be ascertained by his knowledge of the Evangelist's use of sources. The method comes clear if we ask: if Luke had given us just the picture of Jesus that could have been derived from his available models (Mark, Q, and the early kerygma reflected in some of the speeches in Acts), how would this compare with the picture we get in his finished product? Such a question brings the reader of the Gospel to an awareness that the entire framework of the Lucan picture of Christ would be missing if the Evangelist had merely copied his models. Missing would be the birth narratives (Luke 1—2), the narrative of the ascension of Jesus (Acts 1), the lengthy journey of Jesus to Jerusalem (Luke 9:51—19:46), and the distinctive way in which the beginning of the public ministry of Jesus is depicted (Luke 3—4). The overall pattern of Luke's picture of Jesus, therefore, is due to his deviation from his available models. It is to this distinctively Lucan picture of Jesus that we now turn.

The Ascension

In our discussion of the overall pattern of the Lucan picture of Jesus, it is with the climax of the life of Jesus, the ascension, that we begin. In beginning with the ascension we are following two leads. On the one hand, Mediterranean documents frequently, if not generally, have their key point at the center. This is true both for Greco-Roman and for Jewish writings.[12] On the other hand, Luke-Acts seems to fit into this general tendency. At least from Luke 9:51 everything in the Third Gospel moves toward the ascension. Luke 24:50-53 closes the Gospel. Acts 1:9-11 opens the Acts. From Acts 1 everything moves out from the ascension.

The narrative of Acts 1 which describes the ascension as an event distinguishable from the resurrection-exaltation is clearly a reflection of the Lucan hand.[13] It is not derived from any of Luke's known models. Moreover, neither Paul nor the pre-Pauline tradition of I Cor 15:3-5 knows of an ascension separate from the resurrection-exaltation. The Fourth Gospel, the only other Gospel to allude to an ascension, does not really separate it from resurrection-exaltation for in John 20:17-19 it is a part of resurrection day. Indeed, Luke himself knows a tradition which does not separate ascension from resurrection-exaltation.[14] The conclusion is inescapable. Luke stands alone in early Christianity in speaking of an ascension separate from Jesus' resurrection-exaltation, and even he reflects a knowledge of tradition to the contrary.[15]

In the distinctively Lucan understanding of the ascension, the narrative of Acts 1 seems to function as a guarantee device. In the first place, by means of this narrative the Evangelist seeks to guarantee the *corporeality* of the one who ascend. For Luke the ascension is an empirical event, observable to the natural eye of its beholders.[16] Note the language of Acts 1. It is while they are watching ($\beta\lambda\epsilon\pi\acute{o}\nu\tau\omega\nu$ $a\mathring{v}\tau\hat{\omega}\nu$) that Jesus is lifted up ($\epsilon\pi\acute{\eta}\rho\theta\eta$) in vs. 9a. In vs. 9b a cloud takes him up ($\mathring{v}\pi\acute{\epsilon}\lambda a\beta\epsilon\nu$) from their eyes ($\mathring{a}\pi\grave{o}$ $\tau\hat{\omega}\nu$ $\mathring{o}\phi\theta a\lambda\mu\hat{\omega}\nu$ $a\mathring{v}\tau\hat{\omega}\nu$). It is as they are looking intently ($\mathring{a}\tau\epsilon\nu\acute{i}\zeta o\nu\tau\epsilon\varsigma$) that he proceeds into the heaven in vs. 10 ($\epsilon\mathring{i}\varsigma$ $\tau\grave{o}\nu$ $o\mathring{v}\rho a\nu\grave{o}\nu$ $\pi o\rho\epsilon vo\mu\acute{\epsilon}\nu o\nu$ $a\mathring{v}\tau o\hat{v}$). When the two men in white garments address the disciples they ask: why do you stand looking into heaven ($\beta\lambda\acute{\epsilon}\pi o\nu\tau\epsilon\varsigma$ $\epsilon\mathring{i}\varsigma$ $\tau\grave{o}\nu$ $o\mathring{v}\rho a\nu\acute{o}\nu$ —vs. 11)? Then they say that the Jesus who will return will be the one whom "you beheld going into heaven" ($\mathring{\epsilon}\theta\epsilon\acute{a}\sigma a\sigma\theta\epsilon$ ... $\pi o\rho\epsilon vo\mu\epsilon\nu o\nu$ $\epsilon\mathring{i}\varsigma$ $\tau\grave{o}\nu$ $o\mathring{v}\rho a\nu\acute{o}\nu$ —vs. 11). From this language it is clear that Luke regards Jesus' ascension as an act of levitation visible to the natural eye.

This emphasis upon the corporeality of Jesus' ascension is the same as that in the passion narrative where Luke shapes his sources so that the materiality of the events is accented.[17] In Luke 23:55 the Evangelist modifies Mark 15:47 so we are told that they saw the *body* of Jesus laid in the tomb. In Luke 24:3 there is a remark peculiar to Luke: "They did not find the *body*." In Luke 24:22-23, a passage found only in the Third Gospel, the two men, referring back to the empty tomb narrative, say: "Moreover, some women of our company amazed us. They were at the tomb early in the morning and did not find his *body*." In Luke 24:36-43, again a passage found only in this Gospel, Jesus undertakes to prove that he is not a spirit. He says: "See my hands and my feet, that it is I myself; handle me, and see; for a spirit has not *flesh and bones* as you see that I have" (vs. 39). Then Jesus eats a piece of broiled fish before them (vs. 43), something a purely spiritual being would not do (cf. Tob 12:19).

The corporeality of the ascension is guaranteed by the presence of the Galileans who observe it. The two men at the ascension address the witnesses as "men of Galilee" ($\mathring{a}\nu\delta\rho\epsilon\varsigma$ $\Gamma a\lambda\iota\lambda a\hat{\iota}o\iota$) in vs. 11. When Luke gives the names of those who returned to Jerusalem after the ascension (1:13), it is the same group mentioned in Luke 6:14-16 (with the exception of Judas Iscariot, of course), that is, the apostles chosen in Galilee.

This emphasis upon the Galileans who witness the event and thereby guarantee its materiality is also the same as that in the passion narrative where

Luke adapts his sources so that Galileans are present to witness and guarantee the materiality of the events.[18] In Luke 23:49 (Mark 15:40-41) we read: "And all his acquaintances and the women who had followed him from Galilee stood at a distance and saw these things." The Galileans see Jesus crucified and die. In Luke 23:55, instead of Mark's "Mary Magdalene and Mary the mother of Jesus saw where he was laid" (15:47), Luke has "The women who had come with him from Galilee followed, and saw the tomb, and how his body was laid." The Galileans see his body laid in the tomb. In Luke 24:3 we find a sentence peculiar to the Third Gospel: "When they went in they did not find the body." The same Galileans who saw Jesus buried now witness the absence of the body from the tomb. In Luke 24:33-53 the risen Lord appears to the Galileans, that is, to Simon (vs. 34) and to the eleven (vss. 36-43).

Since no one argues a case when there is no challenge, the strong emphasis on the materiality of the passion-resurrection-ascension and the attempt to guarantee such by the presence of eyewitnesses must surely point to a problem which the Evangelist was facing. Some one must have been denying the very points defended. This would mean that Luke was confronted by a docetic tendency. Some one was not only denying the real death-resurrection of Jesus but was also apparently advocating a spiritual ascension. In the face of this challenge the Third Evangelist first sought to guarantee the corporeality of the one who ascended.

In the second place, with the ascension narrative of Acts 1 the Evangelist seeks to guarantee the *continuity* between the one who ascends and the one who suffered, died, and was raised. Luke wants to say that the one who ascends is the one who suffered, died, and then was raised in Jerusalem. His method of doing this is to connect the ascension with the lengthy journey of Jesus to Jerusalem in Luke 9:51—19:46.[19] This so-called "travel section" has been put into its present form by the Evangelist. It is not simply taken over from his sources.[20] Though Mark (9:30; 10:1, 17, 32, 46; 11:1, 11) contains the motif of a journey of Jesus from Galilee to Jerusalem, Luke has considerably expanded the idea. (1) With few exceptions (9:53; 18:31; 18:35; 19:28, 29), the notices of movement (9:57; 10:1, 17, 38; 11:1; 13:10; 14:1, 25) and destination (9:51; 13:22, 33; 17:11; 18:35; 19:1, 11, 37, 41) in the travel section are found in the framework and not in the traditional units themselves. (2) The style of these travel notices is Lucan. (3) These travel notices are included in sections including Mark, Q, and L tradition. This means that the travel section is the result of the Evangelist who brought these three sources together. When we read the travel section of the Third Gospel, therefore, we are in touch with the Lucan mind.

Luke connects Jesus' journey to Jerusalem with his ascension. (1) Luke 9:51, the beginning of the journey, reads: "When the days drew near for him to be received up, he set his face to go to Jerusalem." The future event toward which the journey points is called τῆς ἀναλήμψεως αὐτοῦ. This, of course, is a reference to Jesus' ascension as Acts 1:11(ὁ ἀναλημφθείς) and Acts 1:22(ἀνελήμφθη) show.[21] His going to Jerusalem in 9:51 (τοῦ πορεύεσθαι εἰς Ἰερουσαλήμ) is at the same time his going to heaven (Acts 1:10— εἰς τὸν οὐρανὸν πορευο. μένου αὐτοῦ; 1:11—πορευόμενον εἰς τὸν οὐρανόν).²² (2) In addition, Luke 9:31 says that on the Mount of Transfiguration Moses and Elijah were speaking of Jesus' exodus (ἔξοδον) which he was about to fulfill in Jerusalem (ἤμελλεν πληροῦν ἐν Ἰερουσαλήμ). This is a distinctively Lucan emphasis due to his modification of Mark. Since Jesus' coming into the world is described as his εἴσοδος (Acts 13:24– τῆς εἰσόδου αὐτοῦ), his departure from the world is his ἔξοδος. This, of course, must mean not only his death but also his resurrection and above all his ascension. It is almost an impossibility to read Jesus' exodus otherwise in light of its proximity to 9:51 where Jesus goes to Jerusalem to be received up and its location in a context which foreshadows the ascension.²³

This Lucan connection between Jesus' journey to Jerusalem and his ascension means that for the Third Evangelist the journey is the first part of that ascent to heaven which he calls Jesus' ἀνάλημψις. To regard the journey as the first stage of the ascension means that in Luke the death and resurrection of Jesus are viewed in an ascension framework. They are further stages in the ascent. For Luke the ascension motif includes Jesus' death-burial-resurrection.²⁴ The very structure of the Third Gospel demands such a reading. This is the reason that side by side with the statements about Jesus' exodus and his being received up in Jerusalem there are statements about his death and resurrection in Jerusalem (9:22, 44; 12:50; 13:32-35—death in Jerusalem; 19:31-33—death and resurrection in Jerusalem). The same emphasis is found in the Lucan speeches. In Luke 24:26, a distinctively Lucan speech attributed to the risen Christ, Jesus says: "Was it not necessary that the Christ should suffer these things and enter into his glory?" Here the suffering is integral to the entering into glory. The same theme is also echoed in the speeches of Acts (Acts 2:22-36; 3:15-21, for example). Thus, there is an emphasis in the Lucan ascension tradition that the ascension of Jesus into heaven is the culmination of his journey from Galilee to Jerusalem for suffering, death, and resurrection in the holy city. Ascension is not an escape from human miseries. Rather it is through death to glory. This is the same emphasis in Christology that Luke makes in Acts with reference to the church (cf. Acts 14:22).²⁵

The continuity between the one who ascends and the one who dies and rises in Jerusalem is guaranteed by the presence of witnesses who accompany Jesus from Galilee to Jerusalem via the lengthy journey and then see him die, see him buried, have him appear to them after the resurrection, and see him ascend into heaven.²⁶

Again, since no one defends what is secure, the strong emphasis upon a continuity between the one who dies and is raised and the one who ascends and the attempt to guarantee this by the presence of witnesses throughout points to a problem with which Luke is faced. Someone apparently was saying that the one who ascended was not the one who died and rose. This is no doubt a docetic claim. We know of certain Gnostic systems in early Christianity which tried to support their docetism by a radical interpretation of the ascension. So, for example, the Sethian-Ophites,[27] Basilides,[28] Cerinthus, [29] and possibly the opponents of Paul in I Corinthians.[30]

Examination of the function of the ascension in the Lucan Christology has revealed the Evangelist's concern to prevent the separation between spirit and flesh in the church's Savior. Indeed the second half of the framework of Luke's picture of Jesus (journey and ascension) seems largely to function in an anti-docetic role. By emphasizing the *corporeality* of the one who ascends and his *continuity* with the one who suffered and rose in Jerusalem, the Third Evangelist seeks to guarantee the real humanity of Jesus Christ.

The Baptism

Can this anti-docetic concern, so apparent in the second half of the Lucan framework, be found in the first part of the Evangelist's picture of Jesus? The evangelist not only seeks to show the continuity between the one who died and rose in Jerusalem and the one who ascends. He also seeks to establish continuity between the one who ascends and the one who worked in Galilee. So in Acts 1:11 the witnesses of the ascension are called "men of Galilee." By this form of address the reader is made aware that "this Jesus, who was taken up from you into heaven" (1:11) is the Jesus who was with the disciples in Galilee. The same note is struck in Acts 1:13 where the disciples chosen in Galilee (Luke 6:12-16) are named again. Especially in Acts 1:21-22 do we find this emphasis. Here the qualifications for a successor to Judas are set forth. A witness must have been with Jesus "beginning from the baptism of John until the day when he was taken up from us." As Acts 10:37 indicates, the baptism of John is linked with Galilee. The Lord's public ministry is from his baptism by John to his ascension. But if the Evangelist wants to establish the identity of the one who ascended and the one who was baptized and worked in Galilee, and if he argues against any separation of flesh and spirit in the ascension, does he not thereby lead the reader to expect the same emphasis in his description of the Lord's baptism? It is to the baptism narrative in Luke 3:21-22, therefore, that we now direct our attention.

For the reader of Luke-Acts who has just seen the Evangelist emphasize the corporeal character of the ascent of the Savior in Acts 1, the most striking thing about the baptism narrative of Luke 3:21-22 is the emphasis upon the corporeal character of the Spirit's descent upon Jesus. In Luke's source (Mark 1:9-11), the Spirit descends upon Jesus "like a dove" (vs. 10). Luke has modified Mark at the point, however, so that we read: "the Holy Spirit descended upon him *in bodily form* (σωματικῷ εἴδει), as a dove." Here the Hellenistic mentality which conceived of power in the form of substance[31] is used, as the ascension narrative has shown, to prevent any separation between Spirit and flesh in Jesus. The same Lucan emphasis is found at Jesus' baptism that we found at his ascension.

This emphasis is found not only in the Lucan modification of Mark's baptism narrative but also in the location of certain material immediately following the baptism pericope (Luke 3:21-22). Luke 3:23 reads: "Jesus when he was about thirty years of age, being the son (as was supposed) of Joseph. . . ." Luke 3:23's "when he began his ministry" points the reader to 4:16-30 where the beginning of Jesus' public ministry is treated as a foreshadowing of his later life.[32] Luke 3:23's "as was supposed" points the reader to Luke 1—2 where Jesus' virginal conception is treated. This means that immediately upon reading the narrative of the baptism of Jesus, the reader is referred both forward to the frontispiece of the public ministry and backward to the birth narratives which open the Gospel. It is as though the Evangelist wanted to interpret the baptism of Jesus for the reader by these links. That this is indeed his intention may be seen if we follow his guidelines.

When we look forward to the beginning of Jesus' public ministry in Luke, we find Luke 4:16-30 opening with Jesus in the synagogue. He reads from Isa 61:1-2: "The Spirit of the Lord is upon me, because he has anointed me . . . ." Then he says: "Today this scripture has been fulfilled in your hearing" (vs. 21). By the phrase "when he began his ministry" in 3:23, Luke has referred us to this narrative in which Jesus says that he has been anointed by the Spirit. This is Luke's way of telling the reader what the descent of the Spirit at Jesus' baptism means. It is his *anointing* for the servant's role and work.[33]

When we look backward to the birth narratives to the referant of "as was supposed" we read: " 'And behold, you will conceive in your womb and bear a son . . . .' And Mary said to the angel, 'How can this be, since I have no husband?' And the angel said to her, 'The Holy Spirit will come upon you, and the power of the Most High will overshadow you; therefore the child to be born will be called holy, the Son of God' " (1:31a, 34-35). By the phrase "as was supposed" in 3:23, Luke refers us to the narrative in which the heavenly messenger says that Jesus will be conceived of the Holy Spirit and born Son of God. The birth narrative says that Jesus is begotten Son of God by the Holy Spirit from his conception. This is Luke's way of telling the reader what the descent of the Spirit at Jesus' baptism does not mean. It is not his being begotten Son of God. That is the meaning of his birth.[34]

The introduction (3:23) which the Evangelist constructs for his genealogy, [35] functions together with the Lucan "in bodily form" (3:22) of the baptism narrative to define for the reader precisely what the descent of the Spirit at Jesus' baptism means.

It is possible that the genealogy, together with the temptation story, serves in yet another way to interpret the baptism narrative for Luke's readers. That Luke so intended it seems clear from the location of the genealogy. The Marcan order of events ran: (1) the preaching of John (1:4-8); (2) the baptism of Jesus (1:9-11); (3) the temptation narrative (1:12-13). Luke, however, has separated the baptism and temptation narratives by the insertion of his genealogy tracing Jesus back to Adam. His order runs: (1) the preaching of John (3:3-18); (2) the baptism of Jesus (3:21-22); (3) genealogy (3:23-38); (4) temptation (4:1-13). The formal link between the baptism narrative and the genealogy seems to be that they both end with designations of Jesus as Son.[36]

The genealogy thereby defines the Son of 3:22b as Son of Adam. Luke then returns to the Marcan order by giving an account of Jesus' temptations. It is not the Marcan account, however. Luke rather chooses the longer Q version. At least the formal reason for his preference seems to have been that the Q version uses the designation Son of God whereas Mark's version does not. Thus, he would have two affirmations of Jesus' Sonship (3:22; 3:38) balancing two questions about Jesus' Sonship (4:3, 9). But Luke also apparently alters the order of the Q account of Jesus' three temptations so that they correspond loosely to the temptations of Adam in Genesis 3.[37] In so doing, Luke reinforced the point made in the preceding genealogy. Son of God means Son of Adam, second Adam. It means that this one is fully involved in the historical process and its moral decisions. The genealogy and the temptation story, therefore, form a unit of Son pericopes together with the baptism narrative. By means of this unit Luke has a control over the way his readers will read the baptism story with its declaration that Jesus is God's beloved Son. The one who is declared Son at his baptism is a full participant in our common lot as Sons of Adam.

That this full involvement in a common humanity is not all that the Evangelist means by Son of God, however, is clear from his reference in 3:23 back to the virgin birth. Son of God also implies transcendence over our common lot as well as involvement in it. But it is the humanity of Jesus as Son of God that Luke is at pains to emphasize in the baptism narrative and its context.

Putting our findings together, we conclude that birth narratives, genealogy, temptation narrative, and Nazareth episode in Luke all function as guides for Luke's readers about the meaning of Jesus' baptism. Above all Luke wants to say three things. (1) The Spirit cannot be divorced from matter at Jesus' baptism. The descent of the Spirit is in bodily form. (2) Jesus' baptism is his anointing by which he is equipped for service, not his being begotten Son of God. As Luke sees it, Jesus is Son of God from his birth. (3) When Jesus is declared to be God's Son at his baptism, this means above all else that he shares our full humanity. In these three points we find the same concern of Luke to prevent any separation between spirit and flesh and to guarantee the real humanity of the church's Savior that we found in the ascension narrative. Here again, therefore, we are doubtless dealing with an anti-docetic tendency. That this is so seems clear when we remember that some early Christian Gnostics used the baptism of Jesus as a means to their docetic ends. Compare, for example, the Sethian-Ophites[38] and Cerinthus.[39]

The Occasion

Examination of the framework of the Lucan picture of Jesus reveals that there are two focal points in his narrative, ascension and baptism. The other facets of the framework function as controls on the way the reader understands ascension and baptism. In each case, Luke attempts to prevent any separation of spirit and flesh or any denial of the Savior's humanity. It would seem, therefore, that Luke was faced by some one who wanted to separate spirit and flesh in Jesus Christ by means of an interpretation of his baptism as the moment of the descent of a spiritual reality upon Jesus and the ascension as the moment of the spiritual reality's ascent prior to any suffering or death. Such an inference about the problem confronting Luke leads one to ask whether there was such a problem at the time when Luke-Acts was written.[40]

In the Aegean basin during the last quarter of the first century C.E. there was a variety of Gnosticism exactly like that which we have inferred from Luke-Acts, the Gnosticism of Cerinthus. Our significant information about Cerinthus comes in the final analysis almost entirely from Irenaeus.[41] According to Irenaeus,[42] Cerinthus' christology included: (1) that Jesus was born of Joseph and Mary; (2) that after his baptism, from the Absolute Sovereignty above all, the Christ descended upon Jesus in the form of a dove; (3) that after the descent of the spiritual Christ upon him, Jesus proclaimed the unknown Father and worked miracles; (4) that at the end, the Christ withdrew from Jesus, leaving Jesus to suffer and be raised while the Christ remained impassible since he was spiritual.

Any response to Cerinthus' christology would of necessity stress:[43] (1) that Jesus Christ was one person, thereby rejecting the claim that the spiritual Christ descended upon the human Jesus at the baptism and left him at the end; (2) that Jesus Christ, the one person, was capable of suffering, death, and resurrection. Also, it is possible that a response to Cerinthus would emphasize the virgin birth of Jesus Christ. All of these points that would of necessity fit into any response to Cerinthus are precisely those which we have seen Luke emphasize. The Lucan framework of Jesus' life is best seen as a response to the type of docetism that we meet in a late first century Gnostic like Cerinthus. When the Third Evangelist says that Jesus was born Son of God, anointed by the Spirit, and that he journeyed to Jerusalem where he died and was raised before ascending bodily into heaven, he is saying "No" to a docetism which claimed that the spiritual redeemer descended upon the man Jesus at the baptism and left him before his passion. At least a major facet of Lucan christology is a way of saying to docetism that the church's Savior was really human from first to last.

If the Third Evangelist did construct his christological framework to oppose a docetic point of view which asserted the descent of the spiritual revealer upon the human Jesus at his baptism, as the result of which he performed miracles and proclaimed the unknown Father, and ascended into heaven prior to the passion of the earthly Jesus, then we have a context within which to interpret the meaning-function of three more sets of Lucan correspondences. From an overall perspective the Evangelist's primary concern is to affirm the unity of the total Christ-event from the birth of the Son of God to his corporeal ascension into heaven. This overall concern breaks down into at least three parts. In the first place, Luke wants to affirm the continuity between the one who dies and rises in Jerusalem on the one hand and the one who ascends into heaven on the other. It is into this context that the correspondences between Luke 24 and Acts 1 fit. They are a further strand of evidence tying passion and ascension together. In the second place, the Third Evangelist intends to assert, in a way that goes beyond what one finds in Matthew and Mark, a continuity between the one who works miracles and preaches in Galilee and the one who suffers and dies in Jerusalem. It is within this context that the correspondences between Luke 9 and 22—23 function. They reinforce the point that Luke makes elsewhere in other ways.[44] In the third place, the author of Luke-Acts wants to insure a continuity between the one who works in Galilee and who foresees his passion and the one who ascends in Jerusalem. Within this context the correspondences between Luke 9 and Acts 1 may be understood.

As has become evident in the preceding chapter, the Lucan Evangelist does not use his architectural patterns in isolation to convey his theological aims. Rather it is often the case that once we discern both the Lucan theological tendency and his architectural designs, we can see links between them. Frequently the architecture supports and reinforces theological aims of the author that we have become aware of by other means. To see the interweaving of the artistry and the theology of the Evangelist enables us more adequately to appreciate the Lucan achievement.

The last two chapters have pointed to the alliance with meaning into which eight of the eleven patterns noted earlier fit. What of the other three? What can be said of the correspondences found in Luke 4—8, Luke 9—18, and Acts 15—21? It seems, at least in light of our present knowledge of Lucan theology, that these patterns exist primarily for aesthetic reasons. Of course, the mere fact of repetition has some meaning-function in that it intensifies the emphases of the material. Nevertheless, these three patterns appear to exist largely to ensure or to carry out a balanced architectonic scheme. In Luke-Acts, therefore, architectural design serves both theological and aesthetic ends just as we have seen it do in the Lucan milieu. This is exactly what we would have expected. The Third Evangelist stands before us a man of his time and place. He shares, in this regard at least, in the *Zeitgeist* of the Mediterranean peoples.

FOOTNOTES

[1]Most recently, the works of Ferdinand Hahn, *Christologische Hoheitstitel* (Gottingen: Vandenhoeck & Ruprecht, 1963) and R. H. Fuller, *The Foundations of New Testament Christology* (New York: Scribner's, 1965) emphasize the point. Much of this chapter comes from my article, "An Anti-Gnostic Tendency in Lucan Christology," *NTS* 14 (1968-69) 259-71, and is used by permission.

[2]Opinions regarding the contents of the fragment differ. See C. K. Barrett. *The Epistle to the Romans* (New York: Harper, 1957) 18; A. M. Hunter, *Paul and His Predecessors* (rev. ed.; Philadelphia: Westminster, 1961) 24-26; Fuller, *Foundations of New Testament Christology*, 165-67. On any reading, however, the fragment is adoptionistic.

[3]E. Schweizer, "The Concept of the Davidic 'Son of God' in Acts and Its Old Testament Background," in *Studies in Luke-Acts*, ed. Keck and Martyn, 186.

[4]See Fuller, *Foundations of New Testament Christology*, 216-18, 222-27, for summary and recent bibliography.

[5]This has been a special concern of E. Schweizer. See his "Orthodox Proclamation: The Reinterpretation of the Gospel by the Fourth Evangelist," *Int* 8 (1954) 387-403; *Lordship and Discipleship* (Naperville: Allenson, 1960) especially 104-6; "Two New Testament Creeds Compared," in *Current Issues in New Testament Interpretation*, ed. Klassen and Snyder, 166-77. Also, very briefly, K. Stendahl, *IDB* 1. 426.

[6]A comparison of C. K. Barrett's *Luke the Historian in Recent Study* (1961) with A. T. Robertson's *Luke the Historian in the Light of Research* (New York: Scribner's, 1920) will indicate the legitimacy of speaking of a Lucan Christology. C. F. D. Moule, "The Christology of Acts," in *Studies in Luke-Acts*, 160, says that "it is a commonplace of New Testament criticism that the Gospels are theological documents and, at the very least, reflect the faith of the writers and of their communities."

[7]On reading aloud in antiquity, see H. J. Cadbury, *The Book of Acts in History* (London: Black, 1955) 18, and B. M. Metzger, *The Text of the New Testament* (New York: Oxford, 1964) 13, for evidence.

[8]"The Gospel of Luke was . . . written as *supplementary* instruction for those readers who already belonged to the church. . . . It is assumed that the main outlines of the faith are known to the readers. . . ." Bo Reicke, *The Gospel of Luke*, 47.

[9]Assumed here as elsewhere in the book are the priority of Mark, the existence of some source or sources common to Matthew and Luke commonly designated Q, and the existence of certain traditions peculiar to Luke commonly designated L.

[10]This is the commonly accepted methodology of *Redaktionsgeschichte*. See Hans Conzelmann, *The Theology of St. Luke*, 9-17; G. W. H. Lampe, "Luke," in *PCB*, ed. Rowley and Black, 821; Lampe, "The Lucan Portrait of Christ," *NTS* 2 (1956) 160. In the article in *NTS* 161-64, Lampe, however, argues that the best point of departure in the quest for the Lucan Christology is in the speeches of Acts. Though influenced by both Lucan style and theology, however, these speeches can serve our purposes in an auxiliary way only. (1) They sometimes reflect pre-Lucan Christology (e.g., Acts 2:36; 13:33; 3:17-26. Cf. J. A. T. Robinson, "The Earliest Christology of All," in *Twelve New Testament Studies*, 139-53). (2) They omit references to the birth narratives which are integral to the Third Gospel. See the summary of evidence in P. S. Minear, "Luke's Use of the Birth Stories," in *Studies in Luke-Acts*, 111-30. (3) Also, the travel narrative (cf. Acts 13:31) and the ascension (cf. Acts 2:34) occupy a relatively minor place in the speeches. The speeches, then, represent a mixture of Lucan and non-Lucan elements. This requires that they be sifted carefully in order to sort out the disparate elements. The speeches of Acts, therefore, can serve only to confirm and to complement conclusions drawn from an examination of the Lucan use of sources. They cannot be the starting point in a search for the Lucan Christology.

11Conzelmann, *St. Luke*, 170, is certainly correct when he says that "the special elements in Luke's Christology cannot be set out by a statistical analysis of the titles applied to Jesus." The failure to recognize this fact is a major flaw in the work of S. S. Smalley, "The Christology of Acts," *Exp T* 73 (1962) 358-60, and in that of V. Taylor, *The Person of Christ in New Testament Teaching* (London: Macmillan, 1958) 9-12, and *IDB* 3. 184. Conzelmann's preoccupation with the Lucan eschatology prevents his work from being a thorough consideration of Lucan Christology. The thesis of this Chapter does not automatically exclude Conzelmann's views, but neither does our thesis rest upon the validity of his.

12Cf. ch. 1, n. 62; ch. 5, n. 45.

13A. M. Ramsay, "What Was the Ascension?" *Bulletin of the Studiorum Novi Testamenti Societas* 2 (1951) 45-50.

14Luke 24:26; Acts 2:32-33; 5:30-31, for example. So Ramsay, "What Was the Ascension?" 45; C. F. Sleeper, "Pentecost and Resurrection," *JBL* 84 (1965) 392; A. N. Wilder, "Variant Traditions of the Resurrection in Acts," *JBL* 62 (1943) 313-18. Perhaps the difficult passage, Luke 24:51, should also be included here. Regardless of whether one prefers the longer or the shorter text, the verse still refers to the ascension. Here ascension is a part of resurrection day as in the Fourth Gospel.

15It is better to acknowledge the presence of two views of the ascension in Luke-Acts than to try various expedients to excise one or the other. When J. H. Ropes, *Beginnings of Christianity*, 3. 256-58, suggests that the ascension was not originally present in Luke 24:51 or Acts 1:2, it is just as unconvincing as P. H. Menoud's arguments that Acts 1:3 is a part of two later additions to Luke-Acts, Luke 24:50-53 and Acts 1:1-5, in "Remarques sur les textes de l'ascension dans Luc-Actes," *Neutestamentliche Studien fur Rudolf Bultmann*, ed. W. Eltester, 148-56.

16P. A. van Stempvoort, "Interpretation of the Ascension in Luke and Acts," *NTS* 5 (1958) 37-39; Wilder, "Variant Traditions of the Resurrection in Acts," 310.

17For what follows, see my book, *Luke and the Gnostics*, 30-31.

18*Ibid.*, 29-30.

19Not everyone is agreed on the extent of the journey section. There are at least three current options. (1) 9:51-18:14, so C. F. Evans, "The Central Section of St. Luke's Gospel," in *Studies in the Gospels* (ed. Nineham; Oxford: Blackwell, 1955) 37-53. (2) 9:51—19:27, so W. C. Robinson, Jr., "The Theological Context for Interpreting Luke's Travel Narrative," *JBL* 79 (1960) 20-31. (3) 9:51—19:46, so J. H. Davies, "The Purpose of the Central Section of St. Luke's Gospel," in *Studia Evangelica*, (ed. Cross; Berlin: Akademie-Verlag, 1964) 2. 164-69. The most natural division of the three seems to me to be that of Davies.

20W. G. Kümmel, *Introduction to the New Testament*, 93; W. C. Robinson, Jr., "The Theological Context for Interpreting Luke's Travel Narrative." For what follows, we are especially indebted to Robinson.

21Lampe, "The Holy Spirit in the Writings of St. Luke," in *Studies in the Gospels*, 181.

22J. H. Davies, "The Purpose of the Central Section of St. Luke's Gospel," 164-66.

23J. G. Davies, "The Prefigurement of the Ascension in the Third Gospel," *JTS* n.s., 6 (1955) 230; Conzelmann, *The Theology of St. Luke*, 59; Lampe, "Holy Spirit in the Writings of St. Luke," 182.

24J. H. Davies, "The Purpose of the Central Section of St. Luke's Gospel;" Lampe, "The Lucan Portrait of Christ," 166-67; Evans, "The Central Section of St. Luke's Gospel," 39-40. Evans' argument, however, that ἀνάλημψις of 9:51 must refer to more than just the ascension because of the plural ἡμέρας (cf. Acts 1:21-22) is possible but not entirely convincing.

25Lampe, "The Lucan Portrait of Christ," 167.

26W. C. Robinson, Jr., "The Theological Context for Interpreting Luke's Travel Narrative," 29-30, is primarily concerned with the function of the travel section in relation to the apostles. His thesis is that the Lucan expansion of the motif of transition from Galilee to Jerusalem is solely in the service of the concept of the authenticated witness. It is certainly in the interest of the concept of authenticated witness, but not solely. The witness motif also serves Luke's christology.

[27]Irenaeus, *Against Heresies* 1:30:13-14. In 13 Irenaeus says: "they say that Christ himself . . . departed from him . . . while Jesus was crucified" (*The Ante-Nicene Fathers*).

[28]Irenaeus, *Against Heresies* 1:24:3-6. In 4 Irenaeus says that Basilides believed that Christ "did not himself suffer death, but Simon, a certain man of Cyrene, being compelled, bore the cross in his stead; so that this latter being transfigured by him, that he might be thought to be Jesus, was crucified. . . . For since he [Christ] was an incorporeal power . . . he . . . ascended to him who had sent him." Further on Irenaeus says that Basilides claimed: "If any one . . . confesses the crucified, that man is still a slave . . ." (*The Ante-Nicene Fathers*).

[29]Irenaeus, *Against Heresies* 1:26:1 "But at last Christ departed from Jesus, and that then Jesus suffered and rose again, while Christ remained impassible, inasmuch as he was a spiritual being" (*The Ante-Nicene Fathers*).

[30]J. M. Robinson, "Ascension," *IDB* 1. 246.

[31]Eduard Schweizer, *Spirit of God* (London: Black, 1960) 40-41.

[32]The observation of Lampe, "The Holy Spirit in the Writings of St. Luke," 171, is to the point. "The reading of the prophecy and the announcement of its fulfillment in the mission of Jesus serve as a prologue to the whole of the rest of St. Luke's work. It was, no doubt, in order to use it for this purpose that St. Luke took the story of the Nazareth preaching out of its Marcan context and re-wrote it."

[33]The same point of view is found in the speeches of Acts. Cf. especially Acts 10:38; 4:27. This confirms our interpretation of the baptism following Luke's guidelines in Luke 3:23.

[34]Hans von Campenhausen, *The Virgin Birth in the Theology of the Ancient Church* (Naperville: Allenson, 1964) 25, says: "It is only in Luke that the inner relation of this event to the nature of the child so born is expressly brought out and stressed: just because no human being, no man, but the Holy Spirit, will come over Mary and 'overshadow' her, the 'holy' one thus born will be called the Son of God." Cf. also, Fuller, *The Foundations of New Testament Christology*, 288; Lampe, "The Holy Spirit in the Writings of St. Luke," 168.

[35]It is generally recognized that the parenthesis "as was supposed" in 3:23 is due to the Lucan hand. From our examination it appears that it functions not as an apology for inclusion of the genealogy (so S. M. Gilmour, *Interpreter's Bible*, 8. 82) nor as an attempt to cover up a discrepancy (so Creed, *The Gospel according to St. Luke* [London: Macmillan, 1953] 59), but rather as a guideline for Luke's readers. Our examination makes it probable that the rest of the verse, except for "Jesus, son of Joseph," also is a Lucan composition. Cf. Matt 1:1.

[36]This is true regardless of how one decides the difficult textual question of 3:22. I personally find the recent arguments of Leaney (*The Gospel according to St. Luke*, 111) and Keck (*RevExp* 64 [1967] 473, n. 34) for the Western reading unconvincing.

[37]Most recently, A. Feuillet, "Le récit Lucanien de la Tentation (Lc. 4:13)," *Bib* 40 (1959) 617-31.

[38]Irenaeus, *Against Heresies* 1:30:12-14. In 12 we read: "Jesus . . . was wiser, purer, and more righteous than all other men. Christ . . . descended into him, and thus Jesus Christ was produced." In 14 we read: "They strove to establish the descent and ascent of Christ, by the fact that neither before his baptism, nor after his resurrection from the dead, do his disciples state that he did any mighty works . . ." (*The Ante-Nicene Fathers*).

[39]Irenaeus, *Against Heresies* 1:26:1. "After his baptism, Christ descended upon him in the form of a dove from the Supreme Ruler . . ." (*The Ante-Nicene Fathers*).

[40]The recent attempt of J. C. O'Neill, *The Theology of Acts in Its Historical Setting*, to date the Lucan literature in the second century on the basis of parallels with Justin has proved untenable. Cf. H. J. Cadbury's review in *JBL* 81 (1962) 198. A date in the last quarter of the first century C.E. still remains the most probable option.

[41]R. M. Grant, "The Origin of the Fourth Gospel," *JBL* 69 (1950) 310. In an attempt to determine whether the Fourth Gospel was written against Cerinthus, as Irenaeus claims (*Against Heresies* 3:11:1), Grant shows that our principal sources of information about Cerinthus are: (1) Irenaeus, *Against Heresies* 1:26:1; 3:3:4 (used by Hippolytus, *Refutation* 7:33, and to some extent by Epiphanius, *Heresies* 28; (2) Gaius of Rome (in Eusebius, *The Ecclesiastical History* 3:28:2

used by Dionysus of Alexandria, in Eusebius, *The Ecclesiastical History* 7:25:1-3); (3) The Epistle of the Apostles 1:7. An evaluation of these sources leads Grant to conclude that for all practical purposes we are left with Irenaeus and his followers. As L. E. Keck has observed: "We must bear in mind that even though the new texts from Nag Hammadi are of inestimable value, for many forms of Christianized Gnosticism we are as dependent now as before on what its opponents (i.e., Irenaeus) report" ("John the Baptist in Christianized Gnosticism," in *Initiation*, [ed. Bleeker; Leiden: Brill, 1965] 184).

[42]*Against Heresies* 1:26:1.

[43]The following points are those which Grant, "The Origin of the Fourth Gospel", 313, says the Gospel of John would have to make if it is to be regarded as written against Cerinthus. Whereas these points do not fit the Fourth Gospel, they certainly do fit Luke-Acts. Grant, in part, has seen this. He says: "The idea that the Christ not only did, but had to, suffer is set forth not in John but in Luke (24:26, 46)." (p. 315)

[44]Cf. *Luke and the Gnostics*, ch. 1, "The Authentic Witness," especially 23-27.

CHAPTER VIII

Lucan Patterns and the Genre of Luke-Acts

To this point we have located certain patterns in the Lucan literature expressive of the principle of balance; we have seen such patterns present in the Lucan milieu and rooted in the aesthetic assumptions of Mediterranean peoples; and we have found that many of the Lucan patterns are related in some way or other to key theological positions of the Evangelist as they can be discerned by redaction criticism. It has not yet been determined, however, just exactly how the patterns are related to the genre of Luke-Acts. It is to this question that we turn in our final chapter. The major problem, of course, is to determine exactly to what genre Luke-Acts belongs. The approach made to the problem in this chapter will begin with a comparison of Diogenes Laertius' *Lives of Eminent Philosophers* and Luke-Acts though it cannot end there. The argument will develop in two main parts: first, an analysis of Laertius' *Lives* in terms of contents, form, and function; and second, a comparison of Laertius with Luke-Acts, leading to an explanation of their remarkable similarities.

Diogenes Laertius' Lives

This early third century work professes to trace two philosophic successions, the Ionic in the East and the Italian in the West. The Ionic succession begins in Book 2, the Italian in Book 8. Within the separate schools each master hands down doctrine and authority to his disciples, so that the succeeding generations of philosophers are assimilated to a pedigree or genealogical table. The key figures whom we know as the founders of the various schools—e.g., Aristippus. Plato, Aristotle, Antisthenes, Zeno, Pythagoras, Epicurus—are of particular interest. Many of the generalizations which follow will be primarily about such founders of schools as they are treated by Laertius in his *Lives*. The analysis of the *Lives* which follows will focus upon the contents, the form, and function of such Lives in Laertius' work.

In choosing as the *contents* of his literary endeavor the lives of founders of philosophical schools, Laertius was selecting for subjects individuals who in antiquity were regarded as divine figures. Our model which conceives of such philosophers after the analogy of a modern academician who assists his students to master the tools of a discipline is a modern misconception of ancient realities. The proper model for understanding the role of a founder of a philosophical school in antiquity is a religious, not an academic one.[1] It is said of Pythagoras, for example: "The Pythagoreans derive their confidence in their views from the fact that the first to express them was no ordinary man, but God."[2] Pythagoras was numbered among the gods;[3] was called by the people of Croton the Hyperborean Apollo;[4] was believed to have been born of more than mortal seed.[5] He was viewed as more than an academician. The same is true for Epicurus. Lucretius invokes him throughout his poem in forms borrowed from and clearly intended to recall, the conventional invocation of deity.[6] For Lucretius, Epicurus was the true divinity. He says of his philosophical master: "he was a god . . . a god he was, who first discovered that reasoned plan of life which is now called Wisdom."[7] That this is not merely poetic exaggeration may be seen from both Cicero and Plutarch. In his *Tusculan Disputations* (1:21:48) Cicero speaks of the philosophers who do reverence to Epicurus as a god. Plutarch in his *Reply to Colotes* (1117 B) tells how Colotes "while hearing a lecture of Epicurus . . . suddenly cast himself down before him and embraced his knees," an act reflecting the way statues of gods were supplicated at the time. Indeed in 1117 C, Plutarch makes the act's meaning explicit. Plutarch also cited the words of Metrodorus to Timarchus: "Let us . . . (exchange) this earthbound life for the holy mysteries of Epicurus, which are in very truth the revelation of a god" (1117 B). The popular philosopher, Apolonius of Tyana, is no different. In Philostratus' *Life of Apollonius of Tyana* 8:4, Domitian asks the philosopher why men call him (Apollonius) god. The question is taken seriously by the sage, whose answer indicates that such a belief was widespread opinion, not only about Apollonius but about philosophical masters in general.[8] That Laertius was aware of this attitude towards philosophers is evident throughout the *Lives* (e.g., 8:66, 68, 70; 8:41; 3:45; 2:100). The words about Plato in 3:45, moreover, apparently come from Laertius' own hand.[9] This shows that it was a belief he shared. In choosing to write about great philosophers, therefore, Laertius was selecting as his subject matter the lives of divine figures, men regarded in antiquity as more than human.

The contents of Laertius' *Lives* not only included the lives of founders of philosophical schools but also narratives about the masters' successors and selected other disciples who in actuality formed a type of religious community created and sustained by the divine figure. This, of course, is implicit in the veneration of the master as a divine figure. As a result, scholars frequently speak of the philosophical schools as possessing many of the characteristics of a church. For example, the Epicurean school possessed "a sacred founder, sacred books, a credo of memory verses from those books, congregations of the faithful, and a tradition that was more concerned to preserve and gloss than to build upon and develop the founder's doctrine."[10] The disciples and successors of Epicurus did not desire to rival him but to copy him, to tread in his footprints.[11] He was both the fount of authority and the focus of reverence for the community.[12] Plutarch's words in his *Reply to Colotes* (1117) about the Epicureans' collective behavior are a description of a cult. He speaks of their "roars of ecstasy," their "cries of thanksgiving," their "reverential demonstrations," and "all that apparatus of adoration" resorted to in their "supplicating and hymning" Epicurus. Indeed Plutarch uses the very term "worship" to describe certain acts in the lecture hall (1117 C). Cicero, moreover, speaks of an ongoing banquet (a sacred meal) to honor the founder of the school (*De fin.* 2:31, 101). What can be said of the Epicureans can also be said of the Pythagoreans who seem to have been organized as a mystery cult in the first century, if their subterranean basilica at the Porta Maggiore in Rome is any indication.[13] This religious character of the philosophical schools in antiquity was the reason that early Christians could at times speak of the church as a philosophical school.[14] The similarities were apparent to all. Laertius, moreover, was not unaware of traditions that portrayed a philosopher's followers in cultic terms (e.g., 8:68; 10:18). If Diogenes Laertius' discussion of founders of philosophical schools was a narrative about divine figures, his treatment of their followers was the story of religious communities. Again the academic model is inadequate for understanding ancient philosophical phenomena; only a religious one will do.

The third content component of Laertius' *Lives* consists of summaries of the doctrine of the various schools. Such summaries are given sometimes in the words of the founder, sometimes in the words of his disciples and successors.[15] These three components—the lives of founders of philosophical schools, narratives about the communities that emerged from them, and a summary of the doctrine of the various schools—may be regarded as the essential contents of Laertius' *Lives*. Now we must ask about the *form* into which these contents are cast.

Looking at each individual Life of a founder of a philosophical school, taken as a whole, it is possible to see that usually the three content components function as structural units so that an (a)+(b)+(c) form emerges: (a) life of the founder + (b) narrative about disciples and successors + (c) summary of the doctrine of the school. This pattern is characteristic of five of the seven Lives of founders mentioned earlier.[16] Perhaps due to the available data of his sources, Laertius casts the other two founders' Lives in different forms. In Aristotle's biography (5:1-35), we find the pattern (a)+(c) with an allusion to the (b) part which follows in a series of separate Lives. Antisthenes' biography (6:1-19) contains merely (a) + an extended list of his writings, without a summary of doctrine, though at the end there is also an allusion to his successors who are treated in a series of separate Lives which follow. It is possible to say, however, that whenever Laertius includes a list or narrative about a founder's successors or other disciples in the founder's own biography, the pattern is always (a)+(b)+(c). This pattern, moreover, is the dominant one in his work.

If we take each of these three formal components separately, what do we find? In the first place, we note that the Life of the founder, like other biographies in antiquity,[17] is not strictly chronological but more topical in its arrangement. Moreover, like other biographies in antiquity,[18] it shows no development of character but treats the man as a finished product. In the second place, the succession list or narrative often gives not only the official successors of the founder but also data about selected other disciples at various points in the chain of succession. This formal component may include anecdotes, sayings, and even lists of the writings of a disciple or successor.[19] In the third place, the summary of doctrine may follow a logical, topical arrangement[20] or it may be given in terms of letters and maxims of the founder.[21] Sometimes there is discussion about which books are genuine.[22] Having said this about the form of Laertius' work, we must now ask about its function. What function did Laertius expect such content cast into this form to play?

It is necessary to distinguish the *function* that such component parts would have played outside of Diogenes Laertius' work if they had circulated separately, on the one hand, from the role they play when taken together in his *Lives*, on the other. On the one hand, quite apart from the efforts of Diogenes Laertius, the Life of a philosopher in antiquity was designed as a means of defining the way of life of a given school derived from or associated with him.[23] It served as a call to emulation and sometimes as a defense against attacks upon or misunderstandings of the philosophical way. In like manner, a succession list or narrative was frequently joined to the Life of a philosopher in order to delineate where the true and living tradition of the school was to be found.[24] Moreover, both a list of books deemed to be genuine and a summary of the master's teaching were to insure that one got an accurate rather than an eccentric view of the tradition.

On the other hand, it appears that Diogenes Laertius' combination of ingredients into a virtual catalogue of the philosophical successions was designed to do in a thorough way what each of the components was intended to do if taken separately—that is, to present a way of life (more accurately, various ways of life), and specifically, the authentic or true way of the various schools. In his treatment of Plato, for example, Laertius offers a rationale for his inclusion of an account of the true nature of his discourses, the arrangement of the dialogues, and the method of Plato's inductive procedure in an elementary manner and in main outline. The reason he gives for this treatment is his desire that Plato's life may not suffer by the omission of his doctrine.[25] Furthermore, Laertius says explicitly that Plato's first tetralogy has a common plan underlying it. Plato wishes to describe what the life of the philosopher (i.e., the follower of Plato) will be.[26] From what is said here about his treatment of Plato, it is apparent that the general assumption is that the Life of a philosopher is designed to make clear the way of life of the school. What Laertius needs to justify is his addition to the Life of a summary of Plato's teaching and methodology as another means of communicating the same thing. It is Laertius' belief, moreover, that without the teaching section the Life may suffer. Why this concern with the union of life and doctrine of a philosophical master? Laertius says to justify his treatment of Epicurus that this combination of life and doctrine is "that you may be in a position to study the philosopher on all sides and know how to judge him."[27] This statement must be understood in the context of Laertius' desire to defend Epicurus against attacks, such as, that the philosopher was overindulgent, stupid, wrote with a poor style, and was basically hostile to other people (10:6-14). In the midst of his defense of Epicurus against these charges Laertius says: "And, as we go on, we shall know this better from his doctrines and his sayings" (10:12). He is referring to the forthcoming summary of doctrine in the three letters and forty maxims. Both the Life and the summary of doctrine work for the same ends, to protect the master from false charges. This makes it explicit that Laertius' union of component parts has a similar purpose to that played by each if it were taken separately. Nor should we think it strange that Laertius, who apparently is not a devotee of any one of the schools, should desire to defend the masters from attack or misunderstanding and to present them in a sympathetic light. Elsewhere, in Plutarch's *Against Colotes on Behalf of the Other Philosophers* we find a defense of philosophers of many schools by one who is not a member of most of those he defends. Having noted briefly the contents, form, and function of Diogenes Laertius' *Lives*, it is now time to move on to a comparison of these *Lives* with Luke-Acts.

Comparison of *Laertius' Lives and Luke-Acts*

Although Luke-Acts is grouped with the gospels among early Christian writings, modern scholars seem inclined to place the two volume work within the genres of either history,[28] romance,[29] or aretalogy.[30] The suggestion of Hermann von Soden that Luke developed the Marcan pattern in the direction of the Hellenistic biographies of philosophers has been almost totally ignored by scholars in this century.[31] It will be the purpose of this section of the chapter to test von Soden's hypothesis by means of a comparison between Laertius' *Lives of Eminent Philosophers* and Luke-Acts. This comparison will note both the similarities and the differences in the contents, form, and function of the two documents, asking at the end for some explanation of what has been uncovered.

The similarities between the lives of founders of philosophical schools presented by Laertius and Luke-Acts are remarkable. First of all, as to *contents*, in an earlier chapter we have seen that Luke-Acts presents the story of the church's savior and of the church very much, but not totally, in terms of the popular image of the wandering philosopher in antiquity. When we remember that in antiquity the founder of a philosophical school was not conceived in terms of an academic model but in terms of a religious one as a divine figure, the appeal of the philosophical image for the Third Evangelist becomes apparent. Luke-Acts, as well as Diogenes Laertius, therefore, has for its contents the life of a founder of a religious community, a list or narrative of the founder's successors and selected other disciples, and a summary of the doctrine of the community.

In the second place, in *form* Luke-Acts like Laertius' *Lives* has the life of a founder as the first structural unit, followed by a second, namely, the narrative of successors and selected other disciples. For one who is aware of the differences in the contents of the apostolic speeches in Acts on the one hand and the words of the earthly Jesus in Luke on the other, however, the question cannot help but arise: how are the words of the philosophical founder mentioned in the narrative of his life related to the summary of doctrine of school which follows? Laertius tells us in 7:38: "I have decided to give a general account of all the Stoic doctrines in the life of Zeno because he was founder of the school ... And his tenets in general are as follows." What follows, however, is no more identical with Zeno's words narrated in the context of his life than are the apostles' speeches of Acts with the words of the earthly Jesus in Luke. At the same time, Laertius does not see a lack of identity as discontinuity. Rather, as he says in his treatment of Epicurus (10:12): "And, as we go on, we shall know this better from his doctrines and sayings." The summary of doctrine, while not identical to the words of the earthly founder, was understood by Laertius to be complementary to and in continuity with them. The same is true for Luke-Acts. There is, then, a structural similarity between Laertius and Luke-Acts in the way they relate the summary of doctrine material—whether it be a separate unit as in Laertius or part of the succession narrative as in Acts—to the life of the founder. The summary of teaching is understood as complementary to, rather than identical with, the words of the founder set forth in the context of his earthly life.

Finally, I have tried to show elsewhere,[32] as well as in the previous chapters, that the Lucan writings have their *Sitz im Leben* in the struggle against heresy. Their *function* is to present the authentically Christian picture of Jesus and of Christian faith just as Laertius intended to present the true way of the various successions. In contents, form, and function, therefore, the similarities between Luke-Acts and the lives of the founders of certain philosophical schools in Laertius are remarkable.

There are, of course, differences as well. The chief differences are structural. In the first place, Laertius' *Lives* is a collection of many biographies of philosophers while Luke-Acts is a treatment of the life of a single founder. It is a fact that biographies of philosophers in antiquity developed in two directions: one, that of individual biographies, the other, that of collections of Lives.[33] Luke-Acts obviously belongs to the one, Laertius to the other. In both cases, however, the biography could, and often did, contain both the life of the founder and a succession list or narrative. The Lives of Aristotle offer helpful data. (1) A number of fifth century epitomes of Aristotle's life were in use in neo-Platonic exegesis of the philosopher's works. These contain at least succession lists as part of the biography.[34] (2) These fifth century epitomes depend upon the same original, that of Ptolemy in the early fourth century.[35] (3) Ptolemy's epitome depends in turn upon the late third century B.C.E. Life of Aristotle by Hermippus.[36] (4) Hermippus' biography was intended to extol Aristotle as the founder of the Peripatetic school. It included within itself both a claim that Aristotle was the successor of Plato and an anecdote about Aristotle's selection of a successor to himself.[37] This data allows us to draw three conclusions. First, a single Life of a philosopher with a succession list or narrative could exist apart from a collection of such Lives. Second, the presence of succession information within the Life of a founder of a philosophical school is known as early as the third century B.C.E. and as late as the centuries immediately after Laertius. The pattern (a)+(b) had a long life. Third, Hermippus' attempt to make Aristotle a successor indicates that the biography functioned as a cult-legend. From such observations it seems clear that while Laertius and Luke-Acts share a common pattern, (a)+(b), they represent two different directions the pattern took in antiquity: one, that of collections, the other, that of individual Lives. The collections were literary productions intended for the public. The individual Lives were cult legends intended for use in the ongoing life of the school.

In the second place, Laertius' *Lives* usually consist of three structural units, (a)+(b)+(c), whereas Luke-Acts has only two, (a)+(b). In Luke-Acts there is a summary of doctrine but it is found in the apostolic speeches interspersed throughout the narrative about the disciples, with roots, of course, in the narrative about Jesus. The summary of doctrine does not constitute a separate structural unit in Luke-Acts as it frequently does in Laertius' *Lives*. This difference is not absolute since not all of Laertius' *Lives* have the three structural units either. The Life of Socrates, for example, consists of an (a)+(b) without (c).[38] In those cases where Laertius' *Lives* have the three structural units, an examination of his sources reveals that he has one set for the (a)+(b) components and another for the (c) component. This leads us to draw the conclusion that it was Laertius himself who joined the life and succession material on the one hand to the summary of doctrine material on the other.[39] That Luke-Acts has only (a)+(b) components, therefore, would seem to point to its proximity to Laertius' sources, some of which also apparently consisted of only (a)+(b) components.

In the third place, in Laertius' *Lives* the (b) component is not as fully developed as in Acts. The same observation holds true for the Lives of Aristotle which circulated singly instead of in a collection. The fuller development of Acts consists both in the sheer amount of material in the Lucan narrative about the disciples and successors on the one hand and in the kinds of material used in Luke's second volume on the other (e.g., preface with dedication; speeches; letters; travel narrative with a shipwreck). On the one side, even when a Life of a philosopher includes references to his successors and selected other disciples that constitute more than a list, an episode or two, a few sayings, and a list of a man's writings, if any, is about as much as is given on each follower (cf. Zeno, 7:36-38; Epicurus, 10:22-26). There can be no doubt that the Lucan Acts is more fully developed, containing as it does a mass of material equal to the amount in the Third Gospel. On the other side, the presence of a preface with a dedication, of speeches, and of letters in Acts reminds one of types of material found in historiography while the presence of a travel narrative with a shipwreck in it reminds one of a favorite theme of the ancient romances. What must be made of the more fully developed form of Acts? On the one hand, we must recognize that the mere expansion of content in the (b) component of Acts need not necessarily involve a denial of its participation in the biographical genre. Indeed, it may be just the reverse. When we note that the second part of Acts is devoted almost entirely to "the report of the fate of a single Apostle, Paul,"[40] we must conclude that the biographical spirit has taken over the succession narrative and enlarged it. On the other hand, we must recognize further that the presence of types of material characteristic of genres other than biography need not necessarily involve a denial of Acts' participation in the biographical genre. In the first place, a preface with a dedication, speeches, and letters functioned in biography in antiquity in much the same way that they did in historiography.[41] Their presence, therefore, does not determine to what genre a writing belongs. In the second place, in Acts the hero of the travel narrative with its shipwreck is an historical person as in biography.[42] At the most, one could say that the genre of romance has exercized an influence upon Acts so that a mixed form, a biography with motifs from the romance, lies before us. Such a phenomenon is not unknown in antiquity.[43] The fuller form of Acts' narrative, therefore, is no argument against its participation, as the second volume of Luke's two volume work, in the biographical genre.

There are obvious differences in content, that is, in what the narratives contain and in the way they are shaped. For example, the succession narratives in Laertius do not possess the strong emphasis on bearing witness, spreading the gospel, preaching the word, that we find in Acts. Nor is there to be found in Laertius' narratives the strong Lucan accent on the gift and guidance of the Holy Spirit. There are, in fact, so many of these differences that one cannot enumerate them all here. But is this type of content difference crucial in determining genre? By no means! If this type of differnece were made crucial, then the concept of genre itself would dissolve into nothingness. It would, for example, prevent our speaking of Matthew, Mark, Luke, and John as "gospels" because of the differences due to their individual ideological distinctives. It would also keep us from speaking of both the *Life of Aesop* with its hostility to philosophers and any life of a philosopher treated sympathetically as biographies because of their differences in ideology. Authors combine in their works both their individuality and their appropriation of convention. If we are to use the concept of genre at all, we must use it to group writings on the basis of shared conventions: e.g., these documents treat this type of subject matter, following this kind of pattern, with such and such a function in mind. To share conventions, however, does not mean identity. Individuality is preserved at every point—witness the four canonical gospels—but especially in ideology. Having noted the remarkable similarities between Laertius' *Lives* and having recognized that the differences are not decisive, it is now our task to try to explain the similarities.

Granting the remarkable similarities between these two documents, how are they to be explained? One obvious possibility would be to claim that the latter (Diogenes Laertius) borrowed from the earlier (Luke-Acts). This, however, is a highly unlikely explanation for several reasons. (1) There is no sign of Laertius' knowledge of or indebtedness to Christianity in any way. He seems to move in a separate orbit altogether. (2) Laertius is not likely to have known Luke and Acts as two parts of one work—if we suppose for the sake of argument that he knew them at all—since they had been separated and had circulated independently since at least the middle of the second century and quite possibly before that. (3) We know that biographies of philosophers controlled by the pattern, (a) life of founder + (b) succession list or narrative, existed from pre-Christian times and that at least some of these were used by Diogenes Laertius as sources for his work. Three examples should suffice. First, from Laertius' *Lives* we can reconstruct enough of the work of Sotion, whose *Successions* were written about 200—170 B.C.E., to know that it included at least (a) treatment of a philosopher's life[44] + (b) the succession from the founder.[45] Second, Heraclides Lembus, about 181—146 B.C.E., made an epitome of Sotion's work which contained the same material, only in briefer form.[46] Lembus was also used as a source by Laertius.[47] Finally, another of the sources used in the *Lives* was a comprehensive work on the philosophers written in the first century B.C.E. by Philodemus the Epicurean.[48] It so happens that among the Herculaneum papyri there are at least two (1018, 1021) and possibly a third (1044) which preserve parts of Philodemus' *Successions*.[49] These fragments, taken together with what Laertius says about the document, make it crystal clear that this work included both (a) a treatment of a philosopher's life and (b) the succession from him. Obviously, then, it was not from Luke-Acts, of which he probably knew nothing, but from such *Lives* of philosophers as these that Laertius derived his structural pattern, (a) life of a founder + (b) succession list or narrative. Biographies of philosophers from pre-Christian times—both collections and individual Lives—included these two component parts and Diogenes Laertius was merely perpetuating the pattern.[50] This, of course, explains the pattern of Laertius' *Lives* but it does not yet explain the similarities between Laertius and Luke-Acts.

The most likely option for explaining these similarities between Laertius' *Lives* and Luke-Acts would seem to be the hypothesis of their dependence upon a *common pattern* used in depicting lives of philosophers. The dependence of Laertius upon the pattern, (a) life of a founder + (b) succession list or narrative, is as certain as anything can be, but what of Luke-Acts? We have noted that this was a widespread pattern in biographies of philosophers both in collections and in individual Lives and that it was in existence and in use before the time of the composition of the Lucan writings. There is to my knowledge, moreover, no other example in early Christianity besides Luke-

Acts of the use of the pattern, (a) life of founder + (b) succession narrative. In early Christianity the (a)+(b) pattern of Luke-Acts is unique. Furthermore, I know of no use of this twofold pattern in Judaism for constructing narratives. There is, of course, evidence for a Jewish concept of the successors of Moses.[51] To my knowledge, however, this succession principle in Judaism never produced a Life of Moses, treated as a structural unit, followed by a narrative about his successors, treated as a structural unit, both of which form one whole. Nor can we find the pattern in the Old Testament—e.g., Deuteronomy followed by Joshua through 2 Kings. In the first place, Deuteronomy can hardly be called a Life of Moses. It is a farewell speech. Joshua through 2 Kings, moreover, can hardly be called a succession narrative. In the second place, there is no indication that this segment of the Old Testament was understood in such a way in Judaism near the beginning of the Christian era. For example, in the Hebrew Bible Deuteronomy belongs to the first structural unit, Joshua through 2 Kings to the second. In the LXX order, furthermore, Ruth is inserted between Judges and I Samuel, indicating a break at that point. What is more, in the Greco-Roman world the structural pattern is found only in certain Lives of philosphers. There is no twofold narrative based on such a pattern to be found in the treatment of any other kind of figure—literary, political, or military—insofar as I have been able to determine. In the ancient world the (a)+(b) pattern is found only in certain Lives of philosophers and in Luke-Acts.[51] This is a striking fact. There is furthermore a similarity in purpose between Luke-Acts and the Lives of philosophers following this pattern, whether they be collections or individual Lives. Both are concerned to say where the true tradition is to be found in the present. The most striking similarity, however, is that between the function of Luke-Acts and the individual Lives of philosophers with an (a)+(b) pattern. Both are cult documents intended to be read and used within the community which produced them and in the interests of its ongoing life.[53] When we consider further the evidence of the Lucan employment of the philosophical image in antiquity in depicting Jesus and his followers, the conclusion seems inescapable. Luke-Acts, just as Diogenes Laertius, derived the pattern for his work, (a)+(b), from the widespread use of it since pre-Christian times in portraying the lives of certain philosophers. If so, then Luke-Acts, to some extent, must be regarded as belonging to the genre of Greco-Roman biography, in particular, to that type of biography which dealt with the lives of philosophers and their successors. To this extent, von Soden's judgment is vindicated.

Genre, Patterns, and the Lucan Sitz in Leben

Recognition of the fact that Luke-Acts belongs to that type of ancient biography in which the life of a philosophical founder is followed by a list or narrative of his successors and selected other disciples raises a related question for our study of Lucan style. Is the Lucan employment of the biographical genre related to his use of the law of duality, and if so, how?

Of course, the patterns reflecting the principle of balance are found in many genres in antiquity. Chapter Five has shown us that. The law of duality is found in prose genres as well as in poetic ones. It is operative amid the prose genres in biography as well as in historiography. It is then, certainly not alien to the genre of Luke-Acts as it has been delineated in this chapter. The question for us, however, seems to be: what is there in the particular type of biography employed by the Third Evangelist that calls for the law of duality as a dominant stylistic principle in his work? The answer seems almost obvious. The (a)+(b) structure of a biography that is composed of the life of a founder of a philosophical school plus a record of his successors and selected other disciples innately tends towards balance. The life of the founder is counterbalanced by the record of his followers. The Evangelist's choice of the principle of balance for his basic architectonic scheme, therefore, is integrally intertwined with his adoption of a certain type of ancient biography as the vehicle for his communication.[54]

Both Luke's choice of genre type for his message to the church and his development of the type chosen were rooted in the *Sitz im Leben* of his community. The Lucan community was one that was troubled by a clash of views over the legitimate understanding of Jesus and the true nature of the Christian life. The Evangelist needed to be able to say both *where* the true tradition was to be found in his time (i.e., with the successors of Paul and of the Twelve) and *what* the content of that tradition was (i.e., how the apostles lived and what they taught, seen as rooted in the career of Jesus). The Lucan milieu offered the Evangelist a ready-made vehicle for dealing with the first issue. Faced with the existence of continual clashes not only among the various philosophical schools but also within any given school, the different philosophical communities developed lives of their founders to which were appended lists or narratives of the legitimate line of succession as a means of meeting the need to say where their true tradition was to be found. Such biographies said precisely where the "living voice" was located. The Third Evangelist chose this type of biography because it could do precisely what needed to be done in his church. It would allow him to say that the true tradition in his time was located in certain successors of Paul (Acts 20:17-35). Furthermore, it was the desire to deal with the same problem of heresy in his community that caused the Evangelist to develop the (b) component of his work beyond what it had been in the biographies of philosophers. Luke needed to spell out what the content of the true tradition was. Hence he expanded the (b) component of his work (Acts) both in length and in content so that it would correspond loosely with the content and order of the Third Gospel. In this way Luke could spell out the behavior and teaching of the apostles and present it to his readers as rooted in the life of the founder of the community. In this act of expansion the balance that was innate in his genre preference was developed to near perfection. The Acts truly counterbalanced the Third Gospel.

Once the basic architectonic principle was settled in this way, it was virtually inevitable that the Evangelist would follow the Mediterranean convention of allowing the pattern which controlled the organization of the whole to inform the arrangement of the parts. It is part of the Lucan artistic genius that the law of duality which was made to shape the various parts of the work was also utilized, in most cases, to complement and support the dominant theological emphases of the several sections.

FOOTNOTES

[1]A. D. Nock, *Conversion* (Oxford University Press, 1933) 175-76.

[2]Iamblichus, *Life of Pythagoras* 28:140-42 (quoting Aristotle).

[3]Iamblichus, *Life of Pythagoras* 6:30 (quoting Aristotle); Porphyry, *Life of Pythagoras* 20.

[4]Porphyry, *Life of Pythagoras* 28; Philostratus, *Life of Apollonius of Tyana* 1:1; Aelian, *Various History* 2:26 (quoting Aristotle).

[5]Porphyry, *Life of Pythagoras* 2; Aelian, *Various History* 4:17.

[6]E. J. Kenney (ed.), *Lucretius: De Rerum Natura, Book 3* (Cambridge University Press, 1971) 2-3. A. S. Cox, "Lucretius and His Message," *Greece and Rome*, 2d Series, Vol. 18 (1971) 8, says: "Epicurus plays the part in Lucretian preaching which Jesus does in Christian. . . ."

[7]*De Rerum Natura* 5:1-10. (LCL). Cf. also 3:1-5; 6:1-7.

[8]Cf. *Life of Apollonius of Tyana* 1:4.

[9]Cf. David L. Dungan, *Sourcebook of Texts for the Comparative Study of the Gospels* (2d ed.; Society of Biblical Literature, 1972) 7.

[10]Kenney, *Lucretius*, 2. Aelian, *Various History* 4:17, says of the Pythagoreans that it was not lawful among them to doubt anything Pythagoras said or to question him about it. Rather they had to acquiesce in what he said as to a divine oracle.

[11]Lucretius, *De Rerum Natura* 3:1-5; 5:55. That Diogenes Laertius understood this dimension of a disciple's relation to his master may be seen in *Lives* 4:19: "It would seem that in all respects Polemo emulated Xenocrates . . . . Certainly he always kept his predecessor before his mind. . . ."

[12]Cox, "Lucretius and His Message," 8, who also calls attention to the Epicurean dictum: "Always behave as though Epicurus were watching you." Cf. Leon Robin, *Greek Thought and the Origins of the Scientific Spirit* (New York: Knopf, 1928) 324, 340.

[13]Robert L. Wilken, "Collegia, Philosophical Schools, and Theology," in *The Catacombs and the Colosseum* (ed. S. Benko and J. J. O'Rourke; Valley Forge, Pa.: Judson, 1971) 279.

[14]Adolf Harnack, *The Mission and Expansion of Christianity in the First Three Centuries* (London: Williams & Norgate, 1908) 1. 226; 254-55; 443, n. 2; Wilken, "Collegia, Philosophical Schools, and Theology," 268-91. Wilken's article is unusually helpful. If my thesis holds, however, the origins of the Christians' conceptualization of themselves in school categories go back behind Justin. This is not surprising since Josephus (*Ant.* 18:1:1-6) is evidence that Jews had already thought of themselves in these terms.

[15]*Lives* 7:1:38, 68, 71, 79, 87, 89, 120, 121, for example.

[16]Aristippus (Life—2:65-84; Pupils—2:85-86; Summary of opinions of the Cyrenaic school—2:86-104); Plato (Life—3:1-45; Disciples—3:46-47; Doctrine—3:47-109); Zeno (Life—7:1-35; Successors and other disciples—7:36-38; Doctrine—7:38-160); Pythagoras (Life—8:1-44; Succession—8:45-46; Teachings—8:48-50); Epicurus (Life—10:1-21; Successors and other disciples—10:22-28; Views—10:29-154).

[17]Friedrich Leo, *Griechisch-romische Biographie nach Ihrer litterarischen Form* (Leipzig: Teubner, 1901).

[18]D. R. Stuart, *Epochs of Greek and Roman Biography* (Berkeley: University of California Press, 1928) 178. That the ancient biographer was interested in the man as a finished product and was not concerned with the evolution of his personality is a fact that New Testament scholars need to note.

[19]E.g., 7:36-38; 8:22-26; 2:85-86.

[20]Cf. Zeno, 7:38-150, where the division is into the topics: logic, ethics, and physics.

[21]Cf. Epicurus, 10:29-154, where one finds three letters and a number of maxims.

[22]E.G., Aristotle, 5:22-28; Plato, 3:47-65. When a philosopher did not write, as Socrates for example, obviously there would be no list of writings (cf. 2. ch. 5).

[23]D. R. Stuart, *Epochs of Greek and Roman Biography*, 158-59, 126.

[24]Elias Bickermann, "La chaine de la tradition Pharisienne," *RB* 59 (1952) 49.

[25]*Lives* 3:47.

[26]*Lives* 3:57.

[27]*Lives* 10:29 (LCL).

[28]Arnold Ehrhardt, *The Acts of the Apostles* (Manchester University Press, 1969) 12, says that E. Meyer rightly placed Acts in the same rank with Thucydides, Polybius, and Tacitus as a historian. F. F. Bruce in the Foreword approves. R. L. Wilken, *The Myth of Christian Beginnings* (Garden City, N.Y.: Doubleday Anchor, 1971) 31, cautiously says that whereas Luke-Acts has the closest affinity with the historical works of Greek antiquity, in reality Luke "chose a literary form with no real parallel in ancient literature."

[29]C. K. Barrett, *Luke the Historian in Recent Study* (London: Epworth, 1961) 13-15.

[30]Moses Hadas and Morton Smith, *Heroes and Gods* (New York: Harper & Row, 1965) 101, 161-95.

[31]Hans Freiherr von Soden, *Geschichte der christlichen Kirche, 1: Die Entstehung der christlichen Kirche* (Leipzig: Teubner, 1919) 73.

[32]"The Redactional Critical Quest for Luke the Theologian," in *Jesus and Man's Hope* (2 vols.; Pittsburgh Theological Seminary, 1970) 1. 171-222; *Luke and the Gnostics* (Nashville: Abingdon, 1966).

[33]A. J. Gossage, "Plutarch," in *Latin Biography* (ed. T. A. Dorey: London: Routledge & Kegan Paul, 1967) 47.

[34]Ingemar Düring, *Aristotle in the Ancient Biographical Tradition* (Göteborg: Göteborgs Universitets Arsskrift, 1957) Parts 1 and 2, especially pp. 82, 105, 106, 157, 200.

[35]Düring, *Aristotle*, 469.

[36]Düring, *Aristotle*, 464.

[37]Düring, *Aristotle*, 465-66, 345-46.

[38]*Lives*, 2. ch. 5.

[39]Cf. R. D. Hicks, "Introduction," in LCL, 1. xxii-xxxii.

[40]Helmut Koester, "Romance, Biography, and Gospel," "Working Paper of the Task Force on the Genre of the Gospels, Published by the Society of Biblical Literautre for the 1972 meeting in Los Angeles, 24.

[41](a) For a preface with a dedication in biography, cf. Plutarch's "Theseus," "Demosthenes," and "Dion"; Tacitus' *Agricola*. For a two volume biography with a preface at the beginning of volume two very much like that of Acts, cf. Philo's *Life of Moses*, 2, 1. (b) For speeches used in biography as religious teaching, cf. Iamblichus' *Life of Pythagoras*. C. J. de Vogel, *Pythagoras and Early Pythagoreanism* (Assen: Van Gorcum, 1966) ch. 6, points out how the speeches in this biography are archaic in style. This, then, is not a trait only of speeches in historiography, as suggested by E. Plümacher, *Lukas als hellenisticher Schriftsteller* (Göttingen: Vandenhoeck & Ruprecht, 1972) 38-78. (c) For letters in biography, cf. Porphyry's *Life of Plotinus*, 17, 19.

[42]Koester, "Romance, Biography, and Gospel," 25-26.

[43]On mixed forms, cf. E. I. McQueen, "Quintus Curtis Rufus," in *Latin Biography*, ed. T. A. Dorey, 17-43.

[44]E.g., *Lives* 2:74. Albin Lesky, *A History of Greek Literature* (London: Methuen, 1966) 690, speaks of Sotion as the creator of the form which remained influential up to Diogenes Laertius.

[45]E.g., *Lives* 9:115 (see Index, LCL, Vol. 2, for further references).

[46]*Lives* 10:1 (see Index, LCL, Vol. 2, for further references).

[47]*Lives* 8:7; 8:58.

[48]*Lives* 10:3.

[49]Papyrus 1021 is a catalogue of the heads of the Academic School with some facts about their lives; 1018 is a similar catalogue of the Stoic School. Papyrus 1044 possibly belongs to the same work as the other two. It deals with the heads of the Epicurean School. We know from Diogenes Laertius, *Lives*, 10:3, that Philodemus' work most certainly included such data about Epicurus and his successors. Cf. Walter Scott (ed.), *Fragmenta Herculanensia* (Oxford: Clarendon Press, 1885), on 1021 and 1018; Augustus Traversa (ed.), *Index Stoicorum Herculanensis* (Genova: Istituto di Filologia Classica, 1952) xiii-xvii, for a treatment of 1018; Th. Gomperz, "Ein Brief Epikurs an ein Kind," *Hermes* 5 (1871) 386, for a discussion of 1044.

[50] For others, see R. D. Hicks, "Introduction," in Vol. 1 of LCL.

[51] Cf. ch. 6, notes 47 and 48. For further references, see Wayne Meeks, "Moses as God and King," in *Religions in Antiquity* (ed. J. Neusner; Leiden: Brill, 1968) 365-66, n. 3.

[52] The (b) component of this pattern is missing from the biographical pattern abstracted from traditional narrative by scholars like Lord Raglan ("The Hero of Tradition," *Folklore* 45 [1934] 212-31; *The Hero* [New York: Vintage, 1956]). According to my count, Matthew's account of Jesus conforms to 17 of the 22 points in Raglan's pattern, Mark's to 9 of 22, John's to 7 of 22. The Third Gospel conforms to 13 of the 22 points. With Acts, however, there is a radical departure. It is the presence of Acts which demands an investigation that goes beyond what one finds in Hahn, Rank, Propp, Raglan, and Campbell.

[53] It would be well to remember that reading or reciting literary works in the Greco-Roman world, whether in a religious or secular context, was different from the Jewish and later Christian lectionary system. The system of lections reduced a text to its small component parts. A single reading did not encompass the whole or even a major part of the whole. The practice of reading or reciting tragedy, lyric poetry, speeches, polemical biography, or history, for example, involved lengthy periods of time and encompassed either the whole work or a major part of it (cf. Pliny, *Letters* 7:4; 7:17; 8:21; 9:1; 9:27). In his *Letters* 9:27, for example, Pliny tells of an author who recited part of a historical work on one day for friends and left the remainder for another day. Most likely, the gospels, like the epistles of the NT and the Apocalpse of John, were written to be read originally as wholes. In the case of Luke-Acts, the length may have required two sessions for reading, like the history referred to by Pliny. Such lengthy speech was apparently not unknown to the early Christians' gatherings (cf. Acts 20:7-12). In such reading sessions, the patterns would more likely be perceived than in the later reduction of the gospels to short lections or to modern chapters and verses.

[54] Since, with the exception of Laertius' *Lives*, all of the extant biographies with an (a) + (b) pattern are fragmentary, it is impossible to say with finality that such biographies automatically involve a balanced architecture. To my knowledge, Laertius' work has never been studied from this perspective. Even a superficial reading, however, uncovers the tendency to balance at work in his *Lives*. (a) The Prologue for the work as a whole falls into two major sections which correspond to one another:

A—Barbarians (1)
    B—Egyptians (2)
        C—Persians (3)
            D—Greeks (4)
A'—Barbarians (5)
        C'—Persians (6—9)
            B'—Egyptians (10—11)
            D'—Greeks (12).

This is followed by a summary statement on the twofold origin of philosophy. (b) The rest of Book 1 contains brief biographies of eleven Wise Men. The key to the literary arrangement of these lives lies in the letters which come at the end of all but two of them. For example, in the first life, that of Thales, we find a letter to Pherecydes, the wise man whose life occurs last in Book 1. Furthermore, in the life of Pherecydes there is a letter to Thales, the wise man of the first life. In the same way, the second life, that of Solon, contains a letter to Epimenides, the wise man whose life is next to last. Also, Epimenides' life has a letter to Solon, whose life is second. In this way, lives one and two are linked with ten and eleven to form an inclusion or brackets around the whole unit. With a similar method, lives 3 and 7, lives 4 and 8, lives 5 and 9, and lives 6 and 10 correspond: 3 and 7, 4 and 8, 6 and 10 by means of letters with identical addresses, 5 and 9 by being the only two lives without any letters. The resulting balanced pattern is: A, B[C, D, E, F—C', D', E', F', (=B')] B', A'. (c) Books 2—10 fall into two parts tracing the Ionian and Italian successions, six books for the former, three books for the latter. This balanced scheme that is apparent even to cursory reading points to the probability that a much greater architectonic balance exists and could be brought to light if it were made the object of scholarly attention. The conclusion seems inescapable. This particular genre type tends towards balance as an architectonic principle.

Conclusion

When one takes into account all of the data that has been presented in the preceding pages and tries to conceptualize the Evangelist's technique of composition, what model can he use? It seems to me that only by holding together two models can one truly grasp what must have gone on in the composition of the Lucan literature. I am thinking of both a literary and a pastoral model.

By a literary model I mean a compositional procedure modelled after what we hear in Aristotle's *Poetics* 17:5-10, in Suetonius' *Life of Vergil* 22-23, in Lucian's *How To Write History* 48, and in Pliny's *Letters* 9:36. In this procedure an author begins with an overall conception of the whole, represented on occasion by a preliminary summary sketch divided into its major parts. He then fills out the parts in light of the total conception. Because of his preliminary conception of the whole, the author need not work on the parts in the order in which they ultimately appear in the finished product. In line with the aesthetic conventions of the Mediterranean world, the principles and patterns which inform the whole are utilized by the author to shape the various parts of the whole even down to minutiae. Only such a model is able to grasp certain dimensions of the Lucan achievement.

By a pastoral model I mean a compositional procedure modelled after what we infer from such Pauline letters as 1, 2 Corinthians, Galatians, Philippians, and 1 Thessalonians or from the Johannine apocalypse. In this procedure an author begins with an awareness of a problem or series of problems in a community with which he is concerned and for which he is responsible. He then responds to the occasion, if he cannot do it otherwise, with a writing which deals theologically with the specific problems raised by his church's experience. In line with his pastoral concerns, the writing is shaped even in details by the occasion to which it is a response.

Only by combining these two models, I think, are we able to conceptualize the Evangelist's compositional procedures. It is the churchly situation which motivates the Lucan author to write and it is from a theological perspective that he exercizes his pastoral concern. In writing, however, it is apparently the accepted literary procedure of the day which he follows. This means that there are both theological and aesthetic influences at work on the Evangelist. It also means that his work is both occasional and planned. The author's compositional procedures are not understood until both of these models are taken into account. Looking at our data in summary fashion and from this point of view yields the following results.

The Lucan Evangelist stood within a community that was troubled, among other things, by a concern for the true Christian tradition. Where was it to be found in the present? It was Luke's pastoral concern that motivated him to write. His cultural context presented him with a suitable mode of expression. In the philosophical schools this type of question about where the true tradition was to be found in the present had been answered by a type of biography of the group's founder which included within itself a list or short narrative of the founder's successors and selected other disciples. It was at the end point of this succession that the true tradition was located in the here and now. In terms of this genre Luke spoke as a pastor. At the same time, his theological concern to maintain the normative character of the apostolic age over the ministry of later times caused the Evangelist to expand the narrative of Jesus' successors so that the content of their normative deeds and words would be clear. Luke's theological perspective also dictated that he show that the apostolic deed and word were normative because they were a reflection of the word and deed of Jesus, the founder of the community. The correspondences between the career of Jesus in Luke and the lives of the apostolic figures in Acts, therefore, have their roots in the author's choice of a genre. Balance was inherent in its (a)+(b) pattern. This basic formal pattern, however, was made explicit in Luke-Acts because of the theological perspective of the Evangelist. In Luke's preliminary conception of the whole both literary and pastoral models of activity are present.

The same is true regarding the correspondences between Acts 1—12 and Acts 13—28 on the one hand and the parallel panels in Acts 1—5 on the other. The aesthetic convention according to which an author utilized the patterns which inform the whole to shape its various parts was reinforced in Acts by the theological need to portray the apostolic age as an ideal time. The correspondences in these parts of the whole meet the demands of both literary and pastoral models.

Any attempt to make sense of the compositional procedure involved in the correspondences between Luke 9 and Luke 22—23, between Luke 24 and Acts 1, and between Luke 9 and Acts 1, must also think in terms of two procedural models, literary and pastoral. Redaction critical research has shown that the Evangelist was confronted by a point of view that tended to divide the whole Christ by its advocacy of a descent of the spiritual savior on the human Jesus at his baptism and his ascent prior to the crucifixion, leaving the human Jesus to suffer and die. The Lucan response involved an attempt to link the parts of the Christ event together in an inseparable unity. This theological tendency would utilize the literary proclivity for correspondences in the parts of a balanced whole. The Jesus of Galilee and the Jesus of Jerusalem would be linked with the One who rose from the grave by the correspondences of Luke 24 and Acts 1. The One who ascended would be linked with the One who worked in Galilee by the correspondences between Luke 9 and Acts 1. That theological considerations took precedence in this case over literary ones may be seen in the correspondences between Luke 9 and Luke 22—23. If the Evangelist's balance was to be exact in his two volume work, the first half of Luke needed to be paralleled by the second half of the Gospel as was the Acts. This, however, is not the case. Luke 9 is made to correspond with Luke 22—23 only. This is enough to serve the Evangelist's theological needs but it satisfies his aesthetic requirements in a less satisfactory way. Nevertheless, both literary and pastoral models are needed again to conceptualize Lucan compositional procedure.

In Luke 1—2 we have found two sets of correspondences between John and Jesus. In Luke 3—4 we have noted another. Again the aesthetic compulsion to shape the parts of the whole by the same patterns which control the total literary entity is at work. In league with it is the Lucan theological desire to link John and Jesus closely in salvation history, even though John is subordinate to Jesus. Again, therefore, the patterns serve two separate functions. Again, Luke must be viewed in terms of both literary and pastoral models.

It is only when we consider the correspondences of Luke 4—8 and the chiastic patterns of the journeys of Jesus and Paul that we need only a literary model for an explanation of their presence. In these three cases only, of the formal patterns considered in this work, do we find an absence of overt pastoral concern. In these three cases the concern is primarily aesthetic. In light of ancient literary practice, such a phenomenon, however, is exactly what we would expect.

If we assume a literary model for the Lucan compositional procedure then the Evangelist would not be writing hastily. Nor would he be necessarily composing in a series, from the beginning of the final product unto its end. Rather he would be understood as starting from an overall conception, both literary and theological, and as working on the parts individually and at different times. For example, the Evangelist may, though he need not have, worked on the Acts before he worked on the Gospel or on later sections of either before earlier ones. At the same time, his work was most definitely occasional. It was written not out of literary motives but rather in order to deal with a specific occasion in the life of his church. Luke's effort is both occasional and planned. It is both literary and pastoral. Only in these terms can one make sense of these literary patterns and their relation to the theological tendencies of Luke-Acts.

Index of Passages

OLD TESTAMENT

Genesis
3 .... 47, 118
25:22-26 105
25:23 105

Exodus
5-14 71
7:8-10:27 71

Deuteronomy
19:15 2

1 Kings
3-11 71
6-8 73
7:27-29 73

Psalms
106 50

Isaiah
40 46
40:3-5 46
61:1-2 117

Ezekiel
12:18-19 73
41-43 73

Jonah
1-2 81
1:4-5 72
1:4 71
1:5-6 72
1:6 .... 72, 77
1:7 72
1:8 72
1:9-15 77
1:9-10 72
1:11 72
1:12 72
1:13 72
1:14 .... 71, 72
1:15-16 72
1:15 71
1:16 .... 72, 77

1:17 71
2:1 71
2:2-6 71
2:2 71
2:3 71
2:6-7 71
2:6 71
2:8 71
2:9 .... 71, 72
2:10 .... 71, 77
3-4 82
3:4 72
3:5-8 72
3:6-8 77
3:10 72
4:1-11 71
4:1-3 72
4:1 .... 71, 72
4:2-3 77
4:2 .... 71, 77
4:3 71
4:4-11 71
4:4 72
4:5 77
4:6-11 72
4:8-11 77

Malachi
3:1 97

NEW TESTAMENT

Matthew
1:1 123
3:7-10 46
3:7 46
3:11-12 46
4:1-11 47
5:3-4 42
5:6 42
5:11-12 42
5:13 55

5:15 54	24:37-41 54
5:18 55	24:43-44 55
5:25-26 55	24:45-51 55
5:32 55	25:1-13 55
5:39-42 42	26:57 21
5:44-48 42	28:18-20 62
6:9-13 54	
6:19-21 55	**Mark**
6:22-23 54	1:4-8 117
6:24 55	1:9-11 .... 18, 116, 117
6:25-33 55	1:12-13 117
7:1-5 42	1:14 104
7:7-11 54	1:16-20 .... 40, 41
7:12 42	1:21-34 41
7:13-14 56	1:23 41
7:16-21 42	1:31 41
7:22-23 56	2:1-12 .... 19, 42
7:24-27 42	2:13-28 42
8:5-13 43	2:15-3:6 19
8:5-10 19	2:16 42
8:8 19	2:18 42
8:11-12 56	2:23 42
9:37-38 20	3:7-12 42
10:7-16 20	3:8 42
10:19-20 55	3:13-19 42
10:26-33 55	3:20-22 40
10:34-36 55	3:23-30 40
10:37-38 55	3:31-35 43
11:1-15 41	4:1-9 43
11:12-13 55	4:1 43
11:25-27 53	4:21-25 43
12:11-30 54	4:26-29 40
12:32 55	4:30-32 40
12:38-42 54	4:33-34 40
12:43-45 54	4:35-41 42
13:16-17 53	5:1-20 41
13:31-33 56	5:21-24 43
16:2-3 55	5:25-34 43
17:20 54	5:35-43 43
18:6-7 54	6:45-8:26 .... 28, 33, 62, 66
18:12-14 55	6:1-6 .... 18, 41
18:14 55	6:7-13 27
18:15 54	6:7 62
18:21-22 54	6:8 27
19:28 28	6:14-16 27
22:1-10 56	6:17-18 48
23:4 54	6:30-44 27
23:6-7 54	6:34 62
23:13-14 54	7:1-23 33
23:25-26 54	8:27-33 27
23:27-28 54	8:34-9:1 28
23:29-32 54	9:2-8 .... 28, 61
23:37-39 56	9:2 62
24:26-28 54	9:4 62

9:14-29	28
9:30-32	29
9:30	114
9:33-37	29
10:1	114
10:13-16	52, 53
10:17-30	52, 53
10:17	114
10:32	20, 114
10:46	114
11:1-10	20
11:1	114
11:4-5	41
11:6	41
11:11	20, 21, 114
11:12-14	21
11:15-18	21
11:16-19	42
12:18-27	21
12:28-34	52, 53
14:3-9	20, 42
14:17-21	28
14:22-25	21, 28
14:22	21
14:26-31	28
14:29-31	33
14:32	28
14:32-42	28
14:43-52	29
14:53	21, 22
14:65	22
15:1	22
15:2	22
15:9	22
15:39	22
15:40-41	114
15:47	113, 114
16:1-8	22

Luke

1-2	2, 44, 45, 80, 103, 104, 106, 112, 117, 143
1:1-4	16, 18, 80
1:3	18
1:5-Acts 15	36
1:5-2:52	47, 89
1:5-4:15	47, 48, 105
1:5-38	44
1:5-7	44
1:8-11	44
1:12	44
1:13-17	44, 104
1:18	44
1:19-23	44

1:24-25	44
1:26-27	44
1:28	44
1:29	44
1:31	117
1:30-33	44
1:34-35	117
1:34	44
1:35-37	44
1:36	104
1:38	44
1:39-56	44, 45, 104, 105
1:41	105
1:57-2:52	44, 77
1:57-80	78
1:57	44
1:58	44
1:59-64	44, 78
1:65-66	44
1:68-79	44, 80
1:76	104
1:80	44
2:1-52	78
2:1-7	44
2:8-20	44
2:17-18	44
2:21	44, 78
2:22-38	44, 47
2:39-40	44
2:41-52	44, 47
3-4	44, 45, 47, 89, 103, 104, 105, 106, 112, 143
3:1-20	50
3:1-6	45, 46, 105
3:1-2	46
3:3-18	117
3:4	105
3:4-6	46
3:7-17	45, 46, 47
3:7-9	46
3:7	46
3:9	46
3:10-14	46
3:10	47
3:15-17	46, 105
3:15	47
3:18-20	45, 47, 105
3:21-38	45, 46, 47
3:21-22	18, 117
3:21	16
3:22	16, 46, 47, 116, 117, 118
3:23-28	46, 117
3:23	117, 127, 123
3:31	104

3:38 .... 47, 118

4-8 .... 2, 39, 43, 76, 120, 143

4:16-7:17 .... 39, 40

4:16-30 16, 18, 19, 39, 40, 41, 97, 117

4:1-13 .... 45, 46, 47, 117

4:3 .... 46, 47, 118

4:9 .... 46, 47, 118

4:14-15 .... 45, 47, 48

4:16 95

4:17-21 19

4:21 117

4:25-27 98

4:31-8:56 .... 16, 19, 20

4:31-41 .... 40, 41, 42

4:31 95

4:33 41

4:35 41

4:39 41

4:41 41

4:44 95

5:1-11 .... 40, 41, 42

5:12 95

5:17-26 .... 16, 19, 40, 42

5:17 .... 19, 42

5:27-6:5 .... 40, 42

5:29-6:11 16

5:29 42

5:30 42

5:33 42

5:59-6:11 19

6:1 42

6:12-16 .... 40, 42, 113, 116

6:12 95

6:14-16 113

6:17-49 .... 40, 42

6:17-19 .... 42, 43

6:17 .... 42, 43, 95

6:20-49 42

6:20 43

7:1-10 .... 16, 19, 39, 43

7:1 .... 43, 95

7:3-5 19

7:6 19

7:11-17 .... 16, 19, 39, 43

7:11 95

7:18-8:56 .... 39, 40

7:18-30 .... 39, 40, 41

7:22 41

7:23 41

7:27 97

7:29 41

7:31-35 .... 40, 42

7:34 42

7:36-50 .... 16, 20, 40, 42

8:1-3 .... 40, 42, 43

8:1 .... 43, 95

8:4-8 .... 40, 42, 43

8:4 43

8:16-21 .... 40, 42, 43

8:18-21 43

8:19 43

8:22-25 .... 40, 41, 42

8:26-39 .... 40, 41

8:26 95

8:27 41

8:28 41

8:40-56 41

8:40-42 43

8:40 95

8:43-48 .... 39, 43

8:49-56 43

9-18 120

9 .... 2, 26, 27, 61, 62, 111, 120,
    142, 143

9:1-34 61

9:1-6 .... 26, 27, 61, 62

9:1 62

9:3 27

9:7-9 .... 26, 27

9:9 27

9:10-17 .... 26, 27, 28, 61, 62

9:10 95

9:11 .... 27, 62

9:20-22 .... 26, 27

9:22 .... 97, 115

9:23-27 .... 26, 28

9:23 28

9:28-43 28

9:28-36 .... 26, 28, 61

9:28 .... 61, 95

9:29 61

9:30 .... 61, 62

9:31 .... 16, 61, 62, 115

9:32 .... 61, 62

9:34-35 61

9:37-43 .... 26, 28

9:43-45 .... 27, 29

9:44 .... 97, 115

9:45 16

9:46-48 .... 27, 29

9:51-19:46 .... 51, 95, 112, 114

9:51-19:28 .... 16, 20

9:51-18:14 52,

9:51 .... 16, 17, 20, 121, 112, 114,
    115, 122

9:53 .... 17, 20, 114

9:57 114

10:1-12 .... 16, 20, 78

10:1 .... 20, 114
10:17 114
10:21-18:30 51
10:21-24 .... 51, 53
10:25-37 .... 51, 53
10:25-28 .... 52, 53
10:38-42 51
10:38-42 54
10:38 114
11:1-13 .... 52, 54
11:1 114
11:14-36 .... 52, 54
11:14-16 40
11:37-54 .... 52, 54
12:1-48 .... 52, 55
12:1-12 .... 52, 55
12:13-34 52
12:13-21 55
12:22-34 55
12:35-48 .... 52, 54
12:49-13:9 .... 52, 55
12:49-53 .... 52, 55
12:50 .... 16, 115
12:54-59 .... 52, 55
13:1-5 .... 52, 55
13:6-9 .... 52, 55
13:10-17 .... 52, 56
13:10 114
13:18-30 56
13:18-21 56
13:18-19 40
13:22-30 56
13:22 .... 17, 20, 114
13:31-33 .... 52, 56
13:32-35 115
13:33 .... 16, 17, 20, 97, 114
13:34-35 .... 52, 56
14:1-18:30 51
14:1-6 .... 52, 56
14:1 .... 20, 114
14:7-24 .... 52, 56
14:15 56
14:25-ch. 15 52
14:25-27 .... 52, 55
14:25 114
14:28-33 .... 52, 55
14:34-35 .... 52, 55
15 52
15:1-2 20
15:3-7 55
15:7 55
15:8-10 55
15:11-32 55
16 .... 52, 55

16:1-8 52
16:9-15 52
16:14 20
16:16-17 103
16:16 .... 48, 103, 104
16:19-31 52
17:1-10 .... 52, 54
17:11-37 .... 52, 54
17:11 .... 17, 20, 114
17:25 97
18:1-8 .... 52, 54
18:9-14 .... 20, 51, 54
18:15-17 .... 51, 52, 53
18:15 52
18:16-17 53
18:18-30 .... 51, 52, 53
18:31-34 .... 16, 97
18:31 .... 17, 20, 114
18:34 16
18:35 44
19:1-48 26
19:1 114
19:11 .... 17, 20, 114
19:28-38 20
19:28-29 114
19:28 .... 17, 20
19:31-33 115
19:37 .... 17, 20, 114
19:41 114
19:45-48 .... 17, 21
19:45 20
20:17-18 98
20:17 97
20:27-39 .... 17, 21
20:37 98
20:39 21
22-23 .... 26, 27, 111, 120, 142, 143
22:7-20 .... 26, 27
22:15-20 .... 21, 28, 33
22:15-18 33
22:19-20 33
22:19 .... 17, 21
22:21-23 .... 27, 29
22:24-27 .... 27, 29
22:26 .... 17, 22
22:28-30 .... 26, 28
22:31-34 .... 26, 27, 28
22:31-32 33
22:33-34 33
22:35-38 .... 26, 27
22:35 27
22:37 97
22:39-53 .... 29, 33
22:39-46 .... 26, 28, 33

22:39 28
22:43 33
22:47-53 .... 26, 28, 29
22:51 29
22:54 .... 17, 21
22:63-64 .... 17, 22
22:66-71 97
22:69 97
23:1 .... 17, 22
23:4 17,22
23:6-16 .... 26, 27
23:6-12 .... 17, 22
23:8 .... 17, 22, 27
23:13 .... 17, 22
23:14 .... 17, 22
23:16 .... 17, 22
23:18 .... 18, 22
23:22 .... 17, 22
23:34 97
23:39-43 97
23:41 97
23:46 97
23:47 .... 18, 22
23:49 114
23:55 .... 113, 114
24 .... 18, 22, 59, 60, 145, 111, 120,
    142, 143
24:1-11 .... 22, 139
24:3 .... 113, 114
24:7 97
24:13-32 22
24:21-24 60
24:22-23 113
24:25-27 .... 22, 97, 98
24:26 .... 115, 122, 124
24:32 .... 22, 97
24:33-53 114
24:33-49 22
24:33-34 .... 59, 60
24:34 .... 60, 114
24:36 .... 59, 60
24:39 113
24:36-43 .... 59, 60, 113, 114
24:43 113
24:44-49 .... 22, 60, 97, 98
24:44 22
24:46 124
24:47-48 .... 59, 60
24:47 98
24:49 .... 59, 60, 97
24:50-53 .... 60, 112, 122
24:51-52 .... 59, 60
24:51 122

John
1:1-18 111
4:46-54 19
12:1-8 20
20:17-19 113
20:26-29 60
21:1-10 41

Acts
1-15 .... 25, 32, 36, 37
1-12 .... 23, 24, 25, 26, 31, 32, 89, 142
1-5 .... 1, 2, 13, 35, 36, 37, 38, 39, 43,
    101, 103, 142
1 .... 2, 59, 60, 61, 62, 111, 112, 113,
    114, 116, 120, 142, 143
1:1-12 61
1:1-5 .... 16, 18, 65, 122
1:1-2 59
1:1 .... 18, 98
1:2 122
1:3-4 .... 61, 62
1:3 .... 59, 60, 122
1:4 .... 22, 59, 60, 97
1:6-14 37
1:8 .... 22, 59, 60, 61, 62, 96
1:9-11 .... 60, 61, 62, 112
1:9 .... 59, 61, 113
1:10 .... 61, 62, 113, 115
1:11 .... 61, 113, 114, 115, 116
1:12-26 35
1:12 .... 59, 60, 61, 65
1:13 .... 113, 116
1:14 .... 16, 18
1:15-26 37
1:21-22 .... 24, 116, 122
1:22 114
1:24 .... 16, 18
2 .... 37, 38
2:1-13 .... 16, 18, 35
2:1-4 .... 23, 37
2:14-40 .... 16, 18, 19, 23, 25, 35, 38
2:16-21 97
2:22-23 32
2:24 32
2:25-28 32
2:29 32
2:30-32 32
2:32-36 115
2:32-33 122
2:34 122
2:36 .... 111, 122
2:41-12:17 .... 16, 19
2:41-5:40 49

2:42-4:31 38
2:42-47 .... 35, 38, 101
2:43 35
3-5 .... 37, 38
3:1-10 .... 16, 19, 23, 35
3:12-26 .... 19, 23, 35, 38
3:15-21 115
3:17-26 122
3:17-18 97
3:18 22
3:22-26 97
3:24-25 97
4 39
4:1-8:3 .... 16, 19
4:1-7 36
4:5-12 37
4:8-12 .... 36, 38
4:11 97
4:13-17 35
4:18 .... 36, 102
4:19-20 36
4:21-23 36
4:24-5:42 .... 34, 38, 89
4:24-31 .... 35, 37, 38
4:27 123
4:31 .... 35, 38
4:32-37 101
4:32-35 .... 35, 38
5 39
5:1-11 101
5:5 .... 35, 38
5:11 .... 35, 38
5:12 .... 35, 38
5:13-16 35
5:13 38
5:14 38
5:15-16 38
5:17-28 36
5:28 102
5:30-32 .... 36, 38, 122
5:34-39 .... 24, 36, 38
5:40-42 36
6-7 32
6:1-6 .... 24, 38, 101, 102
6:8-8:4 23
6:8-14 .... 37, 38, 102
6:12-15 97
6:13-14 24
7:1-53 37
7:55-8:3 38
7:56 97
7:59 97
7:60 97

8 32
8:1-4 97
8:1 96
8:4-5 96
8:9-24 24
8:13-24 102
8:14-17 24
8:26 96
8:30-35 97
9 32
9:1-30 38
9:31-11:18 36
9:32-35 16
9:36-43 .... 16, 19, 24
10-11 .... 23, 101
10 .... 16, 19, 96
10:9-16 23
10:25-26 24
10:26-43 37
10:37 116
10:38 123
10:43 97
11 32
11:1-18 .... 16, 20
11:19-26 .... 96, 97
12 24
12:3-4 24
12:4 24
12:5-6 24
12:6-11 24
12:17 24
12:24 24
13-28 ..... 23, 24, 25, 26, 31, 32, 89, 142
13-21 .... 16, 23, 78
13-14 .... 20, 32, 58, 65
13:1-3 .... 23, 25
13:4-12 102
13:4 38
13:6-12 24
13:16-40 .... 23, 25, 37
13:23 .... 32, 97
13:24 .... 62, 115
13:27-39 97
13:27-28 32
13:27 .... 76, 97
13:30 32
13:31 121
13:33 .... 111, 121
13:35 32
13:36 32
13:40-41 98
13:47 98
14:8-13 23

14:13-15 24
14:15-17 23
14:19-23 23
14:22 115
14:23 24
14:26 98
15-21 .... 56, 57, 58, 120
15 .... 23, 32, 101
15:1-18:11 57
15:1-29 .... 57, 58
15:7-11 .... 23, 37
15:15-18 98
15:30-16:15 57
15:36-28:31 .... 32, 36
15:36-21:16 58
15:36-41 101
16-20 .... 20, 32
16:6-10 23
16:10-17 57
16:16-40 57
16:19-39 102
16:24-26 24
16:25-34 58
17:1-15 57
17:2-3 .... 97, 98
17:5-9 102
17:11 97
17:16-34 57
17:22-31 58
18:1-11 57
18:12-21:26 57
18:12-23 57
18:12-17 102
18:24-19:7 57
18:24-28 97
19:1-6 24
19:8-10 57
19:11-20:12 57
19:14-16 58
19:21-21:17 .... 16, 20
19:21 17
19:23-41 102
20:3 16
20:5-15 57
20:7-12 .... 58, 139
20:9-12 24
20:13-21:14 57
20:17-35 .... 34, 58, 95, 99, 102, 135
20:18-19 96
20:20 96
20:22-24 16
20:22 .... 16, 17
20:27 96
20:29-30 102

20:33-35 96
20:37-38 16
21-28 24
21 23
21:1-18 57
21:4 .... 16, 17, 58
21:10-11 16
21:11 58
21:11-12 17
21:12-13 16
21:13 .... 16, 17
21:14 16
21:15-26 57
21:15 17
21:16 24
21:17-20 .... 17, 20
21:17 17
21:20-21 24
21:26 .... 17, 21
21:30 .... 17, 21
21:36 18
23 .... 17, 22
23:2 .... 17, 22
23:6-9 .... 17, 21
23:9 .... 17, 24
23:11 24
23:12-35 24
24 .... 17, 22
24:14-15 98
24:17 20
25 .... 17, 22
25:8 24
25:13-26:32 17
25:13 24
25:23-24 24
25:25 17
26 .... 17, 22
26:6-8 98
26:16 24
26:22-23 .... 97, 98
26:31 17
26:32 17
27:1-28:16 57
27:3 18
27:35 .... 17, 21, 31
27:43 18
28 .... 18, 22, 58
28:23 97
28:25-27 98
28:30-31 24

Romans

1:3-4 111

9-11 75
15:25-27, 31 20

1 Corinthians
8-10 75
15:3-5 113
15:5 60

Galatians
1-2 25
2:4-5 101

1 Timothy
1:5 95
1:11 95
3:14-15 95
3:16 111
4:12 95
6:11 95
6:20 95

2 Timothy
1:12 95
1:13-14 95
2:2 95
3:10-11, 14 95
4:2 95
1:7-8 95
1:9 95
2:1 95
2:7 95
3:8 95
3:14 95

Titus
1:19 95
3:8 95
3:14 95

2 Peter
1:13-15 100
1:16-18 101
1:20-21 101
2:1-22 100
3:2 101

Jude
17-18 101

Revelation
1:13-2:18 75

JEWISH SOURCES
OUTSIDE THE CANON (MT)

1 Enoch
93 71
96:12-17 71

Epistle of Aristeas
127 92

Josephus
Against Apion
1:8 109
Antiquities
18:1:1-6 .... 65, 137

Manual of Discipline
3:13-4:26 71

Mishnah
Erubin
2:6 108
Orlah
2:5 108
Sukkah
2:5 108
3:9 108

Philo
On Abraham
1:3-5 92
Life of Moses
1:162 93
2:1 138

Talmud
b. Ber. 11a 109
b. Ber. 24a, b 108
b. Ber. 38b 108
b. Ber. 39b 108
b. Ber. 62a 108
b. Erub. 93b 109

Tobit
12:19 113

CHRISTIAN SOURCES
OUTSIDE THE CANON

1 Clement
1:2-2:8 101

Clement of Alexandria
Miscellanies
1:14 108
50:7 109

Epiphanius
Heresies
28 123
33:3-7 109

Epistle of the Apostles
1:7 124

Eusebius
Church History
3:28:2 123
3:32:7-8 109
4:22:4 109
7:25:1-3 124

Preparation of the Gospel
9:30 109

Hippolytus
Refutation
7:33 123

Irenaeus
Against Heresies
1:24:3-6 123
1:26:1 .... 123, 124
1:30:12-14 123
1:30:13-14 123
3:2:2 109
3:3:3 94
3:3:4 .... 109, 123
3:11:1 123
4:26:2-5 94

Protevangelium Jacobi
1:1 76
4:1-2 .... 75, 76
5:2 76
9:3 76
11:1-2 76
11:3 76
16:2 75
18:2 76
19:2 76
20:3 76
25 76

Shepherd of Hermas
Vision
3:5:1 109

Tertullian
Prescription Against Heretics
6 109
20 109
21-29 109
30 109
32 109
35 109

GREEK AND ROMAN SOURCES

Aelian
Various History
2:26 137
4:17 137

Aristotle
Poetics
17:5-10 .... 79, 141

Cicero
About the Ends of Goods and Evils
2:31:101 127

Academic Questions
1:34-35 108

Tusculan Disputations
1:21:48 126

Demetrius
On Style
5:250 78

Dio Chrysostom
Discourses
13:9 108
13:10 108
55:4-5 108
70:6 108

Diodorus of Sicily
1:42 65
2:1 65
3:1 65

Diogenes Laertius
Lives of Eminent Philosphers
1:13-15 108
2 125
2. ch. 5 138
2:47 108
2:65-84 137
2:74 138
2:85, 86 137
2:86-104 137
2:100 126
3:1-45 137
3:45 126
3:46-47 137
3:47-65 137
3:57 138
4:19 137
5:1-19 127
5:22-28 137

6:1-20 127
7:1-35 137
7:36-38 .... 130, 131, 137
7:38-160 137
8 125
8:1-44 137
8:7 138
8:41 126
8:45-46 137
8:48-50 137
8:58 138
8:66 126
8:68 .... 126, 127
8:70 126
9:115 138
10:1-21 137
10:1 138
10:3 138
10:6-14 129
10:12 .... 129, 130
10:16-17 108
10:18 127
10:22-28 .... 137, 131
10:22 108
10:29-154 137
10:29 138

Dionysus of Halicarnassus
2 65

Herculaneum Papyri
1018 .... 133, 138
1021 .... 133, 138
1044 .... 133, 138

Herodotus
Histories
2:32-35 85

Homer
Odyssey
11:170-203 81

Horace
On the Art of Poetry
347-352 78
353-355 68

Iamblichus
Life of Pythagoras
6:30 137
28:140-142 137

Livy
1:1:5 109

21 65
31:1:2 65

Longinus
On the Sublime
33:1 78

Lucian
How to Write History
48 .... 79, 141

Lucretius
On the Nature of Things
3:1-5 137
5:1-10 137
5:55 137
6:1-7 137

Plato
Republic
605 a 68

Philostratus
Life of Apollonius
1:1 137
1:4 137
5:21 108
8:4 126

Pliny the Elder
Natural History
30:4 108

Pliny the Younger
Letters
7:4 139
7:17 .... 85, 139
8:21 139
9:1 139
9:27 .... 85, 139
9:36 .... 79, 141

Plutarch
On the Glory of the Athenians
3 84

Reply to Colotes
1117 127
1117B 126
1117C 126, 127

Polybius
2:1 65
3:1 65
4:1 65

Porphyry

Life of Plotinus

17 138
19 138

Life of Pythagoras

2 137
20 137
28 137

Quintilian

12:29-30 108

Seneca

Letters

6:5-6 108
11:9-10 108
16:3 108
25:6 108
52:8-9 108
110:1 108

Suetonius

Life of Vergil

22, 23 .... 79, 141

Vergil

Aeneid

1-6 .... 5, 67

1 77
1:1-4, 5-7 67
1:305-418 68
2 .... 67, 68
2:40-56 68
2:57-198 68
2:199-227 68
4:1-705 68
6:56-123 68
7-12 .... 5, 67
7 77
7:44-45 67
7:286-340 68
7:341-539 68
7:540-600 68
8 .... 67, 68
8:172-183 68
8:184-267 68
8:268-305 68

Xenophon

Memorabilia

1:3:1 108
4:1:1 108
4:3:18 108
4:4:25 108

Index of Authors

Anderson, Hugh, 66
Argyle, A. W., 48
Arndt, W. F., 33
Atkinson, D., 84
Badaway, A., 86
Barrett, C. K., 12, 30, 121, 138
Barrois, G. A., 86
Bassett, S. E., 83, 88
Baur, F. C., 1, 3, 4, 11, 23
Bertman, S., 85
Bickermann, E., 108, 137
Black, M., 48
Blass, F., 88
Bligh, J., 65, 87
Blum, G. G., 109
Blumenthal, M., 87
Boismard, M. E., 87
Bowen, C. R., 49
Bowra, C. M., 83, 84
Bruce, F. F. 30, 31, 32, 48, 109, 138
Brun, L., 11
Bultmann, R., 12, 31, 33, 49, 65, 66
Bundy, W. E., 31, 33, 49
Burke, K., 80
Burkitt, F. C., 48
Burton, R. W. B., 83
Buttrey, T. V., 83
Cadbury, H. J., 1, 2, 3, 11, 12, 13, 25, 30, 32, 48, 121, 123
Caird, G. B., 31, 33, 49, 65
Campenhausen, H. von, 109, 123
Camps, W. A., 83
Carney, J. F., 83
Carubba, R. W., 14, 83
Cerfaux, L., 11, 30, 49
Chadwick, H., 66
Chipiez, C., 87
Clarke, M. L., 108
Clogg, F. B., 30
Cohen, M., 87
Collins, J. J., 87
Conway, R. S., 7, 83

Conzelmann, H., 3, 12, 31, 33, 49, 103, 104, 107, 109, 110, 121, 122
Corbett, P. E., 88
Courtney, E., 83
Cox, A. S., 137
Creed, J. M., 11, 110, 123
D'Alton, J. F., 85
Daube, D., 108
Davies, J. G., 2, 11, 61, 65, 66, 122
Davies, J. H., 122
Davies, W. D., 108, 109
Debrunner, A., 88
Deeks, D., 87
Devambez, P., 85
Dibelius, M., 12, 32, 33, 65
Drew, D. L., 83
Duckworth, G. E., 5, 6, 7, 13, 14, 68, 83, 84, 88
Dungan, D. L., 137
Dupont, J., 13, 31, 32, 48, 49, 65, 87
Düring, I., 138
Easton, B. S., 109
Ehrhardt, A., 138
Ellis, E. E., 109
Evans, C. F., 65, 122
Farrer, A. M., 3, 13, 65, 87
Fenik, B., 83
Fenton, J. C., 4, 12
Feuillet, A., 49, 87, 123
Flender, H., 3, 12, 30, 33, 104, 110
Foakes-Jackson, F. J., 109
Forbes, J., 87
Frankfort, H., 74, 86
Friedlander, L., 85
Fuller, D. P., 66
Fuller, R. H., 121, 123
Funk, R. W., 12, 31, 32, 88
Gaechter, P., 4 12, 49
Gardner, P., 84, 85
Georgi, D., 109
Gerhardsson, B., 108, 109
Geyser, A. S., 49

Gilmour, S. M. 123
Glombitza, O., 12
Goguel, M., 30
Gomperz, Th., 138
Goodman, F. W., 49
Goodenough, E. R., 87, 88
Goodspeed, E. J., 48
Gossage, A. J., 138
Goulder, M. D., 2, 3, 11, 12, 30, 31, 32, 49, 51, 65, 66
Grabar, A., 88
Grant, M., 85
Grant, R. M., 33, 123, 124
Hadas, M., 109, 138
Haenchen, E., 3, 11, 12, 32, 38, 39, 48, 65
Hahn, F., 121
Hanson, R. P. C., 48
Harnack, A., 1, 3, 11, 32, 37, 38, 48, 65, 137
Hastings, A., 30
Hawkins, J. C., 65
Herting, L., 88
Hicks, R. D., 108, 138, 139
Hirsch, E., 31
Hovingh, P. F., 13
Hunter, A. M., 121
Immerwahr, H. R., 5, 6, 13
Isserlin, B. S., 87
Jeremias, J., 31, 38, 39, 49, 65
Jonas, R., 84
Kahler, H., 84
Käsemann, E., 65, 109
Kasser, R., 33
Keck, L. E., 4, 12, 123, 124
Kennedy, G., 85
Kenny, E. J., 137
Kirk, G. S., 83
Kirschbaum, E., 88
Kitto, H. D. F., 85
Klostermann, E., 31
Knox, J., 109
Knox, W. L., 49, 109
Knox, W. L., 49, 109
Koester, H., 138
Kraeling, C. H., 110
Krischer, T., 83
Kümmel, W. G., 3, 12, 31, 32, 65, 122
Lake, K., 109
Lamberton, C. D., 88
Lampe, G. W. H., 30, 31, 33, 49, 121, 123
Landes, G. M., 71, 85, 86, 88
Laqueur, R., 65
Laurentin, R., 2, 11, 49

Leaney, A. R. C., 30, 31, 49, 65, 123
Leo, F., 137
Lesky, A., 138
Licht, J., 85
Liefeld, W. L., 108
LIghtfoot, J. B., 31
Lloyd, R. B., 13
Lowrie, W., 88
Lund, N. W., 85, 87
Machen, J. G., 11, 49
Maiuri, A., 85
Malatesta, E., 4, 12,
Marin, L., 30
Martin, R. A., 37
Martin, V., 33
Mattill, A. J., Jr., 11
McCarthy, D. J., 85
McCloy, F. D., 88
McEachern, V. E., 11
McQueen, E. I., 138
Meeks, W., 139
Mendell, C. W., 83
Menoud, P. H., 31, 66, 122
Metzger, B. M., 48, 121
Meyer, E., 138
Minear, P., 2, 11, 121
Morgenthaler, R., 2, 11, 12, 31, 51, 65
Moule, C. F. D., 121
Murley, C., 83
Myres, J., 5, 6, 13, 83
Nock, A. D., 137
Norwood, G., 83
Oliver, H. H., 104, 110
Olrik, A., 13
O'Neill, J. C., 14, 30, 123
Otis, B., 83, 88
Parrot, A., 73, 87
Pedersen, J., 74, 75, 87
Perrot, G., 87
Perry, B. E., 109
Pesch, R., 72, 85, 86
Plümacher, E., 11, 12, 138
Porten, B., 85
Pryce, T. D., 84
Rackham, R. B., 15, 24, 30, 31, 32
Rad, G. von, 87
Raglan, L., 139
Ramsay, A. M., 122
Ranke, H., 86
Reicke, B., 13, 31, 33, 38, 39, 48, 121
Richardson, L., Jr., 7
Richmond, O. L., 84
Richter, G. M. A., 85

Riddle, D. W., 48
Rigaux, B., 12, 65
Robertson, A. T., 121
Robertson, D. S., 84
Robin, L., 137
Robinson, J. A. T., 31, 48, 121
Robinson, J. M., 123
Robinson, W. C., Jr., 14, 31, 49, 104, 110, 122
Rollins, W. G., 11
Ropes, J. H., 122
Rudd, N., 83
Sahlin, H., 36, 48
Sanderson, M. L., 49
Sandys, J. E., 88
Schloessinger, M. S., 84
Schmithals, W., 109
Schneckenburger, M., 11, 23, 31, 32
Schoenberger, G., 87
Schubert, P., 31
Schürmann, H., 33
Schweizer, E., 121, 123
Scott, W., 138
Scranton, R. L., 80, 88
Shepherd, J. T., 83, 88
Shipley, J. T., 84
Sibinga, J. S., 88
Skutsch, O., 83
Sleeper, C. F., 122
Smalley, S. S., 122
Smid, H. R., 75, 87
Smith, G. A., 78
Smith, M., 138
Smith, W. S., 86
Soden, H. von, 129, 134, 138
Sparks, H. F. D., 11, 48
Stein, R. H., 13
Stempvoort, P. A. van, 66, 122
Stendahl, K., 121
Streeter, B. H., 11
Stuart, D. R., 85, 137
Swain, J. W., 48
Swanston, H., 49

Talbert, C. H., 11, 30, 32, 49, 50, 87, 88, 109, 110, 121, 122, 124, 138
Taylor, V., 65, 122
Terrence, E. L. B., 86
Thiering, B., 14, 85
Thomson, G., 83
Todd, J. C., 49
Torrey, C. C., 36, 37, 48
Toynbee, J. M. C., 84
Tracy, H. L., 83, 88
Traversa, A., 138
Trible, P., 86
Trocme, E., 38, 48, 65
Turner, C. H., 108
Unnik, W. C. van, 12, 109
Vanhoye, A., 4, 12, 88
Vazakas, A. A., 48
Vielhauer, P., 11, 49
Vogel, C. J. de, 138
Vööbus, A., 33
Walker, H. H., 85
Wampler, J. C., 84
Ward, W. A., 87
Webster, T. B. L., 68, 84, 85
Weiss, J., 12
Whitman, C., 5, 6, 13, 83, 88
Wilcox, M., 37, 48
Wilder, A., 122
Wilken, W. L., 137, 138
Wilkinson, V., 30
Williams, C. S. C., 31
Williams, R. R., 31, 36, 37, 48
Willis, J. T., 85
Wilson, J. A., 74, 78
Wilson, S. G., 104, 110
Wink, W., 4, 49
Winter, P., 31, 33,
Wohlberg, J., 83
Woldering, I., 86
Woolcombe, K. J., 49
Zehnle, R. G., 48
Zeller, E., 30, 31
Zwaan, J. de, 48